PACEMAKER®

World Literature

GLOBE FEARON

Pearson Learning Group

Pacemaker® World Literature, Second Edition

REVIEWERS
We thank the following educators who provided valuable comments and suggestions during the development of this book:

Pacemaker Curriculum Advisor: Stephen Larson, formerly of the University of Texas at Austin

Program Reviewers: Jerry Bailis, Reading Specialist, Drexel Hill, Upper Darby School District; Margo McCord, Pewamo-Westphalia Jr./Sr. High School; Nita Noveno, Teacher Consultant, Secondary Literacy Institute, Tearchers College, Columbia University

PROJECT STAFF
Art & Design: Susan Brorein, Sherri Hieber-Day, Dan Trush
Editorial: Meredith Nelson, Susan Poskanzer, Kelly Robinson, Emily Shenk
Production/Manufacturing: Lorraine Allen, Ruth Leine, Karyn Mueller
Marketing: Ken Clinton
Publishing Operations: Debi Schlott

ACKNOWLEDGMENTS
page 4: "The Fly," from *The Toad Is the Emperor's Uncle* by Mai Vo-Dinh. Doubleday & Co. Inc, 1970. Reprinted by permission of Mai Vo-Dinh.

page 12: All pages from "By Any Other Name" from *Gifts of Passage* by Santha Rama Rau. Copyright © 1951 by Santha Rama Rau. Copyright renewed © 1979 by Santha Rama Rau. Reprinted by permission of HarperCollins Publishers, Inc. "By Any Other Name" originally appeared in *The New Yorker*.

page 24: "The Small Cabin" from *Selected Poems 1966–1984*, by Margaret Atwood. Copyright © 1990 Oxford University Press Canada. Reprinted by permission of the publisher. "The Small Cabin" from *Selected Poems 1966–1984* by Margaret Atwood. Copyright © 1975 by Margaret Atwood. Reprinted by permission of Houghton Mifflin Company. All rights reserved.

Further acknowledgments appear on page 468, which constitutes an extension of this copyright page.

Photo and Illustration Credits appear on page 470.

ABOUT THE COVER: The images on the cover are connected to the literature in this book in some way. As you read the literature, think about the images on the cover. See if you can make the connections yourself. Ask yourself what other images from the literature in this book could have appeared on the cover.

ISBN: 0-13-024730-8

Printed in the United States of America

11 12 13 14 15 V0UD 19 18 17 16 15

Globe
Fearon
Pearson Learning Group

1-800-321-3106
www.pearsonlearning.com

Contents

A Note to the Student

In this book, you will read short stories, poetry, autobiographies, a memoir, a play, and much more. These selections represent the experiences of people from many different cultures and backgrounds. You will meet interesting characters. You will be transported to other times and places around the world. You will read about conflicts big and small. These selections cover the experiences of people around the world and their cultures.

Several features will help you along the way. The **Unit Opener** provides you with a snapshot of what you will be reading. It also provides a map that shows the countries the authors in that unit are from. The **Chapter Opener** includes a piece of fine art or a photograph to help set the mood for the chapter. It also lists the **Learning Objectives** and provides a **Preview Activity**. The **Chapter Review** includes summaries of all of the selections in the chapter, a **Vocabulary Review**, a **Chapter Quiz**, and a **Chapter Activity**. Finally, the **Unit Review** covers all of the selections in the unit.

For each selection, you will find a **Before You Read** page. It introduces the **Keys to Literature** with examples, as well as the **Words to Know**. The **Did You Know?** feature will help you build your background knowledge.

As you read each selection, you will find side-column notes that will help you set a purpose for reading, make predictions, understand the Keys to Literature, define confusing words, and think about important questions. In addition, illustrations and photographs visually "tell the story."

For each selection, you will also find an **After You Read** page. It asks key questions to help you think about the selection you just read. In addition, **Learn More About It** sections give you interesting information related to something you just read.

We hope you enjoy reading this collection of World Literature. Everyone who put this book together worked hard to make it useful, interesting, and enjoyable. We wish you well in your studies. Our success is in your accomplishment.

Unit One

This image shows acrobats at an important turning point in their act. What other turning points, or moments of truth, can you think of in life?

Learning Objectives

- Identify a story's settings.
- Define narrative.
- Identify and understand idioms.
- Recognize details.
- Recognize who the speaker of a poem is.
- Identify alliteration.
- Understand what a poem is.

Preview Activity

Think of a time when you learned something new about yourself. What event led up to this moment of truth? Share this information with a friend.

Theme Preview: Moments of Truth

At some point in our lives we have moments when we must honestly face who we are, who we've been, and who we want to become. At these moments, we are "up in the air." Our lives can change because of what happens next or how we suddenly see something in a new way. These moments can force us to be stronger and more confident. In this chapter, you will read about people whose lives come to a turning point, or moment of truth.

Keys to Literature

setting: the time and place of the action in a story

Example: One setting in this story is a farm in Vietnam.

narrative: a story; a report of what has happened

Example: "The Fly" is a narrative that tells what happens when a moneylender tries to get back money he has loaned.

Did You Know?

Many people borrow money from banks. Banks charge a specific percentage fee each month until the borrower pays off the loan. When a person borrows from an individual, like the moneylender in this story, the rules for paying back the loan are not always clear.

Words to Know

marketplace	a place where goods are bought and sold
bamboo	a tropical plant with hollow woody stems
witness	a person who sees or hears something
clever	smart and quick
firmness	steadiness; unchangeable manner
explanations	answers or reasons that make something clear
chuckling	quietly laughing

Genre: Short Story

"The Fly" is a short story. Read more about short stories on page 467 of the Genre Guide.

The Fly

BY MAI VO-DINH, *adapted*

Everyone in the village knew the moneylender. He was a rich and smart man. Having made a great fortune over the years, he settled into an easy life in his big house. The house had a huge garden and was guarded by a pack of fierce dogs. But still he was not happy with all he had. He went on making money by lending it to people all over the county. He charged them a very high rate for the loans. The moneylender was the most powerful man in the area, for many were in debt to him.

One day, the rich man set out for the house of one of his poor farmers. Even though he had been warned many times, the poor farmer could not pay off his debt. Even working himself to a shadow, the poor farmer could barely make ends meet. The moneylender was therefore set on getting his money back. If he

READ TO FIND OUT...
What happens when a rich moneylender tries to trick a young boy?

Predict

What kind of person is the moneylender?

Keys to Literature

The **setting** of a story is where it takes place. In this story, the setting changes a few times. What is the setting here?

Predict

Do you think the moneylender will get his money back?

could not get his money back, he would take some of the poor farmer's best belongings. But the rich man found no one at the farmer's house but a small boy of eight or nine. He was playing alone in the dirt yard.

"Child, are your parents home?" the rich man asked.

"No, sir," the boy replied. He went on playing with his sticks and stones. He paid no attention at all to the man.

"Then where are they?" the rich man asked, rather angrily. Still the little boy went on playing and did not answer.

When the rich man repeated his question, the boy looked up and answered slowly. "Well, sir, my father has gone to cut living trees and plant dead ones. My mother is at the **marketplace** selling the wind and buying the moon."

Think About It

Why do you think the boy tells riddles instead of telling where his parents are?

"What? What in heaven are you talking about?" the rich man commanded. "Quick, tell me where they are, or you will see what this stick can do to you!" The **bamboo** walking stick in the big man's hand surely looked frightening.

Even after he questioned him again and again, the boy gave the same reply. Being very upset, the man told him, "All right, little devil, listen to me! I came here today to take the money your parents owe me. But if you tell me where they really are and what they are doing, I will forget all about the debt. Is that clear to you?"

Think About It

Do you think the moneylender is telling the truth about forgetting the debt? Why?

"Oh, sir, why are you joking with a poor little boy? Do you expect me to believe what you are saying?" For the first time the boy looked interested.

"Well, there is heaven and there is earth to hear my promise," the rich man said. As he spoke, he pointed up to the sky and down to the ground.

But the boy only laughed. "Sir, heaven and earth cannot talk and therefore cannot tell anyone about your promise. I want some living thing to hear your promise."

The rich man caught sight of a fly landing on a bamboo pole nearby. Then laughing inside because he was fooling the boy, the rich man made an offer.

"There is a fly. He can be our **witness**. Now, hurry and tell me what you mean. How can your father be out cutting living trees and planting dead ones? How can your mother be at the market selling the wind and buying the moon?"

Looking at the fly on the pole, the boy began to speak. "A fly is a good enough witness for me. Well, here it is, sir. My father has simply gone to cut down bamboo. He will make a fence with it for a man near the river. And my mother ... oh, sir, you'll keep your promise, won't you? You will free my parents of all their debts? You really mean it?"

Think About It

Do you think the fly is a good witness? Why?

"Yes, yes, I do honestly swear in front of this fly here." The rich man urged the boy to go on.

"Well, my mother has gone to the market to sell fans. She will use the money to buy oil for our lamps. Isn't that what you would call selling the wind to buy the moon?"

The rich man shook his head. He had to admit to himself that the boy was **clever**. However, he thought the little genius still had much to learn. A clever person would never believe that a fly could be a witness to anyone. Saying good-by, the man told the boy he would soon return to keep his promise.

A few days passed. Then the moneylender came back. This time he found the poor farmer and his wife at home, as it was late in the evening. A nasty scene followed. The rich man demanded his money, and the poor farmer said he was sorry and begged for more time. Their fighting woke up the little boy. He ran to his father and told him, "Father, father, you don't have to pay your debt. This gentleman here has made a promise to me. He has promised that he would forget all about the money you owe him."

"Nonsense," the rich man shook his walking stick at both father and son. "Nonsense. Are you going to stand there and listen to a child's stories? I never spoke a word to this boy. Now, tell me, are you going to pay, or are you not?"

The whole matter ended by being brought to the judge in charge of the county. The poor farmer and his wife did not know what to believe. All they could do was take their son with them to court. The boy's **firmness** about the rich man's promise was their only hope.

The judge began by asking the boy to tell exactly what happened. Happily, the boy quickly told about the **explanations** he gave the rich man in return for forgetting the debt.

"Well," the judge said to the boy, "if this man here has made such a promise, we have only your word for it. How do we know that you have not made up the whole story yourself? In a case such as this, you need a witness to prove your story. You have none." The boy stayed calm. He said that, of course, there was a witness to his talk with the rich man.

"Who is that, child?" the judge asked.

"A fly, Your Honor."

"A fly? What do you mean, a fly? Watch out, young man. Daydreams are not allowed in this place!" The judge's kind face suddenly became stern.

"Yes, Your Honor, a fly. A fly which was landing on this gentleman's nose!" The boy jumped from his seat.

Think About It
Why does the judge's face become stern, or harsh?

Think About It

The color of the man's face is compared to a ripe tomato. Why is his face turning red?

"Rude little devil, that's a pack of lies!" The rich man roared in anger. His face was like a ripe tomato. "The fly was not on my nose; he was on the pole...." But he stopped dead. It was, however, too late.

The great judge himself could not help bursting out laughing. Then the crowd burst out laughing. The boy's parents, too, laughed shyly. The boy, and the rich man himself, also laughed. With one hand on his stomach, the judge waved the other hand toward the rich man:

Think About It

What lesson does the boy teach the moneylender?

"Now, now, that's all settled. You, dear sir, have indeed made your promises to the child. Pole or no pole, your talk with this boy did happen after all! The court says that you must keep your promise."

Still **chuckling**, he told all to go.

Meet the Author

MAI VO-DINH *(Born 1933)*

Mai Vo-Dinh was born in Hue, Vietnam. He moved to the United States in 1960 after studying in Paris. He became a citizen of the United States in 1976. Since then, he has written and translated many books.

Mai Vo-Dinh is known not only for his short stories, but also for his poetry and nonfiction. He is an artist as well as a writer. He has illustrated a number of his own books, such as *The Toad Is the Emperor's Uncle* and *The Jade Song*.

Check Your Predictions

1. Look back at the answers you gave for the Predict questions. Would you change your answers? Explain.

Understand the Story

2. Why does the rich man come to the boy's house?

3. Who witnesses the promise?

4. Why does the rich man think he has tricked the boy?

5. Name one of the story's settings.

Think About the Story

6. What makes "The Fly" a narrative? What genre is this narrative?

7. What do you think the moneylender has learned from this experience?

8. If you could change the title of the story, what would you name it? Why?

Extend Your Response

Imagine you are a newspaper reporter covering the court case. Make a list of possible newspaper headlines for an article. At least one headline should tell who and what. Another should grab the reader's attention. Work with a partner to decide which is the best headline.

Keys to Literature

idiom: a phrase or expression that has a different meaning from what the individual words usually mean

> Example: "The pot calling the kettle black" is an idiom. It means you are accusing someone of doing something that you yourself do.

details: pieces of information that help to create a picture for the reader

> Example: *Her rimless half-glasses glittered.*

Did You Know?

This selection takes place at a British-run school in India in the late 1920s. At these schools, most of the students were British, with only a small number of Indians. At that time, Britain controlled the government of India. However, many Indians challenged this control.

Words to Know

Anglo-Indian	English and Indian
headmistress	a female school principal
glittered	sparkled or shined
stubborn	firm; unchanging
civil service	part of the government or public service
twilight	faint light after sunset
whitewashed	painted white
guarded	cautious or watchful

Genre: Autobiography

"By Any Other Name" is part of an autobiography. Read more about autobiographies on page 466 of the Genre Guide.

By Any Other Name

BY SANTHA RAMA RAU, *adapted*

At the **Anglo-Indian** day school in Zorinabad, they changed our names. We were sent to this school when my sister was eight years old. I was five and a half. The first day of school was a hot, windless September morning. Such mornings came often in north India. We stood in the **headmistress's** study. She said, "Now you're the new girls. What are your names?" My sister answered for us. "I am Premila." She turned to me. "This is Santha."

The headmistress had been in India fifteen years. She still smiled at her helpless lack of skill when saying Indian names. Her rimless half-glasses **glittered**. The loose bun on her head trembled as she shook her head.

READ TO FIND OUT...
What happens to make an Indian girl decide to leave her new school?

▶ Zorinabad [zoh-REHN-ah-bad] is a village in India.

Think About It
How does the headmistress feel about Indian names?

"Oh, my dears, those are much too hard for me. Let's give you pretty English names. Wouldn't that be more jolly? Let's see, now Pamela for you, I think." She looked at my sister. "That's as close as I can get. As for you," she said to me, "how about Cynthia? Isn't that nice?"

My sister was always less easily frightened than I was. She kept a **stubborn** silence. I said, "Thank you," in a very tiny voice.

We were sent to that school because my father worked in the area. As an officer of the **civil service**, he had to inspect the villages. His headquarters at the time were in Zorinabad. He made his shorter inspection tours on horseback. A week before the first day of school, we had waved good-by to him. It was a stale, hot day after the rainy season. Such days were normal that time of year. An assistant, a secretary, two bearers, and a man to look after the bedding and luggage were with him. They rode away through our large garden. We turned back into the **twilight** of the house. We could hear the sounds of fans whispering in every room.

Up to then, my mother had refused to send Premila to the British-run school. She used to say, "You can bury a dog's tail for seven years, and it still comes out curly. You can take the British away from home for a lifetime, and they'll still remain narrow-minded." Diplomas from Indian schools were not thought to be any good in those days. In my case the question of school had never come up. It probably never would have if Mother's good health had not broken down. For the first time in my life, she could not go on giving us lessons every morning. So our Hindi books were put away. We were sent to the Anglo-Indian school.

I still remember the first day of school. At that age, if one's name is changed, one becomes almost two people. I remember having a distant interest in the actions of "Cynthia." Yet I certainly did not feel I had to answer for them. So, I followed the thin, stiff back of

▶ A *bearer* is a personal servant. Sometimes bearers carry things.

Keys to Literature

An **idiom** is a group of words or a phrase that has special meaning. *Narrow-minded* means "not accepting of new ideas."

the headmistress down the porch to my classroom. I felt only a brief interest in what was going to happen to me. This was a strange, new place they called School.

The building was Indian in appearance. It had wide porches opening into a courtyard. Indian porches are usually **whitewashed** and have stone floors. These, in the style of British schools, were painted dark brown. In addition, they had mats on the floors. The mats seemed to add to the heat.

I think there were about a dozen Indian children in the school. It held about forty students in all. Four Indian students were in my class. They were all sitting at the back of the room. I went to join them. I sat next to a small, serious girl who didn't smile at me. She had long, glossy-black braids. She wore a cotton dress, but she still kept her Indian jewelry. She wore a gold chain around her neck, thin gold bracelets, and tiny rubies in her ears. Like most Indian children, she had a rim of black powder around her eyes. The cotton dress should have looked strange. All I could think of was asking my mother if I couldn't wear a dress to school, too. It would replace the Indian clothes I now wore.

I can't remember too much about what went on in class that day. However, I do remember how it began. The teacher pointed to me. She asked me to stand up. Then she said, "Now, dear, tell the class your name."

I said nothing.

"Come along," she said, frowning slightly. "What's your name, dear?"

"I don't know," I said, at last.

There were about eight or ten English children in the front of class. They giggled and twisted around in their chairs to look at me. I sat down quickly and opened my eyes very wide. I hoped in that way to dry them off. The little girl with the braids put out her hand. Very lightly, she touched my arm. She still didn't smile.

Predict

Do you think Santha and Premila will like their new school?

Keys to Literature

What **details** tell about the small, serious girl's jewelry?

Think About It

Why does Santha say that she does not know her name?

Think About It

Why is Santha bored?

Most of that morning I was quite bored. I looked briefly at the children's drawings pinned to the wall. Then I watched a lizard hanging to the ledge of the high, barred window behind the teacher. From time to time it would shoot out its long, yellow tongue for a fly. Then it would rest with its eyes closed and its belly throbbing.

It seemed as though it were swallowing several times very quickly. The lessons were mostly about reading and writing and simple numbers. These things my mother had already taught me, so I paid little notice. The teacher wrote on the board words like "bat" and "cat." These seemed babyish to me. Only "apple" was new and hard to grasp.

When it was time for lunch, I followed the girl with the braids onto the porch. The children from other classes were also there. I saw Premila. I ran over to her, as she had our lunch boxes. The children were all opening packages and sitting down to eat sandwiches. Premila and I were the only ones who had Indian food. Our lunch boxes held thin wheat chapatties and some vegetable curry. There were also bottles of buttermilk for us to drink. Premila thrust half of the lunch into my hand. Then she whispered fiercely that I should sit with my class. That was what the others seemed to be doing.

Predict

What do you think will happen next?

The huge black eyes of the little Indian girl looked at my food longingly. I offered her some. But she only shook her head. She plowed through her sandwiches.

I was very sleepy after lunch. At home we always took a nap. This was usually a pleasant time of day.

The bedrooms were darkened against the harsh afternoon sun. I would drift off to sleep to the sound of Mother's voice reading a story. Finally, the shrill, fussy voice of the ayah would wake us for tea.

At school, we rested for a short time on low cots on the porch. After that we were expected to play games.

During the hot part of the afternoon, we played indoors. After the shadows got longer and an evening breeze came up, we moved outside to the courtyard.

I never really grasped the idea of games that were contests. At home, whenever we played a game like tag, I was always allowed to "win." "Because she is the youngest," Mother used to tell Premila. I had often heard her say it. So I had no idea what "winning" meant.

When we played twos-and-threes that afternoon, I let one of the small English boys catch me. This is what I was trained to do. So I was, of course, puzzled when the other children did not return the favor. I ran about for what seemed like hours without catching anyone. I ran about until it was time for school to close. Much later I learned my idea was called "not being a good sport." I therefore stopped letting myself be caught. It was years later that I really learned the spirit of the thing.

Think About It

Why doesn't Santha know what *winning* means?

When I saw our car come up to the school gate, I broke away from my classmates. Rushing toward it, I yelled, "Ayah! Ayah!" It seemed like forever since I had seen her that morning. This wise, loving figure in her white sari had given me so much useless advice. All of it was on how to be a good girl at school. Premila followed more calmly. On the way home, she told me never to do that again in front of the other children.

When we got home, we went straight to Mother's high, white room. There we had tea with her. I quickly climbed onto the bed and bounced on the springs. Mother asked how we had liked our first day in school. I was pleased to be home. I was pleased to have left that odd Cynthia behind. So I had nothing whatever to say about school, except to ask what "apple" meant. But Premila told Mother about the classes. She added that in her class they had weekly tests. These were given to see if they had learned their lessons well.

I asked Premila, "What's a test?"

Premila said, "You're too small to have them. You won't have them in your class for donkey's years." She had learned the phrase that day. Now she was using it for the first time. We all laughed loudly at her wit. She also took Mother to one side to say we should take sandwiches for lunch. Not, she said, that she minded. But they would be simpler for me to handle.

That whole lovely evening I didn't think about school at all. I dashed barefoot across the lawns with my best friend, the cook's son. Together we ran to the stream at the end of the garden. We quarreled in our usual way. Then we waited for the night to bring out the smell of flowers. I listened closely to his stories of ghosts and demons. By dark I was too scared to cross the garden alone. The ayah found me. She shouted at the cook's son. Then she scolded me. She hurried me in to supper. It was a wonderful evening.

Keys to Literature

Donkey's years is an **idiom**. What do you think it means?

Think About It

What is the real reason Premila asks for sandwiches?

It was a week later that our lives changed suddenly. It was the day of Premila's first test. I was sitting in the back of my class. As usual, I was only half listening to the teacher. I had started a rather **guarded** friendship with the girl with braids. Her name turned out to be Nalini (Nancy, in school). The other three Indian children were already fast friends. Even at that age, one thing was clear to us. Becoming friends with the English children was out of the question. Sometimes during the class, my new friend and I would draw pictures. We would show them to each other secretly.

The door opened sharply, and Premila marched in. At first, the teacher smiled at her kindly. Then she said, "Now, you're little Cynthia's sister?"

Premila didn't even look at her. She stood with her feet planted firmly apart. Her shoulders were stiff as she spoke straight to me. "Get up," she said. "We're going home."

I didn't know what had happened. I could tell that it was a turning point of some kind.

"Bring your pencils and your notebook," she said.

I went back for them. Then together we left the room. The teacher started to say something just as Premila closed the door. But we didn't wait to hear what it was.

In total silence we left the school and started to walk home. I asked Premila what the matter was. All she would say was, "We're going home for good." It was a very tiring walk for a child of five and a half. I dragged along behind Premila. My pencils were growing sticky in my hand. I can still remember looking at the dusty hedges and tangles of thorns. They lay in ditches by the side of the road. I also remember smelling the faint perfume of the trees. I wondered if we would ever get home. Now and then a horse-drawn cart passed us. The women in their pink and green silks stared at us as we trudged along the road. A few workers and women

Predict

Why do you think Premila is taking her sister home?

Keys to Literature

What **details** help you see how brave and confident Premila is?

Predict

What do you think will
happen when Santha and
Premila arrive home?

with baskets of vegetables on their heads smiled at us.
But it was nearing the hottest time of the day.
Therefore, the road was nearly empty. I walked more
and more slowly.

I shouted to Premila from time to time. "Wait for
me!" I yelled in a voice that became more and more
cranky. She spoke to me only once. That was to tell me
to carry my notebook on my head. It would shield me
from the sun.

When we got home, the ayah was just taking lunch
into Mother's room. She immediately started asking us
questions. Her questions were all about what we were
doing back here at this hour of the day.

Mother looked surprised and very concerned. She
asked Premila what had happened.

Premila said, "We had our test today. She made me
and the other Indians sit at the back of the room, with
a desk between each one."

Mother said, "Why was that, darling?"

"She said it was because Indians cheat," Premila added. "So I don't think we should go back to that school."

Mother seemed far away. She was silent for a long time. At last she said, "Of course not, darling." She sounded displeased.

We all shared the curry she was having for lunch. Afterwards I was sent off to the beautiful bedroom for my nap. I could hear Mother and Premila talking through the open door.

Mother said, "Do you think she understood all that?"

Premila said, "I shouldn't think so. She's a baby."

Mother said, "Well, I hope it won't bother her."

Of course, they were both wrong. I understood it perfectly. I remember it all very clearly. But I put it happily away because it had all happened to a girl called Cynthia. I was never really very interested in her.

Think About It

Why is Premila upset by the teacher's comment?

Think About It

What do we learn about Santha at the end of the story?

Meet the Author

SANTHA RAMA RAU *(Born 1923)*

Santha Rama Rau was born in Madras, India. Most of her schooling was at home. When she was six, her family moved to England. As a young woman, she attended Wellesley College in Massachusetts, where she started her first book.

Her travels around the world led to writing several travel books, for which she is well-known. She also wrote the play version of E.M. Forster's *A Passage to India*, which was made into a film. In addition, she has authored an Indian food cookbook and has written for the *New Yorker*, the *New York Times*, and *Vogue*.

Check Your Predictions

1. Look back at the answers you gave for the Predict questions. Would you change your answers? Explain.

Understand the Autobiography

2. What is the first thing that happens to Premila and Santha on their first day of school?

3. How does Mother feel about British-run schools?

4. How would you describe Premila?

5. What causes Premila to walk out of school?

Think About the Autobiography

6. What detail(s) from the autobiography tell(s) you what the headmistress is like?

7. What idiom does Mother use to say that the British are not accepting of new ideas?

8. Why do you think the author chose to include this story in her autobiography?

Extend Your Response

In this story, Santha thinks of herself as two people. Imagine that you could have another self. What would he or she be like? Write a short description of this self and what he or she does.

Learn More About It

COLONIAL INDIA

India, which is located in South Asia, is one of the largest countries in the world. Over one billion people live there. It has a rich history and was the home of one of the most sophisticated ancient cultures. Today it has a democratic government that was elected by the Indian people. But this was not always true.

Gandhi and others marching to the sea to peacefully protest an unfair tax on salt.

For about 200 years, India was a colony of Great Britain. Great Britain ran the government there. In 1877, Queen Victoria became the empress of India. The British were pleased to have India as a colony. It gave them many resources, such as cotton and spices. However, many Indian people were not happy with British rule. Some fought against it with violence.

Others, such as Mohandas Gandhi, worked for independence peacefully. Gandhi was a lawyer who led Indians to protest British rule. Some Indians quit their government jobs, for example. Others blocked streets to make their beliefs known. Others took their children out of British-run schools. Gandhi himself did not eat for long periods to force the government to change its ways. The government was afraid that if Gandhi starved, the Indian people would rise up against them. He became a symbol for peaceful protest. Eventually, the British government did begin to accept that Indians wanted to rule themselves. However, it was not until 1950 that India became fully independent.

Apply and Connect

How is what Premila does in "By Any Other Name" similar to what Gandhi encouraged people to do?

Keys to Literature

speaker of the poem: the one who is describing or telling about something in the poem

> Example: The speaker of the poem often uses pronouns such as *I* and *we*.

alliteration: the repeating of consonant sounds that begin words

> Example: The <u>w</u>eather <u>was</u> <u>w</u>indy and <u>w</u>arm.

Words to Know

gradually	slowly
crumple	crush into a ball or pile
collapsing	caving in or falling down

Genre: Poetry

"The Small Cabin" is a poem. Read more about poetry in the Learn More About It on page 26 or on page 467 of the Genre Guide.

The Small Cabin

BY MARGARET ATWOOD

READ TO FIND OUT...
What happens to the small cabin?

The house we built **gradually**
from the ground up when we were young
(three rooms, the walls
raw trees) burned down

5 last year   they said

I didn't see it, and so
the house is still there in me

among branches as always   I stand
inside it looking out

10 at the rain moving across the lake

but when I go back
to the empty place in the forest
the house will blaze and **crumple**
suddenly in my mind

15 **collapsing** like a cardboard carton
thrown on a bonfire, summers
crackling, my earlier
selves outlined in flame.

Left in my head will be

20 the blackened earth: the truth

Where did the house go?

Where do the words go
when we have said them?

Keys to Literature

The **speaker of the poem** is the person who tells the poem. This speaker refers to her family as *we*.

What is the repeated letter sound, or **alliteration**, that the poet uses in line 15?

Meet the Author

MARGARET ATWOOD *(Born 1939)*

Margaret Atwood was born in Ottawa, Canada, and studied in both Canada and the United States. From an early age, she knew that she wanted to be a writer. Her first book of poetry was published by the the time she was 22. Soon, her poetry and fiction had captured the attention of readers around the world.

Atwood is now one of Canada's best-known writers. Her novels, including *Bodily Harm*, *The Handmaid's Tale*, *The Blind Assassin*, and *Oryx and Crake*, have won many awards worldwide. Atwood's writing often deals with serious issues, including the roles of women in society or how technology affects society.

Learn More About It

GENRE STUDY: POETRY

Poetry is arranged in separate lines on a page. Poetry usually has rhythm and may also rhyme. Poems that do not rhyme, like "The Small Cabin," are written in free verse. There is no regular pattern to the way the lines sound.

Poetry uses descriptive, almost musical language and often expresses strong feelings. Some poems describe people, places, or real events. Other poems tell stories or describe fictional events. Poets choose their words very carefully to give a certain feeling, or mood, to a poem.

Understand the Poem

1. Who built the cabin?

2. What happens to the cabin?

3. What words does the speaker use to describe what happens to the cabin?

4. What letter is used in the alliteration to describe the burning cabin?

Think About the Poem

5. Who are the "earlier selves outlined in flame"?

6. How does the speaker feel about the cabin burning down?

7. What do you think the poet means by the last two lines of the poem?

Extend Your Response

Think of a place you know that has changed over time. Draw a picture of how it used to look. Then draw a picture of it as it looks now.

Summaries

The Fly A rich moneylender visits a poor family that owes him money. The parents aren't home. Their clever son answers the man's questions with a riddle. The man promises to forget the debt if the boy will explain the riddle and reveal where his parents are. The man thinks he has tricked the boy. Instead, the boy tricks him and the man has to keep his word.

By Any Other Name Premila and Santha are sisters who live in India. On their first day at the Anglo-Indian school, the headmistress gives them British names to use at school. There are only a few other Indian students at the school. At first, the sisters try to fit in. Premila, however, refuses to stay in a school where teachers are prejudiced against Indian students.

The Small Cabin The speaker remembers a small cabin that her family built when she was young. The house stood in a forest near a lake. The small cabin has burned down. The speaker finds it difficult to believe the cabin is no longer standing. When she visits the site of the cabin, though, she can imagine it burning, and her memories with it.

clever
explanations
stubborn
glittered
collapsing

Vocabulary Review

Complete each sentence with a word from the box. Use a separate sheet of paper.

1. The firemen were able to rescue everyone in the building that was _____.
2. Her jewelry _____ in the sunlight.
3. Sam had many _____ for not completing his homework.
4. The _____ boy was the first to solve the puzzle.
5. The _____ horse refused to go up the mountain path.

Chapter Quiz

Write your answers in one or two complete sentences.
Use a separate sheet of paper.

1. The Fly What does the moneylender do when the boy reminds him of his promise when he returns to the house?

2. The Fly How does the boy trick the moneylender into telling the truth?

3. By Any Other Name What does the headmistress do when the girls first arrive at school?

4. By Any Other Name Why does Premila quit school?

5. The Small Cabin What happened to the cabin?

6. The Small Cabin What happens when the speaker goes back to the place where the cabin stood?

Critical Thinking

7. By Any Other Name How would you describe Premila and Santha?

8. The Small Cabin Why do you think the memory of the small cabin is important to the speaker of the poem?

Chapter Activity

"The Small Cabin" is about a place that was meaningful to the speaker of the poem. Write a poem or a paragraph describing a place that has meaning to you. Be sure to tell what it looks like and how you feel about it.

Shoki the Demon Queller, detail by Kawanabe Kyosai

Who do you think these characters are? Why are they in conflict with each other?

Chapter 2 / Conflict

Learning Objectives

- Understand conflict in a story or poem.
- Recognize the rising action of a story.
- Recognize who a story's narrator is.
- Identify the first-person point of view.
- Recognize a story's mood.
- Understand the meaning of irony.

Preview Activity

Think of a time that you had a conflict with yourself or someone else. Tell what happened in a few paragraphs. What did you learn from the conflict? Did it take your life in a new direction? Why or why not?

Theme Preview: Conflict

In our lives we often face conflict, or struggle. We may be in conflict with other people, with nature, or even with ourselves. Conflict is challenging but can also give us a chance to learn something new. In this chapter, you will read about conflicts people have with themselves and others. These conflicts take the characters' lives in new directions.

Keys to Literature

conflict: a problem that needs to be solved in a story

 Example: In this story, there is a conflict between Arachne and Athena. Arachne believes that she is the best weaver. The goddess Athena thinks she is the best weaver.

rising action: the buildup of excitement in a story

 Example: For a long time, people compare Arachne's weaving skill to the goddess Athena's. Finally the two have a contest to see who is the better weaver.

Did You Know?

The ancient Greeks told many myths about gods and goddesses. They believed that these gods were a lot like humans, but with special powers. In this myth, the goddess Athena acts out of jealousy, like a human.

Words to Know

loom	a machine on which cloth is woven
shuttle	a card or spool that moves thread back and forth to weave cloth
immortal	living forever
challenged	called to a fight or contest
dazzling	bright
insult	something said that hurts someone's feelings

Genre: Myth

 "Arachne" is a myth. Read more about myths on page 467 of the Genre Guide.

$\mathcal{A}$rachne

RETOLD BY OLIVIA E. COOLIDGE

READ TO FIND OUT...
Who is the most talented weaver in all of Greece?

▶ Arachne [uh-RAK-nee]

Arachne was not beautiful or well-born. But she became famous all over Greece.

Arachne lived in a little village with her father, who dyed wool. Her father was very skillful at this. He made many different and wonderful colors. He was famous for the clear, bright red he made. This was the most beautiful of all the colors used in ancient Greece.

Arachne was even more skillful than her father. She spun the wool into a fine, soft thread. She wove the thread into cloth on the high **loom** in their cottage.

Arachne was small and pale from all the work she did. Her eyes were light, and her hair was a dusty brown. Yet she was quick and graceful. Her rough fingers moved so fast it was hard to follow them.

Weavers (16th century) by Jacopo Bassano (workshop of)

Soon Arachne was known all over Greece. No one had ever seen work like hers before. They had never seen thread so soft and even, or cloth so fine. They had never seen weaving so beautiful.

People used to come from far and wide to see Arachne working. Even the nymphs would come from the streams or the forests to peek shyly through the cottage door. They would watch in wonder as Arachne worked. They watched Arachne throw the **shuttle** from hand to hand between the hanging threads. They would watch her draw out the long threads of wool as she sat spinning.

▶ Athena [ah-THEEN-uh] is the Greek goddess of wisdom and the arts.

People would say to each other, "Surely Athena herself must have taught her. Who else would know the secret of such great skill?"

Arachne was used to being wondered at. She was very proud of her skill. Praise was all she lived for. It made her angry when people thought Athena had taught her.

Arachne would turn to the crowd of people and say, "I have my skill because of hard practice. I work from early morning until night. As for Athena's skill, how could it be greater than mine? If she came down to compete with me, she could do no better than I."

Keys to Literature

This is the first hint of the **conflict** between Athena and Arachne.

One day when Arachne spoke this way, an old woman answered her. She was a gray old woman and very poor. She leaned on a staff, looking at Arachne through the crowd of people. The old woman said, "Foolish girl! How dare you say you are equal to the **immortal** gods? I am an old woman. I have seen many things. Take my advice and ask pardon of Athena. Be happy that your spinning and weaving is the best that mortals can do."

Arachne said, "Stupid old woman! Who gave you the right to speak to me this way? It is easy to see you were never good at anything. That is why you come here in rags to watch my skill. If Athena dislikes my words, let her answer me. I have **challenged** her to a contest. But she, of course, will not come."

At these words, the old woman threw down her staff. She grew tall and beautiful. She was dressed in long robes of **dazzling** white. The crowd of people was terribly afraid. They knew this was Athena herself.

Arachne turned red. She had never really believed the goddess would hear her. But she would not give in. She pressed her pale lips together with pride.

Arachne led Athena to one of the great looms. Arachne stood before the other loom. Without a word, they began to work. They threaded the long wool strands that hung from the rollers. Between these strands, the shuttles moved back and forth. Many colors of wool were ready for them to use: white, gold, red, and others. The colors Arachne's father made were as wonderful as the cloth she wove.

Soon the room was almost silent. There was the creaking of the looms as the threads were pressed into place. Another sound was the breathing of the crowd of people. They were excited.

The crowd began to see that the skill of Arachne and Athena was almost equal. But the goddess was the quicker of the two.

Arachne also noticed how quickly the goddess was working. She had never matched her skill against anyone like this. She saw the goddess working quickly, calmly, and always a little faster than herself. Instead of being frightened, she became angry. An evil thought came into her head.

Think About It

How does Athena trick Arachne?

Keys to Literature

What is the **rising action** in this paragraph?

Predict

Who do you think will win the contest? Why?

Arachne Transformed into a Spider by Athena (18th century) by anonymous

Meanwhile, on Athena's loom, a pattern of many pictures was growing. At each side of the cloth were branches of Athena's favorite tree, the olive. In the middle, figures began to appear. The crowd saw that Athena was weaving a warning to Arachne.

In the center was Athena herself. She was competing with Poseidon for the city of Athens. But in the four corners were mortals who had tried to compete with the gods. Terrible things had happened to them.

▶ Poseidon [po-SIDE-duhn] is another Greek god. Athena won a contest against Poseidon. She then claimed Athens as her own special city.

Athena finished a little before Arachne. She stood back to see what the young woman was doing. On Arachne's loom were scenes showing evil things the gods had done. The pictures showed how gods tricked young women. They showed how gods came to Earth pretending to be poor people.

When Athena saw this **insult**, her gray eyes blazed with anger. She tore the cloth in half. Then she hit Arachne across the face.

Arachne stood there, feeling anger, fear, and pride. She said, "I will not live under this insult."

She grabbed a rope from the wall. She made it into a noose. She would have hanged herself, but Athena stopped her.

The goddess touched the rope and touched Arachne. She said, "Live on, evil girl. Live on and spin. You shall spin and so shall your descendants. You will remind people that it is not wise to compete with Athena."

The body of Arachne shrank up. Her legs grew tiny. She became a little dusty brown spider on a thin thread.

All spiders are descendants of Arachne. As the Greeks watched them spin their fine thread, they remembered that even the most skillful of mortals must not try to be equal with the gods.

Predict

Are you surprised that Athena allows Arachne to live? What do you think will happen next?

Meet the Reteller

OLIVIA E. COOLIDGE *(Born 1908)*

Olivia Coolidge was born in London, England. As a young woman, she studied at Oxford University. After teaching in Germany and England, she moved to the United States to teach. After World War II, she focused on her writing. Her fiction and nonfiction for young adults soon captured the attention of readers and critics.

Coolidge once explained that her purpose for writing was to "give a picture of life" as well as to "excite, amuse, and interest" readers. Her book about ancient Greek leaders, *Men of Athens*, was awarded a Newbery Medal.

Learn More About It

WEAVING

People have been weaving since ancient times. They may have started by weaving river reeds to form baskets.

This reconstruction shows what an ancient loom might have looked like.

Most weaving takes shape on a loom. The loom holds vertical threads tightly. These threads are called the warp. A shuttle sends horizontal thread back and forth across the loom. The horizontal threads are called the weft. They go over and under the warp. By sending the shuttle over and under different numbers of warp threads, a weaver can form patterns and pictures. Weavers then use a beater to push weft threads tightly together.

We can see the skill of ancient weavers in weavings that still exist today.

Check Your Predictions

1. Look back at the answers you gave for the Predict questions. Would you change your answers? Explain.

Understand the Myth

2. What skill is Arachne known for in Greece?

3. What causes Athena to be angry with Arachne?

4. What warning does Athena weave into her cloth?

5. How is the story's conflict resolved?

Think About the Myth

6. Why do you think Athena allows Arachne to live?

7. What incident is part of the rising action?

8. What makes this story a myth?

Extend Your Response
Imagine you are a god or goddess with amazing powers. Tell what you can do. Then write a story about a conflict with a mortal. What happens?

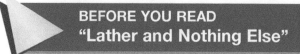

Keys to Literature

narrator: the person telling the story

Example: When you tell the story, you are the narrator.

first-person point of view: when a narrator tells the story using *I* to refer to himself or herself

Example: *When I saw who it was, I started to shake.*

Words to Know

wearily	in a tired way
rebels	people who are working against the ruling government
mangled	cut and bruised
dedicated	devoted
humbly	with meek or modest feeling
cowardly	lacking courage

Genre: Short Story

"Lather and Nothing Else" is a short story. Read more about short stories on page 467 of the Genre Guide.

Lather and Nothing Else

BY HERNANDO TÉLLEZ, *adapted*

READ TO FIND OUT...

What does the barber do when the feared leader of the army enters his shop?

Predict

Look at the art and the title. What do you think this story will be about?

He came in without a word. I was sharpening my best razor. When I saw who it was, I started to shake. But he did not notice. To cover my fright, I went on sharpening the razor. I tried the edge with the tip of my thumb. Then I took another look at the blade in the light.

Meanwhile, he was taking off his bullet-trimmed belt with a pistol holster hanging from it. He put it on a hook in the closet and hung his cap above it. Then he turned full around toward me. Loosening his tie, he remarked, "It's hot as the devil. I want a shave." With that he took his seat.

I guessed he had a four-days' growth of beard.

Keys to Literature

The **narrator** in this story is a barber. How does the narrator refer to himself?

This story is told from the **first-person point of view**. A character in the story tells the story.

They were the four days he had been gone rounding up our men. His face looked burned, tanned by the sun.

I started to work carefully on the shaving soap. I scraped some slices from the cake and dropped them into the mug. Then I added a little warm water and stirred with the brush. The lather soon began to rise.

"The fellows in the troop must have just about as much beard as I," he said. I went on stirring the lather.

He said, "But we did very well, you know. We caught the leaders. Some of them we brought back dead. Others are still alive. But they'll all be dead soon."

"How many did you take?" I asked.

"Fourteen. We had to go pretty far to find them. But now they're paying for it. Not one will escape; not one," he said.

He leaned back in the chair when he saw the brush full of lather. I had not yet put the sheet on him. I was very troubled. Taking the sheet from the drawer, I tied it around his neck.

He went on talking. He seemed to believe that I backed the present government.

"The people must have gotten a scare the other day," he said.

"Yes," I replied. I finished tying the knot behind his neck. His skin smelled of sweat.

"Good show, wasn't it?" he asked.

"Very good," I answered. Now I turned my attention to the brush. The man closed his eyes **wearily**. He waited for the gentle touch of the cool lather.

I had never had him so close before. The day he made us file through the schoolyard, our paths had crossed briefly. We were to look upon the four **rebels** hanging there. But the sight of those **mangled** bodies kept me from looking at the man in charge of it all. Now I had him in my hands.

Think About It

Why does the man close his eyes "wearily"?

It was not a bad face certainly. The beard, which aged him a bit, was not ugly. His name was Torres. Captain Torres.

I started to lay on the first coat of lather. He kept his eyes closed.

"I would love to catch a nap," he said. "But there's a lot to be done."

I lifted the brush. Then, trying to sound casual, I asked, "A firing party?"

"Something like that," he replied, "but slower."

"All of them?"

"No, just a few."

I went on lathering his face. My hands began to shake again. The man could not be aware of this. That was lucky for me. But I wished he had not come in. Probably many of our men had seen him enter my shop. With the enemy in my house, I felt a kind of duty.

Think About It

What detail tells you that Captain Torres makes the narrator feel nervous?

Keys to Literature

Because the story is told from the **first-person point of view**, we know exactly how the narrator feels.

▶ The razor the barber uses is a straight razor. It is long and thin. It looks more like a knife than like the razors used today.

I would have to shave his beard like any other beard. I would be careful and neat, as though he were a good customer. His skin should not ooze a single drop of blood. I would see to it that the blade did not slip in the small folds of skin. The skin would be left clean and soft. When I passed my hand over it, not a single hair should be felt. Yes. I was secretly a rebel. Yet I was also a **dedicated** barber, proud of my work. That four-day beard was a challenge.

I took up the razor and opened the blade. Then I began working downward in front of one ear. The blade worked perfectly. The hair was tough and hard; not very long, but thick. Little by little the skin showed through. The razor gave out its usual sound as it scraped layers of soap and bits of hair. I paused to wipe it clean. Then I sharpened the blade once more. I am a careful barber.

The man had kept his eyes closed. Now he opened them. He put a hand out from under the sheet. He felt the part of his face that rose from the lather.

"Come at six o'clock this evening to the school," he said.

"Will it be like the other day?" I asked, stiff with horror.

"It may be even better," he replied.

"What are you planning to do?" I asked.

"I'm not sure yet. But we'll have a good time," he replied.

Once more he leaned back and shut his eyes. I came closer, the razor held high.

"Are you going to punish all of them?" I meekly asked.

"Yes, all of them," he said.

The lather was drying on his face. I must hurry. Through the mirror, I took a look at the street. It seemed about as usual. There was the grocery shop with two or three people inside. Then I took a quick look at the clock. Two-thirty.

I kept moving the razor down. He had a blue beard, a thick one. He should let it grow like some poets or priests. It would suit him well. Many people would not know him. That would be a good thing for him. I thought this as I went gently over his throat. At this point, you really had to handle your blade with skill. That's because the thin hairs often fall into small folds of skin. It was a curly beard. The skin might open a tiny bit and let out a drop of blood. A good barber like myself builds his good name by not letting that happen to his customers.

This was surely a special customer. How many of ours had he sent to their death? How many had he cut to pieces? It was best not to think about it. Torres did not know I was his enemy. Neither he nor the others knew it. It was a secret known to very few. This made it possible for me to tell the rebels about Torres's actions. I could tell them what he planned to do when he went to hunt rebels. So this was going to be very hard to explain. How was it that I had him in my hands and let him go, alive and clean-shaven?

His beard had now almost disappeared. He looked years younger than when he had come in. I suppose that always happens to men in barber shops. Under my razor, Torres was refreshed. Yes, I am a good barber, the best in this town. I say this **humbly**.

A little more lather here under the chin near the large vein. How hot it is! Torres must be sweating just as I am. But he is not afraid. He is a calm man. He is not even thinking of what he will do to his prisoners later. I, on the other hand, clean him with this razor. I am careful not to draw blood. I cannot keep my thoughts in order.

Think About It
Why is the narrator a good barber?

Think About It
Why do you think no one knows that the barber is a rebel?

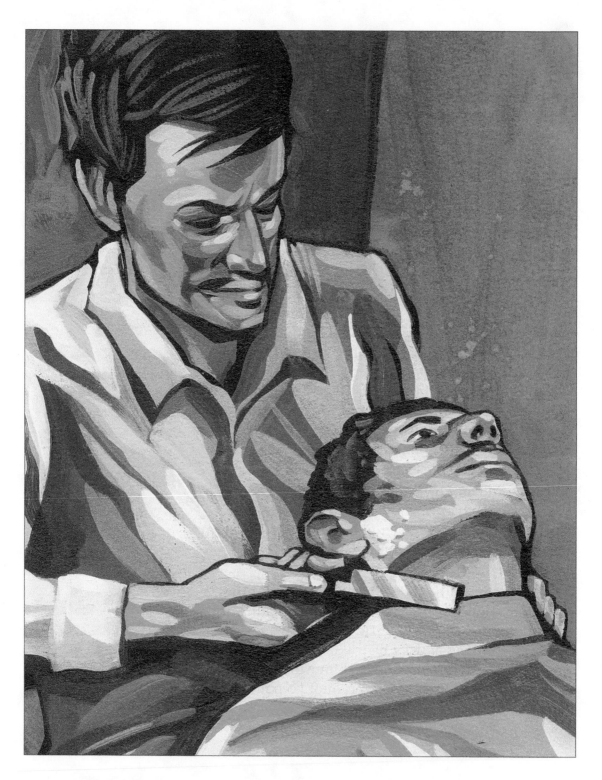

Curse the hour he came into my shop! I am a rebel but not a murderer. It would be so easy to kill him. He has it coming, or does he? No! No one deserves what it costs those who become killers. What is to be gained by it? Nothing. Others and still others keep coming. The first kill the second. Then these kill the next. In the end everything becomes a sea of blood. I could cut his throat, so, swish, swish! He would not even have time to moan. His eyes are shut. He would not even see the shine of the razor or the gleam in my eye.

But I'm shaking like a murderer. From his throat a stream of blood would flow on the sheet. It would run over the chair on my hands then onto the floor. I would have to close the door. But the blood would go on flowing. Along the floor, warm, long-lasting, and unstoppable until it reached the street. A small red river.

I'm sure that with a good, deep cut, he would feel no pain. He would not suffer at all. What would I do then with the body? Where would I hide it? I would have to flee, leave all this. I would find a home far away, very far away. But they would follow until they caught up with me. The murderer of Captain Torres. He slit his throat while he was shaving him. What a **cowardly** thing to do.

Others would say, "The hero of our people. A name to remember. He was the town barber. No one knew he fought for our cause."

So, which will it be? Murderer or hero? My fate hangs on the blade of this razor. I can turn my wrist a little and press the blade in. The skin will part like tissue, like rubber. There is nothing softer than a man's skin. The blood is always there, ready to burst out. A razor like this cannot fail. It is the best one I have.

But I don't want to be a murderer. No, sir. You came in to be shaved. I do my work with honor. I don't want

Predict

The barber is thinking about killing Captain Torres. Do you think he will do it?

Think About It

Why would slitting Torres' throat be a cowardly thing to do?

Think About It

If you were the narrator, what would you choose to do?

to stain my hands with blood. Just with lather and nothing else. You are a killer. I am only a barber. Each one to his job. That's it. Each one to his job.

The chin was now clean and soft. The man got up and looked at himself in the glass. He ran his hand over the skin. He felt its freshness, its newness.

"Thanks," he said. He walked to the closet for his belt, his pistol, and his cap. I must have been very pale. I felt my shirt soaked with sweat. Torres put on his belt, tightened the buckle, and patted his gun. After smoothing his hair out of habit, he put on his cap. From his pants pocket he took some coins to pay for the shave. He started toward the door. At the door he stopped and turned toward me.

"They told me you would kill me. I came to find out if it was true. But it's not easy to kill. I know what I'm talking about."

Think About It

Are you surprised by what Captain Torres says? Why?

Meet the Author

HERNANDO TÉLLEZ *(1908–1966)*

Hernando Téllez was both a writer and a politician. He was a member of Colombia's parliament. He also represented Colombia for UNESCO. UNESCO is the United Nations Educational, Scientific, and Cultural Organization.

"Lather and Nothing Else" is his most famous story. This story shows Téllez's skill as a writer. It also shows how politics affected his writing. During much of Téllez's lifetime, Colombia's government and the rebels fought for the control of the country. Today, Colombia continues to struggle with political problems.

Check Your Predictions

1. Look back at the answers you gave for the Predict questions. Would you change your answers? Explain.

Understand the Story

2. How does Captain Torres make the barber feel?

3. What does the narrator take pride in?

4. What conflict does the narrator face?

5. How does Torres surprise the barber at the end of the story?

Think About the Story

6. Why does the narrator make the decision that he does?

7. How does the first-person point of view help us to understand the short story?

8. What do you think the narrator will do now that the captain knows he is a rebel?

Extend Your Response

Suppose Captain Torres is the narrator. Retell the story from his point of view. Tell what he is thinking and why. Be sure to describe the barber as Captain Torres might have seen him.

Keys to Literature

mood: the feeling you get from reading a story

> Example: *Windy winter night* and *uneasy* suggest a mood that is tense and gloomy.

irony: a result that is the opposite of what is expected; it is often unfortunate.

> Example: In a famous story, a man sells his favorite watch to have enough money to buy his wife a comb. However, the wife sells her hair to buy her husband a watch chain.

Did You Know?

The Carpathian [kahr-PAY-thee-uhn] Mountains are in central Europe. Many wild animals, such as bears, deer, wolves, and boars, live in the forests in the eastern part of the Carpathians.

Words to Know

game	wild animals hunted for sport or for food
lawsuit	a disagreement brought to court
generations	spans of time between the birth of parents and the birth of their children
feud	a long quarrel between families
civilized	educated or having manners
hesitated	stopped for a moment
clumsiness	awkwardness
possibility	chance

Genre: Short Story

"The Interlopers" is a short story. Read more about short stories on page 467 of the Genre Guide.

The Interlopers

BY SAKI, *adapted*

READ TO FIND OUT...
What do two men in a dark forest learn about conflict?

In a forest somewhere in the eastern Carpathians, a man stood. It was a winter night. He watched and listened like a man who is hunting. But the **game** he looked for was not usually hunted. Ulrich von Gradwitz searched the dark forest for a human enemy.

The forests of von Gradwitz were large and well supplied with game. The small strip of steep woods on its border, however, was not known for good hunting.

There was not much game. But it was the most carefully guarded area of von Gradwitz's land.

▶ Ulrich von Gradwitz [OOL-rihk vawn GRAHD-vihtzh]

Predict

What do you think the conflict in this story will be?

▶ Georg Znaeym
[GAY-awg ZAI-ehm]

A famous **lawsuit**, in the days of von Gradwitz's grandfather, took it from a neighbor. The neighbor was a small landowner with no legal right to the land. They lost the case. But they did not agree with the court's ruling. As a result, there were many fights that followed over hunting rights. It caused a bitter feeling between the families. This feeling lasted for three **generations**.

The **feud** became personal once Ulrich became head of his family. The man he hated most in the world was Georg Znaeym. Znaeym was the head of the neighboring family. The feud might have died down. The families might have reached an agreement. But both men continued to fight each other. As boys, they thirsted for each other's blood. As men, each prayed bad luck might fall on the other.

On this windy winter night, Ulrich called together his men to watch the dark forest. They were to keep a lookout for prowling thieves. The deer usually kept under cover during a storm. Tonight, however, these creatures were uneasy. Instead of sleeping as usual, they were running like driven things. Clearly there was something troubling in the forest. Ulrich could guess from where it came.

Keys to Literature

This paragraph sets the **mood** of the story. It is gloomy and tense.

He walked away by himself. The men on lookout duty were waiting on the crest of the hill. Ulrich wandered far down the steep slopes into the wild tangle of bushes. He looked through the tree trunks for sight or sound of the thieves. He thought to himself what it might be like if he came across his enemy, Georg Znaeym. To meet him alone, that was his chief thought. As he stepped round the trunk of a huge tree, he came face to face with the man he wanted to see.

The two enemies stood glaring at one another for a long, silent moment. Each held a rifle. Each had hate in his heart and murder on his mind. The chance had

come to play out the hatred of a lifetime. But a **civilized** man cannot easily bring himself to shoot down his neighbor. One kills in cold blood and without a word only for a crime against his home and honor.

While the men **hesitated**, there was a splitting crash over their heads. Before they could leap aside, a huge falling tree thundered down on them. Ulrich von Gradwitz found himself stretched on the ground. One arm lay numb beneath him. The other was held in a tangle of branches. Both legs were pinned beneath the fallen mass. His heavy boots had saved his feet from being crushed. His broken bones were not as serious as they might have been. Yet it was clear that he could not move until someone came to free him. The falling twigs had slashed the skin of his face. He winked away some drops of blood from his eyelashes. Only then could he get a view of the disaster.

Predict

What do you think will happen next?

At his side lay Georg Znaeym. He was so close to Ulrich, the two men could have touched. Georg Znaeym was alive. He was also helplessly trapped. All round the men lay thick piles of splintered branches and broken twigs.

The men were glad to be alive. But they were angry at being trapped. It brought on mixed feelings. Solemn thanks and sharp oaths came to Ulrich's lips. Georg was nearly blinded by blood dripping across his eyes. He stopped struggling for a moment. He listened. Then he gave a short, mad laugh.

Think About It

What would you do if you were trapped under a tree with your enemy?

"So you're not killed as you ought to be. But you're caught, anyway," Georg cried. "Caught fast. Ha! What a joke. Ulrich von Gradwitz is trapped in his stolen forest. There's justice for you!"

He laughed again.

"I'm caught in my own forest land," returned Ulrich. "When my men come to free us, you will wish you were in some other spot. Caught hunting on a neighbor's land. Shame on you."

Georg was silent for a moment. Then he answered quietly.

Think About It

Why does each man want his men to arrive first?

"Are you sure your men will find much to free? I have men, too. They were in the forest tonight. They will be here first. They will do the freeing. They will drag me out from under these branches. With a little **clumsiness** on their part, they might roll this huge trunk on you. Your men will find you dead. To make it look good, I will send my regrets to your family."

"Good," snarled Georg, "good. We'll fight this out to the death. You, I, and our men. No outsiders will come between us. Death and hell's fires to you, Ulrich von Gradwitz."

"The same to you, Georg Znaeym," said Ulrich. "Land thief, game grabber."

Both men spoke with the bitter **possibility** of losing. Each knew that it might be a long time before his men found him. It was a plain case of who would come first.

Both had given up the useless struggle to get free. The mass of wood held them down. Ulrich tried only to bring one partly free arm to his coat. He hoped to reach his water. Even after he reached it, it was a long time before he got any water down his throat. But what a heaven-sent swallow it was! It was winter, and little snow had fallen as yet. Because of this, the captives suffered less from the cold than might be expected. Even so, the water was refreshing to the injured man. He looked across at his enemy with a small throb of pity. Georg could just barely keep the groans of pain and weariness from his lips.

"Could you reach this water if I threw it over to you?" asked Ulrich suddenly. "One should be as well off as possible."

"No, I can hardly see anything. There is so much blood caked around my eyes," said Georg. "In any case, I don't take water from an enemy."

Ulrich was silent for a few minutes. He lay listening to the low whistle of the wind. An idea was slowly growing in his brain. It became stronger every time he looked across the branches. In the pain Ulrich was feeling, his old hatred seemed to be dying.

"Neighbor," he said at last. "Do as you please if your men come first. It was a fair deal. But as for me, I've changed my mind. If my men come first, you shall be the first to be helped. You will be treated as my guest. We have fought like devils all our lives. Fought over this stupid strip of forest. A place where the trees can't even stand up in the wind. Lying here tonight, thinking, I've learned we've been fools. There are better things in life than winning a quarrel over land.

Think About It

Why does Ulrich decide to give Georg some water?

Think About It

Why do Ulrich's feelings toward Georg begin to change?

Neighbor, if you will help me to bury the old quarrel, I—I will ask you to be my friend."

Georg Znaeym was silent for a long time. Ulrich thought perhaps he had fainted from his injuries. Then Georg spoke slowly and in jerks.

"How the market square would stare and talk if we rode into the town square together. No one living can remember seeing a Znaeym and a von Gradwitz having a friendly talk. What peace there would be among the forest folk if we were to end our feud. If we were to make peace among our people, no outsider could meddle. You would spend nights under my roof. I would feast with you at your castle. I would never fire a shot on your land except as your guest. You could shoot with me down in the marshes where the wild birds are. In all the countryside, none could stop us if we chose to make peace. I thought I would hate you all my life. Now I think I have changed my mind about things. You offered me water.... Ulrich von Gradwitz, I will be your friend."

For a time both men were silent. They turned over in their minds the great changes of this sudden friendship. In the cold, gloomy forests, the wind tore in gusts at the branches and trees. The two men lay and waited for the help that would bring freedom. Each prayed secretly that his men might be the first to arrive. Then he might be the first to attend to the enemy that was now a friend.

Presently, as the wind dropped for a moment, Ulrich broke the silence.

"Let's shout for help," he said. "In this lull, our voices might carry."

"They won't carry far through the trees and brush," said Georg. "But we can try. Together, then."

The two raised their voices in a long hunting call.

They listened. There was no answer. "Together again," said Ulrich a few minutes later.

"I heard something that time, I think," said Ulrich.

"I heard nothing but the deadly wind," said Georg.

There was silence again for some minutes. Then Ulrich gave a joyful cry.

"I can see figures coming through the wood. They are following the way I came down the hill."

Both men raised their voices in as loud a shout as they could gather.

"They hear us! They've stopped. Now they see us. They're running down the hill toward us," cried Ulrich.

"How many of them are there?" asked Georg.

"I can't see clearly," said Ulrich. "Nine or ten."

Predict

Whose men do you think have arrived?

"Then they are yours," said Georg. "I had only seven out with me."

"They are making all the speed they can. Brave lads," said Ulrich gladly.

"Are they your men?" asked Georg. "Are they your men?" he said again eagerly. Ulrich did not answer.

Keys to Literature

The ending of the story is an example of **irony**. What did you expect to happen?

"No," said Ulrich with a laugh. It was the silly laugh of a man who is suddenly very afraid.

"Who are they?" asked Georg quickly. He strained his eyes to see what the other wished he had not seen.

"Wolves."

Meet the Author

SAKI *(1870–1916)*

Saki's real name was H. H. Munro. He called himself Saki after a character in a Persian poem. He was born in Burma, in Southeast Asia. Burma was then a British colony. He was raised in England, however. As a young adult, he returned to Burma briefly to work as a police officer. But after getting ill, he returned to England. There he began his true profession: writing.

Saki is well known for humor in his stories. He was a master of irony, as shown in "The Interlopers." Saki was also a reporter. As a reporter, he traveled around Eastern Europe. This may have inspired the setting for "The Interlopers." His most famous works include the short story collections *Reginald* and *Beasts and Super-Beasts* and the novels *Unbearable Bassington* and *When William Came.*

Check Your Predictions

1. Look back at the answers you gave for the Predict questions. Would you change your answers? Explain.

Understand the Story

2. Why is Ulrich in the forest?

3. How do Ulrich and Georg feel about each other when they meet in the forest?

4. How do Ulrich and Georg become trapped in the forest?

5. What happens when the two men call for help?

Think About the Story

6. What role does nature play in the conflict between Ulrich and Georg?

7. What kind of mood does Saki create in this short story? Give examples from the story.

8. Why is the ending an example of irony?

Extend Your Response

Imagine that the two men are rescued. Write a paragraph telling what happens in the weeks after they are rescued. How has their relationship changed? What do people in the town think?

Summaries

Arachne Arachne is a young maiden in Greece. She is known for her beautiful weaving. People come from all over Greece to see her work. Arachne is proud of her skill. She thinks she can weave as well as the goddess Athena. Arachne's pride angers Athena. Arachne challenges Athena to a weaving contest. Athena teaches Arachne a lesson about having too much pride.

Lather and Nothing Else The narrator is a skilled barber who takes pride in his work. The barber is also a secret rebel. He does not approve of the army leaders who run the government. When the captain of the army visits his shop, the barber struggles with his feelings. He must choose between killing the captain and giving him a good shave.

The Interlopers For many years, the von Gradwitz and Znaeym families have disagreed about who owns a piece of land. Ulrich von Gradwitz and Georg Znaeym are bitter enemies. One night, the two men happen to meet in the forest. They are trapped by a fallen tree. While they are trapped, both men learn that their fight with each other is foolish. However, they have a new struggle to face.

challenged
dazzling
humbly
cowardly
hesitated
possibility

Vocabulary Review

Match each word in the box with its meaning. Write the word next to its meaning on a separate sheet of paper.

1. lacking courage
2. bright
3. stopped for a moment
4. called to a fight or contest
5. with meek or modest feeling
6. chance

Chapter Quiz

**Write your answers in one or two complete sentences.
Use a separate sheet of paper.**

1. Arachne What is Arachne's main fault?

2. Arachne How does Athena punish Arachne?

3. Lather and Nothing Else Why does the barber shake?

4. Lather and Nothing Else What choice does the barber make?

5. The Interlopers Why are Georg and Ulrich enemies?

6. The Interlopers Who discovers Georg and Ulrich in the forest?

Critical Thinking

7. Arachne In what way is Arachne responsible for her punishment from Athena?

8. The Interlopers Why do Ulrich's and Georg's feelings change?

Chapter Activity

Imagine that the barber and the captain from "Lather and Nothing Else" were trapped under a tree like the men in "The Interlopers." What do you think might happen? Rewrite "The Interlopers" with the barber and the captain as characters.

Unit 1 **Review**

On a separate sheet of paper, write the letter that best completes each sentence below.

1. In "The Fly," the boy proves that the moneylender is not telling the truth by

   A. telling the judge that his parents were not home.
   B. making the moneylender angry.
   C. telling a riddle.
   D. asking his parents to pay him.

2. In "By Any Other Name," Premila and Santha leave the school because

   A. the headmistress gives them new names.
   B. Premila has not studied for her test.
   C. Santha is the only student who eats Indian food.
   D. Premila's teacher says that Indians cheat.

3. The cabin in "The Small Cabin"

   A. burns down.
   B. is rebuilt.
   C. is sold.
   D. is deserted.

4. In "Arachne," Arachne suffers from having too much

   A. beauty.
   B. talent.
   C. pride.
   D. money.

5. The barber in "Lather and Nothing Else" has to decide whether to

   A. join the rebels.
   B. kill the captain.
   C. cut the captain's hair.
   D. join the army.

6. In "The Interlopers," the two men learn

   A. how to track down an enemy.
   B. how foolish the feud is.
   C. how to avoid each other.
   D. how dangerous the other's men are.

Making Connections

On a separate sheet of paper, write your answers to the following questions.

7. Which selection in this unit did you like best? Explain. Give examples.

8. Which character in this unit did you think was the most intelligent? Explain why.

Writing an Essay

Choose one selection from the unit and rewrite the ending. If the selection is a poem, change the last few lines. If the selection is fiction or nonfiction, change the last paragraph.

Unit Two

The Snowstorm, detail by Francisco de Goya y Lucientes

What challenge are these people facing? How do you think they feel?

Learning Objectives

- Understand what plot is.
- Understand a character's motivation.
- Understand what a folktale is.
- Identify details.
- Recognize the theme of a story.
- Name the setting of a story.
- Identify the effects of repetition in a story.

Theme Preview: Challenges

Life is full of challenges. Some challenges require physical strength. Others call for intelligence, mental toughness, or strength of character. The stories in this chapter show how characters deal with different challenges. Seeing how these characters solve their problems—or why they fail—can help us learn more about ourselves and our world.

Keys to Literature

plot: the action of a story or a play. Most stories have a problem, and at the end, a solution.

> Example: The first major event in this story's plot is when the women ask the king for help.

motivation: the reason why a character behaves as he or she does

> Example: The women ask the king for help because they are tired of paying for weddings.

Did You Know?

Tourists still visit the two small mountains in Cambodia that inspired this tale. Known as "Man Hill" and "Woman Hill," they sit close together in Kampong Cham province, overlooking the Mekong River.

Words to Know

proposed	offered marriage to someone
custom	a way of doing things or a practice that's gone on for a long time
ministers	people who help run the government of a country
lantern	a covering for a light with see-through openings
slender	thin

Genre: Folktale

"The Mountain of the Men and the Mountain of the Women" is a folktale. Read more about folktales in the Learn More About It on page 75 or on page 466 of the Genre Guide.

The Mountain of the Men and the Mountain of the Women

RETOLD BY TOUCH NEAK AND ALICE LUCAS, *adapted*

Long ago, in the Kampong Cham province of Cambodia, marriage was very different from how it is today. In those days, girls **proposed** to boys. If the boy said yes, the girl had to pay for the wedding. She also had to buy expensive gifts for the boy.

This **custom** went on for many years. The young women thought it was very unfair. They were not as strong as the young men. It was harder for them to make money.

All over the country, girls talked about this problem. They decided to go to the king. At that time, Jayavarman the First was king of Cambodia. He was the king who had brought together two kingdoms: the kingdom of the north and the kingdom of the south. He made them into the mighty Angkor Empire.

The king had made great cities. His buildings had beautiful stone carvings. He was a very good king. The girls trusted that he would help them. But one girl reminded them that the king himself was a man. Men liked the marriage custom very well.

Another girl said, "We must trick the king. We must think of a way to get him to change the marriage custom!" So the girls made a secret plan. The young women who were the best speakers traveled to the city of Angkor to visit the king.

READ TO FIND OUT...
Why would young women want to compete with young men in building a mountain?

▶ Kampong Cham
[KAHM-pahng CHAHM]

Keys to Literature

The women's problem is the beginning of the story's **plot**. The problem starts the action.

▶ Jayavarman
[JY-ya-VAR-muhn]

The young women met with the king Jayavarman. They bowed and said, "Most high Lord, we ask that you listen to our story. We girls are weak compared to the strong men of our country. Yet we are the ones who must propose marriage to a boy. And we must pay for the wedding! We must buy fine gifts for him and his family! It is very hard for us to do these things. Why not have the boys propose marriage to us? It would be easier for them to pay for the wedding and the gifts. Do you not agree?"

King Jayavarman was silent for a long time. He looked down at the bowed heads of the girls. At last he said, "Perhaps you are right, beautiful daughters of the Khmer. But what am I to do? This is the custom of our land. How can I change the Khmer way of proposing marriage?"

The boldest girl raised her head and spoke. She pressed her hands together to show respect. She said, "Great leader of the Khmer people, may we tell you of a plan?"

The king nodded.

Keys to Literature

Motivation is why a character acts a certain way. Here, the king thinks before he answers. If he agrees with the women, the men might not honor him as much. This may be his motivation for not agreeing with the women right away.

▶ The Khmer [kuh-MARE] were one of the first groups of people to live in Cambodia.

The girl said, "Call all the young men and women of our country together. Tell each group they will build a mountain to show respect for you. Give them five days to finish the task. On the morning of the fifth day, the work must stop. Count the days from the time the Morning Star rises in the dark sky. That is the time before the sun shows its face.

"When the Morning Star rises on the first day, the work must begin. When the Morning Star rises for the fifth time, the work must stop."

The king liked the idea of having two mountains built to honor him. There were not many mountains in Kampong Cham province. The king thought he could stand on the top of these mountains and be closer to heaven. He could also watch for enemies from the mountain top. Since he himself was a man, he believed the men would win this contest.

The king agreed to the girls' plan. The next day, his **ministers** called all the young people to the king's palace. As they bowed before him, the king said, "The young women are unhappy with our country's marriage customs. They want the men to propose to them and pay for the wedding!"

The young men laughed at such a foolish idea.

The king shouted, "Silence! To be fair to the girls, I have made a plan. Listen carefully." The king told the young people about the plan to build two mountains. He explained how the days would be counted by the rise of the Morning Star.

Then the king said, "Come with me. I will show you where to build." He walked along the east bank of the Mekong River. He showed them the place where the mountains were to be built.

The king said, "Tomorrow, as the Morning Star rises, I will beat the royal drum. That will be the signal for work to begin. You may work both day and night for

Predict

The Morning Star is the planet Venus. It shines just above the horizon before sunrise. How do you think it will be important to this story?

Think About It

Folktales often teach us about human nature. In this tale, the king says the plan is his idea. What does that tell you about the king?

five days. But remember: When the Morning Star rises for the fifth time, you must stop work. Do you understand?"

The young men and women nodded.

The king said, "When the day is light, I will come to see your work. If the men have built a higher mountain, the women must keep the marriage customs we have now. But if the women's mountain is higher, the customs will change. The men will propose to the women and pay for the wedding and the gifts."

When the king had left, the men laughed and joked about the plan. They said, "No woman can do such hard work. We will win easily. Let us go home and rest so we are ready to work tomorrow."

That night, while the men were sleeping, the women met. They were afraid they might lose unless they started work right away. Quietly, they walked to the building place by the river. They dug the dirt to make it loose. The next day it would be easy for them to dig up big stones. They would roll the stones together to make the base of their mountain. When the women finished, they hid their work with branches. No one would guess they had already started.

When the Morning Star rose the next day, the king beat the royal drum. The work began. The men worked all day. The women worked all day, too. When evening came, the men rested and drank cool drinks. They were sure they were ahead of the women. But the women kept working all night. They took turns resting for only short periods of time.

The Morning Star rose on the second day.

The women stopped working and had a meeting. The men saw them sitting and talking. They said, "Ha, look at those lazy women. We don't have to work too hard." That night, while the men slept, the women worked.

Keys to Literature

How do you think the men's attitude will affect what happens in the **plot**?

Predict

Who do you think will win the contest? Why do you think so?

On the third day, as the Morning Star rose, some of the women went to the market. They bought thin, clear paper, string, and a candle. Some other women went to the forest to cut bamboo.

The men said, "Look, some women are going to the market. Others are going to the woods to get out of the hot sun." The men stopped their work, too. They sat in the cool shade. On the third night, the women worked while the men slept.

On the fourth day, the men saw the women sitting beside their small mountain. The men said, "Look at those foolish women! They must be chewing betel nuts instead of working!" The men worked for a while, then rested under a tree.

▶ Many Asians chew betel nuts, just as Americans chew gum.

What do you think the women had been doing? They had been making their own Morning Star! They cut the bamboo into thin pieces. They arranged the pieces in the shape of a star. They tied the corners together with strong grass. Then they covered the star with clear paper. Now the star looked like a **lantern**. They tied a long string to their star. Then they hid it in the grass.

That night the women worked again while the men slept. But after only a few hours, they took the star lantern from its hiding place. They put the candle inside. The evening breeze lifted the lantern high in the sky.

The women began to cry. They said, "Oh no, the Morning Star has risen for the fifth time. We must stop building. Oh, we have certainly lost the race."

The men said, "Listen to those crying women. We have certainly won the race. Let us sleep a little longer. We will rest for a big celebration tomorrow."

So the men went back to sleep. The women worked for the rest of the night. When the true Morning Star rose, they stopped.

When the sun came up, the king and his ministers came to look at the mountains. The king saw the women's tall mountain with its **slender** peak.

The king saw the men's mountain. It had a strong, wide base. But it was flat on top. It had no peak at all! It was plain to see the women had won.

The king kept his word. This was his order: "From this day on, it must be the man's responsibility to propose to the woman. He must buy fine gifts for her and her family. And he must also pay for the wedding feast. In this way, the men of the Khmer Kingdom will honor the women."

If you travel up the Mekong River on the way to the Kampong Cham, you will see two mountains. One is the Mountain of the Men. The other is the Mountain of the Women. You will see for yourself which mountain is higher and more beautiful.

Keys to Literature

The women cry and say the Morning Star has risen. What is their **motivation** for doing this?

Think About It

Do you think the men will be surprised about the new rules? Why?

Check Your Predictions

1. Look back at the answers you gave for the Predict questions. Would you change your answers? Explain.

Understand the Folktale

2. This folktale explains how something changed long ago in Cambodia. What changed?

3. What challenges do the women face?

4. What tricks do the women use to win the contest?

5. What is the first thing the women do to help them win the contest?

Think About the Folktale

6. Why do you think the king agrees to hold a contest?

7. The men and the women view the contest in different ways. What are the differences?

8. The women in this folktale do many clever things. Do you think they are fair to the men? Why?

Extend Your Response

Imagine you could be a radio sports reporter, watching the contest between the men and the women. What would you be saying into the microphone during the most exciting part of the contest? Write a script telling what you would say.

Learn More About It

A folktale is an old story that has passed from one generation to the next. In olden times, people didn't write down the stories. They just told them over and over. This is how folktales become part of a culture.

Because people passed folktales by word of mouth, there are often many versions of the same story. People have written down some folktales only in modern times. Many folktales have been lost over the centuries. Recording them may help keep them for future generations.

Folktales are a type of oral literature. Some other types of oral literature are fables, fairy tales, legends, and myths. Folktales deal with everyday characters and may have repetition and rhyme. Fables usually tell stories about animals. They often teach people a lesson or moral. Fairy tales often feature a person who reaches an amazing goal. A legend often hints about what is important to a culture. It may tell about a brave heroine or hero who helps a society in some way. A myth often explains how things in the world came to be. For example, some myths tell why the moon is in our sky. Others tell how the world began or how the ocean was created.

Apply and Connect

Do you think "The Mountain of the Men and the Mountain of the Women" is a good story to tell aloud? Why or why not?

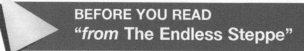
Keys to Literature

details: pieces of information that help create a picture for the reader

> Example: *They had no heat, no floors, and no glass in the windows.*

theme: the main idea of a story, play, or poem

> Example: The theme of this story is that the way you treat people can make a big difference in their lives.

Words to Know

steppe	a large area of flat grassland
manure	animal waste
whitewash	a mixture used like paint to make something white
cubbyhole	small shelf or cupboard used for storing things
pumice	a type of rock, sometimes used to scrub away dead skin
gauze	very thin cloth used for bandages
outcast	a person whom other people do not accept
cast off	thrown away; sent away

Genre: Autobiography

The Endless Steppe is an autobiography. Read more about autobiographies on page 466 of the Genre Guide.

from The Endless Steppe

BY ESTHER HAUTZIG, *adapted*

READ TO FIND OUT...
What happens when Esther is forced to live with Vanya the bum?

Spring came to the **steppe** of Siberia. When I think of spring there, I always think of the thick mud. When the snow melted, the steppe became an ocean of mud. Walking through it was like walking through knee-deep molasses. It took energy to pull a foot up from the bottom of this mud. Often one of my shoes would get stuck. I would have to go back and look for it.

Mud or no mud, I was happy in spring. I had a friend to whisper and gossip with—Svetlana. I played tag and hopscotch. Svetlana and I helped each other in school. She helped me with grammar and spelling. I helped her with ideas for writing. Going to school in Siberia was wonderful. Coming back home to the hut was not.

▶ Svetlana [SVEHT-lah-nah]

Think About It

Who is the *I* in this autobiography?

There were ten of us living in the hut—several other people beside our family. When summer came, the heat was terrible. The hut was an awful little oven with the ten of us inside it. Our tempers rose.

Father decided to look for a new place for our family to live.

On the north side of the village, there were some empty huts. They were empty for a reason. They had no heat, no floors, and no glass in the windows. But they were empty. Father asked the village housing chief if we could live in one of the huts.

A miracle happened. We were allowed to move into one of the empty huts. Our family would be alone at last.

That little hut became my dream house. Every day, after working in the potato patch, I went to the hut and cleaned it. Also, we picked up **manure**, mixed it with clay, and made new bricks. We fixed or replaced the old bricks in the walls. Father got some **whitewash** at his job. We painted the walls with it. Someplace or other, we found glass for the windows.

Father made an outdoor stove out of bricks for summer cooking. We could cook our own little flour cakes or soup. We wouldn't have to line up with other people to eat.

There was a public bath in the village. To go there was Mother's dearest wish. We would have to save up for such a treat. It would mean eating a little less for a week or two. But wouldn't it be wonderful to feel clean before we moved into our own home?

The bath was a small building with two doors—one for women and one for men. We found that Mother was not the only woman who wanted to be clean. The line was long. The wait would be a couple of hours, at least. We waited.

There were two rooms in the bath. One had faucets along the walls. The other was a steam room. In there, you used twigs to rub and clean yourself.

Think About It

How can you tell that the hut means a lot to Esther and her family?

Keys to Literature

Details are pieces of information that help readers picture a story's events, people, and places. Esther and her mother waited at least two hours for a bath. What does this detail tell you about life in Siberia?

We were sent to the faucet room. We were given a
cubbyhole for our clothes, a bowl, and **pumice**. We
filled our bowls at the faucet, sat down on a stone bench,
and scrubbed ourselves. The water was hot. Mother was
delighted. Now we were really ready to move.

Outside our hut, there was a small piece of land that
no one seemed to be using. We would turn it into a
vegetable patch. We had potatoes, tomato plants, and
corn seed.

Things were hard to come by in this land.
Whenever something came your way, you took it.
Svetlana's father had gotten a large amount of **gauze**
from a hospital. (I did not know how he had gotten it.
I did not want to ask.) Svetlana asked me if I wanted
some. I said yes. I would use it for curtains.

Svetlana said, "You're going to use white hospital
gauze for curtains, Esther?"

I said, "You will see."

Predict

What will Esther do with
the gauze?

I began to save onion peels. I asked Svetlana to do the same. In school, we had learned that if you boil onion peels in water, you get a yellow dye.

When I had a big pile of onion peel, I boiled it in water. The water became a pot of pale yellow dye. I put the gauze in this and let it stay for several hours. It worked! The gauze was now a pretty yellow. I dried it out in the sun and then I made my curtains.

The hut was heaven. We ate when we wanted to. We slept when we wanted to. At night we would sit outside and watch the Siberian sky. There was always something to see. We would sit there quietly, quietly.

It was too good to last.

One day the village housing chief came to our hut when I was alone. He told me that the next day someone would be coming to live with us.

I said, "Who is it going to be?"

The housing chief said, "Vanya the bum."

This was awful.

▶ Vanya [VAHN-yah]

I had been taught never to call anyone names. But everyone called this man with one leg, "Vanya the bum." He was the village beggar. People said he stole. Now this dirty bum was going to live with us.

When I gave the news to my parents, they couldn't believe it either.

Father said, "Vanya, the bum...?"

Predict

How will Mother treat Vanya the bum?

Mother coughed. That was a signal to my father. She did not like the way he was speaking. She said Vanya should not be called a bum. In fact, he should not be called Vanya, either. He must have a proper name. When we met him, we should introduce ourselves as usual.

Father agreed. He gave the old speech about not judging people by the way they looked.

I stood on one foot and then the other, listening. To me, Vanya the bum was coming to live with us.

The idea made me scared and sick.

The next evening, Vanya the bum stood at our open door.

He said, "May I come in?"

Mother said, "Of course you may."

Father went toward him. He said, "Good evening."

I felt Mother's eyes on me. I said, "Good evening. My name is Esther Rudomin. What's yours?"

He said, "Vanya."

His eyes went from Father to Mother and back to me.

He added, "My name is Ivan Petrovich, my child." There was a tiny spark in his eyes.

Father said, "Welcome to our house, Ivan Petrovich."

The change from village bum to Ivan Petrovich did not happen overnight. At first he was a shadow from the dark world of the homeless, an **outcast**. He left very early in the morning. When he came home, he went right to his corner of the hut. He talked very little. He would eat bits of food he had picked up, then go to sleep.

After a few weeks, he began to change. He started to eat with us. He would share whatever food he brought.

Then he began to talk. Ivan Petrovich was a shoemaker from the Ukraine. He had read many books. But once he had talked too much or talked too carelessly. Maybe he had been misunderstood. He had been sent to prison in Siberia. He never knew why. When they finally let him out of prison, he had only one leg left. He had gone from village to village, begging.

Soon he began to wash himself. That made us happier than I can tell. He began to comb his beard. He began to walk tall. He became Ivan Petrovich.

Think About It

The family is not happy that Vanya is moving in with them. Why do they use such good manners to greet him?

Keys to Literature

What **details** show that Vanya thinks of himself as an outcast?

As Ivan Petrovich began to look at himself with new eyes, so did the people in the village. They did not think of him as a bum anymore. They thought of him as just another human being **cast off** on the great steppe of Siberia.

One day he disappeared. He left one morning as always but did not come back that night. That was the last time we saw Ivan Petrovich, who used to be called Vanya the bum.

Meet the Author

ESTHER HAUTZIG *(Born 1930)*

Esther Hautzig was ten years old when the Soviet Union invaded Poland and forced her family to move to Siberia. Hautzig spent five years there. In 1947, she sailed to America. She wanted to be a teacher. However, she couldn't get a job because of her accent. Instead, she worked for a company that published children's books.

The Endless Steppe is Hautzig's most famous book. It has been printed in many languages and won the Jane Addams Book Award. That award goes to books that honor peace, justice, and world community. Hautzig wrote several books with crafts and recipes from her life in Siberia. She also wrote other stories about her childhood. Hautzig believes each life story is important to tell. She encourages children to keep journals and tell their own unique stories.

Check Your Predictions

1. Look back at the answers you gave for the Predict questions. Would you change your answers? Explain.

Understand the Autobiography

2. What are the challenges Esther's family must face in Siberia?

3. What details tell you that the new hut is better than the old one?

4. What happened to turn Ivan Petrovich into a bum?

5. What is challenging about living with Vanya?

Think About the Autobiography

6. How would you describe the family in this story?

7. What lesson about people does Vanya's story teach?

8. Why do you think the author wrote her autobiography?

Extend Your Response

Write three rules about how to treat other people that you would enforce in a perfect world. Write how the world would be different if everyone followed your rules.

Learn More About It

SIBERIA

Siberia is an area in northern Asia. All of Siberia is in Russia. It is extremely cold most of the year. Life can be very hard in Siberia.

A railroad being built in Siberia during the early 1900s.

Much of Siberia's northern arctic land is covered with tundra. Tundra is a mucky soil. Land under its surface is icy. It is frozen even in the summer. No trees grow there. Only mosses, small shrubs, and lichens can survive. Lichen is a mix of fungus and algae.

Siberia has high mountains. It also has the deepest lake in the world—Lake Baikal. The steppes, or grasslands, are in the southwest. Siberia's richest soil is in the steppes. Farmers grow oats, wheat, and barley. They raise sheep, cattle, and reindeer.

Siberia has many natural resources. It has oil and coal. It also has minerals like gold, tin, and diamonds. Much of Russia's timber comes from Siberia.

Russian rulers used to send people to prison and labor camps there. It was hard to escape into the harsh cold. In recent years, the government has looked for ways to attract people to Siberia. That is because it needs workers to develop its rich resources.

Apply and Connect
Esther Hautzig lived in the fertile Siberian steppes. How might her life have been different if she'd lived in the northern regions of Siberia?

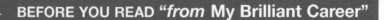

BEFORE YOU READ *"from* My Brilliant Career*"*

Keys to Literature

setting: the time and place of the action in a story

> Example: This story's setting is Possum Gulley, Australia, in 1890.

repetition: words or sentences used over and over to create a feeling or mood

> Example: *This was life—my life! This was my career, my brilliant career!*

Did You Know?

The outback is the vast inland part of Australia. Few people live in the outback. It is dry and very hot in summer. It was settled mostly by farmers raising cattle and sheep in the 1800s.

Words to Know

veranda	a large, open porch
drought	a long period of time with no rain
tripod	a stand with three legs
lever	a rod or bar used to lift things
weariness	tiredness
career	the work a person chooses to do in life
bulwarks	strong supports

Genre: Novel

My Brilliant Career is a novel. Read more about novels on page 467 of the Genre Guide.

from My Brilliant Career

BY MILES FRANKLIN, *adapted*

Possum Gulley, Australia, 1890

My father called to me, "Sybylla, what are you doing? Where is your mother?"

I said, "I'm ironing. Mother's taking care of some chickens. What do you want?"

It was two o'clock in the afternoon. The thermometer hanging in the shade of the **veranda** said 105 degrees.

READ TO FIND OUT…

Why does Sybylla long to get away from the family's farm?

Keys to Literature

The first line tells the basic **setting** of this story. What does the third paragraph tell about the setting?

Predict

How will they get the cows back onto their feet?

Father said, "I see Blackshaw coming across the flat. Call your mother. You bring the leg-ropes. I've got the dog-leg. Come at once. We'll get these cows back on their feet. Poor devils—they're so weak they're falling down. We might as well kill them now. But there might be rain by the next moon. This **drought** can't last forever."

I called my mother, got the leg-ropes, and started off. I pulled my sunbonnet closely over my head. Clouds of dust were blowing from the west. I needed to protect my eyes.

The dog-leg that father was talking about was three poles about eight or ten feet long. They were strapped together to make a **tripod**. Father had made the dog-leg to help us lift cows that had fallen down.

We stood the tripod up on the ground. Across the top of the tripod, we placed a longer pole. We used this as a **lever**, putting our weight at one end to lift the cow at the other end. The cow was tied to the lever with leg-ropes. One rope went around the cow near its front legs. The other rope went close to its back legs.

Think About It

Why do you think some cows are used to the dog-leg?

New cows were not used to the dog-leg. We had a hard time with them. But the cows who were used to it would help themselves. Up they would go, nice as a daisy.

The only trick to the dog-leg was to pull the pole back quickly, before the cow could move. Otherwise, the ropes would trip the cow, and it would fall again.

On this afternoon we had six cows to lift. We struggled hard and got five cows back on their feet. Then we walked to where the last cow was lying. It was a stony spot on the side of a hill. There was no shade.

Blackshaw turned her around by her tail. Mother and I fixed the dog-leg and got the ropes ready. We got the cow up, but the poor animal was so weak that she fell down again.

Keys to Literature

The details here tell more about the **setting**. What is it like?

Keys to Literature

Why does the author use **repetition** of the words *weary* and *weariness*?

Think About It

Does the narrator really think her career is brilliant?

▶ A *peasant* is a poor farm worker.

We decided to let her rest a few minutes before trying to lift her once more. There was not a blade of grass to be seen. The ground was too dusty to sit on. We were so hot and tired, we could not say more than one word to each other. We waited in silence in the blazing sun. We closed our eyes to shut out the dust.

Weariness! Weariness!

Weariness was on my mother's delicate face. Weariness was in my father's dusty face. Blackshaw was weary and said so. He wiped the dust from his face. His sweat had turned the dust to mud. The poor cow lying at our feet was weary.

All of nature was weary. It seemed to sing a sad, tired song with the hot wind. The wind was like the breath of a furnace. It roared among the trees.

Everything was weary, everything but the sun. He felt his power. He was never tired. He would never let up. He swung boldly in the sky, looking down on his helpless victims.

Weariness! Weariness!

This was life—my life! This was my **career**, my brilliant career! I was fifteen—fifteen!

It seemed that in a few short hours I would be as old as the adults who stood around me. I looked at them as they stood there. They were weary. They were on their way down the other side of the hill of life.

When they were young, I'm sure they had dreamed of the better life. Maybe they had even known a better life. But here they were. This had been their life. This was their career. It would probably be mine, too. My life—my career—my brilliant career!

I say nothing against the lower life. Peasants are the **bulwarks** of every nation. For someone who has a peasant's soul, it is a good, honest life. When times are good and the seasons are kind and gentle, a peasant's life is a grand life. But to me the life of a peasant is awful. The people around me work from morning until night. Then they enjoy their hard-earned sleep. They have only two things in their life—work and sleep.

Work and sleep were not enough for me. There was a third part in me which cried out to be fed. I longed for the arts. Music was a great love of mine. I borrowed every book in the neighborhood. I stayed up late to read them when I should have been sleeping. Since I slept less, my work was harder for me than for other children my age.

That third part of me was the strongest part. I live a dream-life with writers, artists, and musicians. Hope whispered sweet, cruel lies to me. It told me that one day my dream-life would be real. That dream-life was like a shining lake I could see in the distance. The lake called to me to come and sail on its silver waters.

Think About It

Do you think Sybylla will ever reach her "shining lake"?

Meet the Author

MILES FRANKLIN *(1879–1954)*

Miles Franklin grew up on her family's cattle ranch in Australia. She stole hours away from her chores to write. *My Brilliant Career* was Franklin's first book. She wrote it when she was a teenager. When it was published, she became an instant celebrity!

Franklin was a social worker as well as a writer. She cared deeply about human rights. She worked with women's groups in Chicago and London. She also nursed soldiers in Greece during World War I. Then Franklin moved back to Australia. She wrote many books about pioneer life there. Today, the Miles Franklin Literary Award is an important honor for fiction writers.

Check Your Predictions

1. Look back at the answer you gave for the Predict question. Would you change your answer? Explain.

Understand the Story

2. What is the setting of the story?

3. Quote one line from the story that shows this author is writing in first-person point of view.

4. What is the challenge the farmers face in this story?

Think About the Story

5. How is Sybylla like the other characters?

6. How is Sybylla different from the other characters?

7. How does the setting influence Sybylla's life?

8. The author repeats the words *weary* and *weariness* many times. What feeling or mood does this create?

Extend Your Response

The selection is part of a novel called *My Brilliant Career*. If you were writing this novel, what would happen next? Explain in a few sentences.

Summaries

The Mountain of the Men and the Mountain of the Women The young women of Cambodia are tired of proposing marriage and paying for weddings. To solve this problem, they convince the king to arrange a mountain-building contest to decide who proposes and pays. Through hard work—and clever tricks—the women win the contest.

The Endless Steppe Esther remembers growing up in Siberia. She and her family are pleased to be able to move into a small hut. Then they are told that Vanya the bum must move in with them. Although they do not like the idea, they are polite and respectful. In time, their kindness helps Vanya regain his self-respect.

My Brilliant Career Sybylla and her parents lead a hard life on their farm in Australia. Sybylla longs for more in life. Yet she realizes there is a huge distance between her present life and the life she dreams about.

Vocabulary Review

For each sentence below, write *true* if the underlined word is used correctly. If it is not used correctly, change the underlined word to make the sentence true. Use a separate sheet of paper.

1. The nurse wrapped the wound with some <u>gauze</u>.
2. The young man had lost weight and was now quite <u>slender</u>.
3. Our pond overflowed last summer because of the <u>drought</u>.
4. It was our <u>custom</u> to celebrate Mothers' Day with a dinner.
5. My sister's favorite <u>career</u> was reading the comics on Sunday.

Chapter Quiz

**Write your answers in one or two complete sentences.
Use a separate sheet of paper.**

1. The Mountain of the Men and the Mountain of the Women
   Why do the women think the marriage custom is unfair?

2. The Mountain of the Men and the Mountain of the Women In
   what two ways is the women's mountain better than the
   men's mountain?

3. The Endless Steppe Why is the first hut so uncomfortable?

4. The Endless Steppe Why does Mother insist that they use
   the name Ivan Petrovich, instead of Vanya?

5. My Brilliant Career What job does the family have to do
   together during this story?

6. My Brilliant Career What does Sybylla say are the only two
   things peasants do?

Critical Thinking

7. The Mountain of the Men and the Mountain of the Women
   What lesson do you think the men should have learned
   from losing the contest?

8. The Endless Steppe Why do you think Esther goes to all that
   trouble to dye and sew gauze into curtains?

Chapter Activity

What do you imagine happened to Ivan Petrovich, who used
to be Vanya the bum? In a couple of paragraphs, tell what
you think happens to him next.

The Life Line, detail by Winslow Homer

What is the hero doing in this painting? Why do you think the painting is called The Life Line?

Learning Objectives

- Understand who the hero of the story is.
- Recognize dialogue.
- Identify characters and their character traits.
- Recognize how suspense is used.
- Understand what a climax is.

Preview Activity

Think of people whom you admire, who have achieved the impossible. Discuss these heroes with a partner. What makes them heroes?

Theme Preview: Heroes

Heroes have existed throughout the ages. Some have saved lives. Some have built nations. Some have taken great risks for their beliefs. Heroes make the world a better place. In this chapter, you will meet heroes who put their own lives in danger to save the lives of others.

Keys to Literature

hero: the main character in a story who acts with great courage or kindness

> Example: Munjurr is the hero in this story.

dialogue: conversation between characters in a story or play; words that characters actually say

> Example: *Munjurr said, "Come fish with me, Nurru."*
> *Nurru said, "The waves are high today...."*

Did You Know?

Aboriginal Australians are the native peoples of Australia. Stories and art are a very important part of their culture. Especially important are stories about the Dreamtime. These stories tell of a time when a magical group of beings created the world.

Words to Know

wallaby	a small kangaroo
reef	a ridge of coral in the sea
whirlpool	fast-moving water that turns in a circle
ancestor	a person who lived long ago and is related to someone living many years later
grieve	to feel or show great sadness
messenger	person who carries news or other information

Genre: Myth

"The Heroic Fisherman" is a myth. Read more about myths on page 467 of the Genre Guide.

The Heroic Fisherman

RETOLD BY LOUIS A. ALLEN, *adapted*

In the Dreamtime, in the country of the Manggalilji people, there lived a great fisherman called Munjurr. In his canoe made of bark, he went far out to sea. He speared kingfish and dugong for the people of his camp. Munjurr was wise in the ways of wind and tide. When the waves rolled high, he alone could steer his canoe between them. Sometimes the surf was so rough others were afraid to fish in it. But Munjurr would calmly paddle through the waves to the fishing grounds beyond.

One morning, Munjurr came to the campfire of his friend, Nurru. Nurru was the best drone piper in the camp. Nurru was practicing power notes on his didjeridu. He was getting ready for a ceremony that would be held before the moon died.

Munjurr said, "Come fish with me, Nurru."

READ TO FIND OUT...

What happens when two friends go fishing in rough ocean waters?

▶ Manggalilji
[mahn-gah-LIHL-jee]

Keys to Literature

Munjurr [MUN-jur] is the **hero** in this myth. Look for details that tell the qualities that make him great.

▶ A drone is a single sound. Nurru [NYOO-ryoo] plays one very powerful long note on his drone pipe, or didjeridu [dij-uh-ree-do].

Keys to Literature

Dialogue is the exact words characters say to each other. In this dialogue you learn about Munjurr and Nurru. How are the characters different from each other?

Think About It

People in the Dreamtime call the sun Walu [WAH-lyoo]. What time of day is it?

Nurru said, "The waves are high today. The canoe will tip over."

Munjurr said, "This is a fine time to catch the big fish. When the surf runs high, they come close to shore."

Nurru said, "Let us hunt the **wallaby**. Tomorrow, when the wind dies, we can fish."

Munjurr said, "You are known as a brave man, Nurru. You and I will bring back a great catch today. Our friends will be proud that we were the only ones who faced such rough waters. If we run into trouble, you can sound a power song on your didjeridu to help us."

Munjurr had touched Nurru's pride. Nurru followed Munjurr to the beach. They pulled the canoe from the bushes and checked to make sure it was watertight. Then they splashed into the surf and quickly began to paddle.

Almost at once, a great wave caught them. It took all of Munjurr's skill to steer through the waves, which were like mountains. But slowly Munjurr moved away from the dangerous shore and into the calmer waters that were beyond the **reef**. There the two men turned their attention to fish.

Walu, the Sun Woman, had just started moving across the sky when Nurru suddenly grabbed Munjurr's arm.

Nurru said, "A whale! It comes this way."

Munjurr looked. A large whale was moving toward them. Water ran down its sides as it cut through the sea. The story of deimiri, the whale spirit, was often told around the camp fires. Munjurr remembered hearing of deimiri's three mouths. Two of those mouths were in the whale's tail. He also remembered how the whale tipped over the canoes of fishermen.

Munjurr shouted to Nurru, "Paddle hard!"

The great whale came toward them. It came faster than they could get away. When they could see the whale's eyes, Nurru picked up his drone pipe and blew a power song with all his might. The whale was almost beneath them. Then suddenly it dove down under the water. The water became a spinning **whirlpool**. It sucked the canoe into its center. The canoe tipped over, and the men were thrown into the sea.

Munjurr saw the spears pop up to the surface of the water. He swam toward them. He was quick, but they floated beyond his reach. Nurru tried to grab his drone pipe, but it floated away.

Finally, Munjurr grabbed a paddle. He pointed toward the shore. He shouted to Nurru, "This way." He began to swim. He held onto the paddle so he could rest when he grew tired.

Predict

What do you think will happen to Munjurr and Nurru?

Nurru swam also but more slowly. As the two men came close to shore, the surf grew rough. Even Munjurr had to rest on his paddle. But Nurru could not rest. His arms grew heavy and slow. His feet hardly moved. He began to sink.

Keys to Literature

How does Munjurr show that he is a **hero**?

Munjurr turned and saw what was happening to his friend. He swam toward Nurru and shoved one end of the paddle at him. Munjurr said, "Take hold of the paddle!"

Nurru grabbed the paddle. But it was too light to hold up both men. Munjurr let go of his end of the paddle. He said, "Hold onto it!" Then he swam away.

The last rays of Walu, the Sun Woman, were sinking when the tide carried Nurru onto the beach. He lay there, hardly breathing. He still held the paddle in his hands.

But Munjurr did not return. Not that day, or the next, or even the day after that. His people searched the beaches but did not find him. The waves had taken his body. They carried it far out to sea. His spirit had gone to the Sky World. There, Barama, the powerful creator **ancestor**, waited to greet him.

Barama said to Munjurr, "When you saved Nurru, you lost much. You lost your family, your friends, and the land of your birth. But you will not **grieve** for them. I will make you my **messenger**. You are to carry my words to the people on earth and bring back their messages to me. In this way, you will be happy."

Munjurr made his camp beside the Milky Way, the great river that flows across the Sky World. He made a canoe like the one he had used on earth. He paddled it on the river and fished as happily as before. From time to time, Barama sent Munjurr to earth with messages. When he made these journeys, Munjurr always came back happy.

Below, in the land of the Manggalilji, wet season followed dry. Dry season followed wet, until Nurru's eyes grew dim. His shoulders stooped. His feet no longer went far from the camp fire. One morning, when the surf ran high and the winds blew strong, Nurru's spirit joined the spirit of Munjurr. In that great river the Milky Way, they fish forever. Sometimes they hunt the turtle and water birds that make their homes along its banks.

Think About It

Why does Barama think that Munjurr will be happy as a messenger?

Think About It

What happens when Nurru dies?

Check Your Predictions

1. Look back at the answer you gave for the Predict question. Would you change your answer? Explain.

Understand the Myth

2. What dialogue tells how Munjurr convinces Nurru to go fishing?

3. What happens to Munjurr after the boat sinks?

4. What happens to Nurru at the end of the myth?

Think About the Myth

5. What kind of man is Nurru?

6. What makes Munjurr the hero of the myth?

7. Do you think Munjurr is happy in the Sky World? Why?

8. What makes this story a myth?

Extend Your Response

Think about which character you are more like: Munjurr or Nurru. In a paragraph, explain what makes you like that character.

Learn More About It

ABORIGINAL AUSTRALIAN CULTURE

Aboriginal Australians have lived in Australia for thousands of years. They lived there long before the British and Europeans arrived in the 1600s and 1700s. Aboriginal Australians include many different groups with many different traditions. Yet the groups share similar beliefs, songs, and myths.

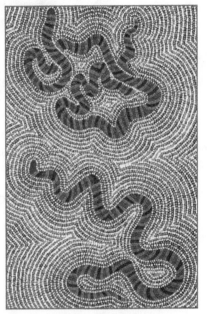

The Snake Dreaming is an important Aboriginal story in the Dreamtime. Here the artist uses traditional dots, lines, and circles to show the snakes.

Dreamtime

One shared belief is the Dreamtime. Dreamtime was the beginning of the world and the beginning of time. It is when spirit ancestors came up from within the earth. Spirit ancestors created all life. Spirit ancestors still remain in some places. Those places are sacred to Aboriginal Australians.

Art

Aboriginal art has many traditional designs. The designs appear in paintings and carvings. Artists put the designs on rocks, wood, and other surfaces. They may also paint their own bodies. The designs have dots, circles, and lines. This artwork honors the spirit ancestors and all they created.

Didjeridu

The didjeridu may be one of the world's oldest instruments. It is a very long wooden flute. Aboriginal Australians use the didjeridu to imitate nature's sounds. The instrument may sound like a bird. It may sound like the rain. The instrument often accompanies traditional chants and songs.

Apply and Connect

Nurru was a skillful player of the didjeridu. What sounds in nature do you think Nurru might have imitated? Explain your answer.

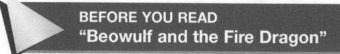

Keys to Literature

character: a person in a story

Example: Beowulf is the main character in this story.

character traits: qualities that a person has, such as bravery or honesty

Example: *The king at that time was Beowulf, a fair man, strong of arm and strong of heart.*

Words to Know

slithered	slid; moved like a snake
goblets	heavy drinking cups with stems
wake	a track left behind
armor	a covering that protects a fighter in battle
bellowed	shouted very loudly
writhed	squirmed; twisted and turned
engulfed	covered completely

Genre: Epic

"Beowulf and the Fire Dragon" is a retelling of an epic. Epics are usually poetry. This epic is not in poetic form because it is retold. Read more about epics on page 466 of the Genre Guide.

Beowulf and the Fire Dragon

BY ANONYMOUS, *retold*

READ TO FIND OUT...
What happens when an aging king sets out to fight a dragon?

Long ago, so long that no one knows when, someone hid a treasure in a cave by the sea. Perhaps a great family had been beaten in war. Perhaps they hoped one day to reclaim their gold. However, this was not to be. Instead, years passed and the riches lay in the cave, forgotten in the darkness.

The first one to find this treasure was not a man, but a beast. A fire dragon, looking for a dark place to nest, climbed a hill beside the sea waves and discovered the cave. It spied a gleam of gold and **slithered** inside. There it saw a pile of jewels and helmets, a tumble of coins, **goblets**, and armbands. The dragon fell in love with the gold, as dragons do. It pushed itself amongst the treasure and wrapped its scaly tail around it. Then it fell asleep atop the golden heap.

The dragon slept for three hundred winters and three hundred springs.

Keys to Literature

The fire dragon is a major **character** in the story.

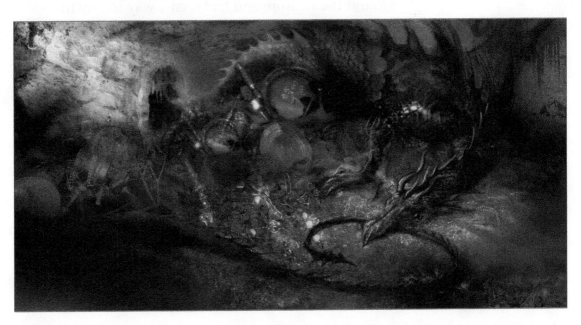

When the beast awoke, the smell of a human filled his cave. While the dragon was dreaming, a slave had found the treasure and had seen a way to buy his freedom. This slave had snatched one gold cup and run for his life.

Predict

What will the fire dragon do next?

The fire dragon sensed at once that part of its beloved gold was missing. Anger boiled in its black heart. Smoke seeped from its nostrils. The creature waited impatiently for nightfall. Then it spread its huge, leathery wings. It took to the sky, scales glowing in the moonlight.

The dragon took its revenge then. Its fiery breath lit the night sky like a bright banner. It set the countryside ablaze. Farms and barns went up in flames. Each night, the creature attacked more people's homes. Each morning it winged its way back to the cave, leaving only black, smoking ruins in its **wake**.

Soon even the king's great hall was burned to ashes. The king at that time was Beowulf, a fair man, strong of arm and strong of heart. As a youth, he had battled a terrible monster from the swamps known as Grendel. He'd killed it with his bare hands. Beowulf defeated his enemies in many battles. People loved him for his strength and courage. But he was not a man eager for war. For fifty years, he had ruled the Geats in peace.

Now Beowulf was an old man. Even so, he knew that it was his duty to keep his people safe. He must kill the dragon.

The king sent for the man who made his **armor**. "My wooden shield is no use against a fire-breathing dragon," he said. "Make me a shield of iron."

Then he called together a dozen of his best fighters. "Come," he said. "We will meet this terror that flies by night. We will challenge him face to face, and we will slay him." The slave who stole the goblet had told his story far and wide. Beowulf ordered the man to take them to the dragon's den. The soldiers were afraid, but they followed their king.

"Stay back," Beowulf told them. "I will meet this hell-born creature by myself." But first, he sat upon a tall rock for a time. Looking out to sea, he told them of his life—of his happy boyhood, and of all his manly deeds since then. Somehow, Beowulf knew that he had reached the end of his time on this earth. This battle would be his last. He said goodbye to each man there. Then he strode forward bravely to meet his fate.

From the black mouth of the dragon's cave a stream flowed. It bubbled, steaming hot. Beowulf stood beside it and drew his sword. He **bellowed** a war cry, which rang and echoed on that hill above the sea.

The earth shook in reply. The dragon, swollen with fury, dragged its gigantic body free of the cave. It **writhed** and twisted. Sparks shot from its furnace-hot mouth. The bright light reflected off its shining scales.

Keys to Literature

Character traits are the qualities a person has. What are some of Beowulf's character traits?

▶ The Geats were people who lived in southern Sweden.

Predict

What will happen to Beowulf?

Think About It

Why does the earth shake?

Through this blast of heat, Beowulf leapt forward. He rammed his sword at the creature, but the blade just bounced off those metal-hard scales. The fire dragon screamed its hatred and attacked with claw and tooth. Fire poured from its mouth.

At that, Beowulf's men groaned and shook with fear. Their feet flew as they ran for cover.

Only one remained behind. This was Wiglaf, a youth whose grandfather had battled the wicked swamp-monster at Beowulf's side many years before. Wiglaf tried to call the others back. He reminded them of their promise to serve Beowulf always. But his words didn't stop the cowards. So young Wiglaf threw on his helmet and rushed forward alone to fight beside his king.

At the sight of yet another hated human, the dragon launched a second wild attack. Red flame **engulfed** the fighters. Wiglaf's shield fell in ashes to the ground. Seeing that, Beowulf raised his iron shield higher. Wiglaf ducked behind it.

Beowulf's armor glowed red-hot. Still, he dove in for another strike. This time, his sword hit the dragon's skull. Blood gushed, but the sword's bright blade shattered. The sword fell to pieces in the mighty warrior's hand.

Quick as a snake then, the dragon struck. It sank its razor-sharp teeth into Beowulf's throat and held on. Beowulf was soaked in his own blood. Still he didn't give up. He groped for the knife in his belt.

Desperate to help his king, Wiglaf jumped forward. He sank his sword deep in the dragon's belly. But it was Beowulf who dealt the death blow. He brought his knife down and stabbed the vile beast in the side. Heaving and screeching, the fire dragon sank to the ground.

Only then did Beowulf give in to his own pain. Clutching his throat, he fell.

Keys to Literature

What are Wiglaf's **character traits**?

Think About It

Many strong action verbs, such as *launched*, help describe the action. What are some others?

Wiglaf rushed to fill his helmet with water from the stream. He bathed Beowulf's face and neck and helped him to drink. The old warrior's body was covered with burns, and his throat still bled. Both men knew that death was near. Wiglaf was burned as well. Not a hair remained on his head; every one had been scorched off by flames. Worse than that, he was heartsick, seeing his king so wounded.

"Do not grieve so," Beowulf told him. "I have lived long and well. I have no regrets. Hurry now and bring me the treasure from the cave. I wish to see it."

Think About It

Why do you think Beowulf tells Wiglaf not to grieve?

Wiglaf passed the dead hulk of the dragon and entered the cave. When he returned, he held a heap of treasure in his arms. He dumped the glittering, gleaming pile of jewelry, cups, and coins at the king's feet.

"Ah," Beowulf said quietly. "That pleases me. My people will be wealthier because of what we did this day." Beowulf asked Wiglaf to promise to bury him on the hill and to build a tall stone monument over the grave. "It will remind my people of a king who loved them," he said. Wiglaf promised.

Then with great effort, Beowulf took the golden collar of kingship from his neck. "You are the last and best of us," he told Wiglaf. He handed him the bloody collar. "Rule strongly and well, as I have tried to do," he said. He waited for Wiglaf's answer.

Wiglaf nodded once.

Then Beowulf, the mighty warrior, drew his last breath on this earth.

▶ The collar is like a crown—a symbol showing who is king.

Think About It

What do Beowulf's words show about what kind of person he is?

"Beowulf and the Fire Dragon"

Check Your Predictions

1. Look back at the answers you gave for the Predict questions. Would you change your answers? Explain.

Understand the Story

2. Why does the dragon suddenly cause trouble?

3. Who are the main characters in the story?

4. Why does Beowulf need an iron shield?

5. Why does Beowulf feel he has to fight the dragon himself?

Think About the Story

6. Why do you think the author decided to have Beowulf, rather than Wiglaf, kill the dragon?

7. Is Wiglaf a good choice to be the next king? Why?

8. What makes Beowulf an epic hero?

Extend Your Response

What if you were in charge of ridding your city, town, or county of an angry fire dragon? How would you go about it? Write a plan.

Keys to Literature

suspense: a feeling of uncertainty about what will happen next in a story. Suspense can keep readers curious and interested.

Example: Mystery novels are filled with suspense.

climax: the high point of a story when the outcome is decided

Example: The climax of a murder mystery is usually when the killer is discovered.

Did You Know?

Elephants in Africa usually have two tusks, which are long and toothlike. Each tusk can be about six feet long. A few elephants, such as the one in this folktale, have only one tusk. This may be because they were born without it or because it was damaged.

Words to Know

baboon	a type of large monkey
gazelle	a small, fast antelope
tusk	a long, curving tooth that usually grows in pairs out of the sides of the mouths of certain animals
gulp	a large swallow or sip
flesh	the soft parts of an animal's body that are covered with skin
groaned	made a deep, pained sound
bleats	the cries of a goat, sheep, or calf

Genre: Folktale

"Unanana and the Elephant" is a folktale. Read more about folktales on page 466 of the Genre Guide.

Unanana and the Elephant

RETOLD BY KATHLEEN ARNOTT, *adapted*

READ TO FIND OUT...

What happens when an elephant steals a poor woman's children?

▶ Unanana
[yoo-nah-NAH-nah]

Many, many years ago there was a poor woman called Unanana. She had two beautiful children. People always noticed their smooth skin and bright eyes.

Early one morning, Unanana went into the bush to collect firewood. She left her children playing with a little cousin.

The children were playing when they heard a noise in the grass. It was a curious **baboon**.

The baboon said, "Whose children are those?"

The cousin said, "They belong to Unanana."

The baboon said, "Well, well, well! I have never seen such beautiful children before."

The baboon disappeared, and the children went on playing. Later the children heard a twig crack. They looked up and saw a **gazelle** staring at them.

The gazelle said, "Whose children are those?"

The cousin said, "They belong to Unanana."

The gazelle said in her soft voice, "I have never seen such beautiful children before." Then the gazelle disappeared into the bush.

The children were getting a drink when they heard a noise. It was a leopard.

The leopard said, "Whose children are those?"

The cousin's voice shook with fear. She said, "They belong to Unanana." She backed up slowly toward the door of the hut. She was afraid the leopard might jump at her.

But the leopard was not interested in a meal. He said, "I have never seen such beautiful children before."

Keys to Literature

Just before each animal appears, the children hear a little noise. This creates a mood of **suspense**.

The children were afraid of these animals who kept asking questions. They called loudly to Unanana. But she did not come. Instead, a huge elephant with one **tusk** came out of the bush.

Predict

What do you think the elephant will do?

The elephant said, "Whose children are those?"

The cousin said, "They … they belong to Unanana."

The elephant said, "I have never seen such beautiful children before. I will take them with me." He opened his mouth wide. He swallowed Unanana's two children in one **gulp**.

The little cousin screamed and ran into the hut.

Soon Unanana came home. When she heard what happened, she said, "Did the elephant swallow them whole? Do you think they might be alive in his stomach?"

The cousin cried loudly. She said, "I don't know."

Unanana said, "There's only one thing to do. I must ask the animals if they have seen an elephant with one tusk. But first of all I must get ready."

Unanana cooked a big pot of beans. She put the pot on her head and got her large knife. She told the little cousin to look after the hut. Then she went off into the bush to look for the elephant.

Soon Unanana found the elephant's tracks. She followed them a long way, but she could not find the elephant. As she walked through some tall trees, she met the baboon.

Unanana begged, "O baboon, help me! Have you seen an elephant with one tusk? He has eaten both my children. I must find him."

The baboon said, "Keep going along this track. You will come to a place with high trees and white stones. There you will find the elephant."

Unanana went along the track for a very long time. Suddenly, a gazelle leaped across her path.

Unanana said, "O gazelle! Help me! Have you seen an elephant with only one tusk? He has eaten both my children. I must find him."

The gazelle said, "Keep going along this path. You will come to a place with high trees and white stones. There you will find the elephant."

Unanana said, "O dear! It seems such a long way. I am so tired and hungry." But Unanana did not eat the food she carried. That was for her children.

Unanana went on and on. She saw a leopard sitting outside his cave. He was washing himself with his tongue.

Unanana said, "O leopard! Have you seen an elephant with only one tusk? He has eaten my children. I must find him."

Think About It
Another mother might scream and cry when she heard that her children were swallowed by an elephant. What does Unanana do?

▶ Unanana meets all the animals in the same order in which they appeared to her children. This repetition is a feature of a folktale.

The leopard said, "Keep going on this track. You will come to a place where there are high trees and white stones. You will find the elephant there."

Unanana said to herself, "My legs will not carry me much further."

She went on a little more. Suddenly she saw high trees ahead. Below the trees were large white stones spread out on the ground.

Think About It

How can Unanana tell that this is the right elephant?

Unanana said, "At last!" She hurried forward. A huge elephant lay in the shade of the trees. He had only one tusk.

Unanana came as close to the elephant as she dared. She shouted, "Elephant! Elephant! Are you the one who has eaten my children?"

The elephant said, "O no! Keep going straight on this track...." But he did not finish what he was saying. Unanana ran up to him, waving her knife.

Unanana screamed, "Where are my children? Where are they?"

The elephant opened his mouth. He did not even bother to stand up. He swallowed Unanana and the pot of beans in one gulp. This was just what Unanana wanted.

Think About It

What makes Unanana a hero?

Down, down, down Unanana went in the darkness. She reached the elephant's stomach. What a sight she saw there! The walls of the elephant's stomach were like hills. There were small groups of people camped on the hills. There were dogs and goats and cows and her own two children.

The children said, "Mother! Mother! How did you get here? Oh, we are so hungry."

Predict

What do you think that Unanana will do next?

Unanana took the pot off her head. She began to feed her children the beans. All the other people crowded around. They begged for just a little food.

Unanana said to them, "Why not get your own food? It is all around you."

She took her knife and cut large pieces of **flesh** from the elephant. She built a fire in the middle of the elephant's stomach and cooked the meat. Soon everyone was eating elephant meat, even the dogs and goats and cows.

The elephant **groaned** so loudly that he could be heard all over the bush. Animals came to the elephant to find out what was the matter. The elephant told them, "Ever since I swallowed a woman called Unanana, I have felt bad inside. I don't know why."

The pain got worse and worse. Finally, the elephant dropped dead. Then Unanana took her knife and cut a door between the elephant's ribs. The dogs, goats, cows, men, women, and children walked outside. They shouted with joy to be free.

Keys to Literature

The **climax** is when the outcome of the story is decided. The climax here is when Unanana opens the elephant's ribs and frees the people and animals inside.

The animals thanked Unanana with moos, barks, and **bleats**. The human beings gave Unanana all kinds of presents. With so many presents, Unanana and her children were not poor anymore.

Meet the Reteller

KATHLEEN ARNOTT *(Born 1914)*

Kathleen Arnott was born in England. After college, she became an elementary school teacher. Her teaching led to her interest in writing. During her twenties, she traveled to Nigeria, Africa, where she taught both children and adults. There, she was surprised to find that the stories students were reading were not set in Africa. So she began writing fiction that focused on Nigerian and African culture. Arnott has also written several English collections of African folktales. In this way, she has been able to introduce African stories and folktales to non-African readers.

"Unanana and the Elephant"

Check Your Predictions

1. Look back at the answers you gave for the Predict questions. Would you change your answers? Explain.

Understand the Folktale

2. What happens to Unanana's children?

3. What does Unanana do to help her children?

4. What is the climax of the story?

5. How is Unanana rewarded for what she has done?

Think About the Folktale

6. What builds suspense in the story?

7. What detail or details tell you that Unanana is clever?

8. Do you think this folktale would be easy to remember and tell aloud? Why or why not?

Extend Your Response

Discuss with a friend what you might have done if you were Unanana. Was her solution the only solution? Were there other ways she could have saved her children?

Chapter 4 / Review

Summaries

The Heroic Fisherman One day Munjurr and Nurru are fishing. A whale makes a whirlpool that tips their canoe. Munjurr could save himself, but instead he gives Nurru the only paddle to float on. Nurru makes it to shore alive. Munjurr's spirit goes the Sky World. There, the creator ancestor makes Munjurr a messenger so he will not miss earth.

Beowulf and the Fire Dragon A fire dragon is terrorizing the countryside. Beowulf, the king, marches to its cave with his men. When the fighting begins, Beowulf's men are frightened. All of them run away except for Wiglaf, who helps his king. Beowulf kills the dragon but is also killed.

Unanana and the Elephant While Unanana is away, an elephant swallows her children. Brave Unanana acts quickly. She tricks the elephant into swallowing her. Once inside the elephant, she sees other people and animals as well as her children. Unanana cuts her way out of the elephant. Her children and the other people and animals are safe and free.

messenger
ancestor
grieve
armor
gulp
groaned

Vocabulary Review

Match each word in the box with its meaning. Write the word next to its meaning on a separate sheet of paper.

1. to feel or show great sadness
2. a person who lived long ago and is related to someone living many years later
3. a large swallow or sip
4. a person who carries news or other information
5. made a deep, pained sound
6. a covering that protects a fighter in battle

Chapter Quiz

Write your answers in one or two complete sentences.
Use a separate sheet of paper.

1. The Heroic Fisherman Why does the canoe tip over?

2. The Heroic Fisherman What does Munjurr do to save Nurru?

3. Beowulf and the Fire Dragon Why is the fire dragon a problem?

4. Beowulf and the Fire Dragon What is Beowulf's last act as king?

5. Unanana and the Elephant What is unusual about the elephant in this folktale?

6. Unanana and the Elephant Why is Unanana no longer poor at the end of the story?

Critical Thinking

7. Beowulf and the Fire Dragon Do you think Beowulf would have been wiser to let younger and stronger men kill the dragon? Why or why not?

8. Beowulf and the Fire Dragon *and* The Heroic Fisherman In what ways are Munjurr and Beowulf similar?

Chapter Activity

Who do you think is the greatest hero in this chapter?
Write a few paragraphs about this character and explain
why he or she is the greatest hero.

Unit 2 **Review**

On a separate sheet of paper, write the letter that best completes each sentence below.

1. In "The Mountain of the Men and the Mountain of the Women," the women are unhappy with
   A. how hard they must work.
   B. their place in society.
   C. how marriage is proposed.
   D. the size of the mountains in their country.

2. In *The Endless Steppe,* Vanya the bum is changed by the family's
   A. kindness.
   B. cooking.
   C. intelligence.
   D. expensive gifts.

3. The narrator in *My Brilliant Career* feels that she needs
   A. stronger cows.
   B. more out of life.
   C. a good night's sleep.
   D. new dog-legs.

4. In "The Heroic Fisherman," Munjurr saves Nurru by giving him a
   A. fishing pole.
   B. canoe.
   C. fish.
   D. paddle.

5. In "Beowulf and the Fire Dragon," almost all of Beowulf's men prove to be
   A. cowards.
   B. strong.
   C. brave.
   D. enemies.

6. In "Unanana and the Elephant," Unanana saves her children and
   A. her cousin.
   B. the leopard.
   C. the other people and animals inside the elephant.
   D. the other animals who ask about her children.

Making Connections

On a separate sheet of paper, write your answers to the following questions.

7. Many of the selections in this unit are folktales. Explain what makes them folktales.

8. Many of the characters in this unit faced a challenge or problem. Which problem do you think was the most difficult? Explain why.

Writing an Essay
Which of the characters in this unit is most like you or someone you know? Explain why and give examples.

Unit Three

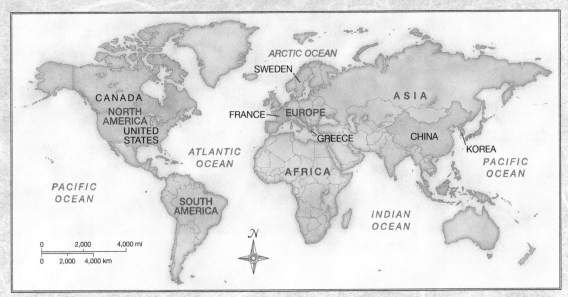

The Paupers' Meal on a Winter Day in Paris by Norbert Goeneutte (1854–1894)

What good deed does this painting show?

Chapter 5 Good Deeds

Learning Objectives

- Recognize a story-within-a-story.
- Understand plot.
- Understand the meaning of symbolism.
- Identify external conflict.
- Understand the difference between a short story and a novel.
- Identify foreshadowing.
- Recognize the omniscient point of view.

Preview Activity

Think of a good deed you have performed or a good deed someone did for you. What happened? How did you feel about it? Share your story with a classmate.

Theme Preview: Good Deeds

Good deeds are acts of kindness that come from open hearts. They can be simple acts, such as giving food to the poor. They can also be acts of heroism, such as risking one's own life. Regardless, good deeds change both the givers and the receivers. The stories in this chapter are about people whose lives are changed forever by good deeds.

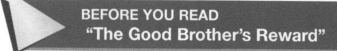
Keys to Literature

story-within-a-story: a story told inside another story. A character from the outer story tells the inner story to another character.

> Example: In "The Good Brother's Reward," the grandmother tells a story to her grandson.

plot: the action of a story or play. Most stories have a problem and, at the end, a solution.

> Example: A poor girl trades her family's horse for a magic apple. She plants the apple seeds. They grow into trees with golden apples.

Did You Know?

In Korea, grandparents, parents, children, uncles, and aunts all usually lived together in one home before the 1900s. The oldest male was the head of the family. Everyone else was expected to obey his wishes.

Words to Know

shelter	a place to live
huddled	crowded closely
porter	a person who carries things for other people
sprouted	began to grow
gourds	fruits with thick skins or rinds
brim	the top edge of a jar or container

Genre: Folktale

"The Good Brother's Reward" is a folktale. Read more about folktales on page 466 of the Genre Guide.

The Good Brother's Reward

RETOLD BY FRANCES CARPENTER, *adapted*

READ TO FIND OUT...
How could helping a baby bird change a person's whole life?

Another family had come to join the others who lived in the crowded houses inside the Kim courts. Another brother of the Master had fallen into bad luck. He had brought his wife and many children to seek the **shelter** of these tiled roofs.

"Why do they come to live with us?" Yong Tu asked his grandmother. "Why didn't they stay in their own house?" The boy was not sure he liked having his cousins there. They wanted to spin his tops and fly his kites. There were so many that Yong Tu's own little sister seldom had a turn now on the swing in the Inner Court.

Think About It
How does Yong Tu feel about his cousins?

"Bad luck found them, blessed boy," the old woman explained. "Where should they come but to their rich brother? How could he do anything but make them welcome? Our gates are always open to guests. Even a stranger is offered food here. How then could a brother be turned away?

▶ The homes of wealthy people in Korea were often built with an open space, or courtyard, in the middle.

"If this custom is broken, my young dragon, trouble surely would follow. Have I ever told you the tale of the two brothers? One was good, and the other was greedy. Do you know how each was rewarded? No? Then sit down beside me and listen well.

Keys to Literature

The grandmother helps Yong Tu by telling him a tale. This begins the **story-within-a-story**.

"Once long ago there were two brothers. One was rich. The other, like your uncle, had fallen into the hands of bad luck. When their father died, the oldest son took all the family riches. He kept them for himself. He didn't fill his father's place as the head of the house and look after his younger brother. Instead, he put his brother out of the gate to seek shelter and food and clothes for his family wherever he might.

"To give these brothers names, let's call the older, greedy one Koh Sang Chip. The younger one might have been named Koh Sang Hun. In the fine Koh family houses, Sang Chip lived alone with his wife. No children blessed his selfish days. Sang Hun, on the other hand, lived with his wife and several sons. They shared a little mud hut. Its old grass roof had huge holes in it. The rain fell through the holes and onto the family as if straight from the sky. At night those poor young people slept on their ragged straw mats on a cold dirt floor. They kept warm only by lying **huddled** together.

Keys to Literature

The **plot** begins when Sang Hun needs to find a way to feed his family. What is the first thing that happens?

"By weaving straw shoes and by doing whatever jobs he could find, Sang Hun barely managed to keep his little family alive. His children often cried out for food. Even the rats complained. They told their neighbors that there was not one grain of rice in the house to steal.

"'Send our youngest son to ask help from your rich brother,' Sang Hun's wife said one day to her unhappy husband. 'Surely when he sees that small boy's hungry look, he will give us some food. He has so much.'

"But that greedy rich brother turned the boy away from his gate. 'I have food enough only for the people in my house,' he said roughly. 'My rice and my bean flour are both locked up in a storeroom. My bran I shall keep for my own cows. Any extra grain must go

to my chickens. If I give you scraps from our table, my dogs will be angry. Go before they bite you!'

"When the little boy returned home, he felt ashamed. He did not want to tell his uncle's cruel words. The boy only said, 'I have brought nothing. My uncle was not at home.'

"'Well,' said his mother, 'I will sell these shoes off my feet. Their straw soles are still good. They will bring enough cash for a little rice. Then we can have supper.'

Think About It

Why does the boy lie to his parents?

"But that night luck found its way to the good brother. Sang Hun had been gathering wood on the mountainside. When he returned home, he brought along a rich treasure. This treasure was a plant root. It was from the medicine plant called insam (ginseng). Even the King and Queen drank insam soup in the spring. The medicine sellers paid Sang Hun much money for this root. His wife's shoes could now be bought back. Together with her husband, she could again look for work.

"Sang Hun's wife found a job cleaning rice. The husband worked as a **porter**. With a wooden frame on his back, he carried loads for the rich people of the village. So they got through the winter.

"Spring came, and the swallows flew back from the south. They built their nests under the straw roof of Sang Hun's little house. Soon baby birds filled the nests. One day while Sang Hun was weaving sandals in his yard, he saw a great roof snake. It slid out from below the straw toward the little birds. Before the man could drive the snake away, it had gobbled up all but one of the young birds. That one had fallen out of the nest and onto the hard ground. When the man picked it up, he saw that one of its tiny legs was broken.

"Gently, big-hearted Sang Hun tied up the swallow's leg. He made braces from dried fish skin. The children fed the bird and nursed it until it could hop about once more. Its tiny leg was crooked, but it seemed strong enough. Soon the bird began to fly about, chirping with joy.

"The days began to grow short and the autumn nights began to grow cooler. The little bird with the crooked leg hopped once more across Sang Hun's yard. It was chirping and chirping as if to say good-bye before it flew off to the south.

"The next spring the swallow with the crooked leg came again. It landed on Sang Hun's hand. Into his palm it dropped a strange seed. On one side of the seed the man's name was written in golden brush strokes. On the other side were the words 'Plant me! Water me!'

"This little bird with the crooked leg could not talk. Still, my grandmother always told me that the seed was sent to Sang Hun by the King of the Birds. It was a reward for saving the baby swallow from the roof snake and for healing its broken leg.

"Well, that seed **sprouted** and grew. Its plant climbed high up to the grass roof of that little house. Three huge **gourds** hung upon its thick vine. About the middle of the Ninth Moon, the man spoke to his wife about them. 'We shall cut the gourds down today. We can eat their soft flesh, and we can make water bowls out of their hard shells.'

Predict

What will grow from this seed?

▶ The moon travels around the Earth in about a month. The Ninth Moon is in September or October.

"When Sang Hun sawed the first gourd open, the couple saw a strange sight. Two servants stepped out of it. They carried a fine table covered with silver bowls and bottles. 'This bottle contains a drink that gives a man long life,' the servants said to Sang Hun. 'This bottle holds a drink that makes the blind see. This one will bring back speech to one who can't talk.'

"The man and his family were silent with wonder as they sawed open the second gourd. At once their yard was filled with shining chests, with rich silks and rolls of shining white linen. Then the third gourd was opened. From it came an army of carpenters with tools and strong pieces of fine wood. Before the stunned man's eyes rose houses with tiled roofs. These were followed by stables for horses and storehouses for grain. Into his gates came a long train of oxen. The animals were loaded with furniture and with rice and other good food. There was enough to fill his storage jars to the **brim**. Servants, horses, and all that a rich man's house holds came to Sang Hun. It all came from these three magic gourds.

"Now, news travels fast. It was not long before Sang Hun's older brother heard of his good fortune. The greedy man came quickly to find out how it had happened. Good Sang Hun told him the story of the swallow with the crooked leg. Sang Chip decided to try the same magic himself.

"With his cane he struck at every little bird he met during his trip home. He killed many, but at last he broke one little sparrow's leg. The cruel man caught it easily. He tied up the sparrow's leg with braces from the dried skin of fish. He kept the bird inside his house until it could hop again. He did just what Sang Hun had done. But there was no kindness in Sang Chip's cruel actions. There was no chirping of thanks when

Keys to Literature

How does Sang Chip's greediness affect what happens next in the **plot**?

that sparrow flew away from his courts. I am sure it chirped loudly enough when it told the King of the Birds about cruel Sang Chip, who had broken its leg.

"When this sparrow with the crooked leg came back in the spring, it brought a seed for this brother, too. Greedy Sang Chip watched with joy when the green vine from it began to climb the side of his house. But the plant grew far too fast. It grew and it grew until it choked his entire home. Its great creeping vines pulled loose his roof tiles. Rain poured in upon all his treasures. It cost him a great sum of money to have his roof fixed.

"Instead of three gourds there were twelve on his plant. These were giant balls almost as big as a huge kimchi jar. When the Ninth Moon came around, Sang Chip had to pay a carpenter hundreds of dollars to open these gourds.

"Here were troubles indeed. Out of the first gourd stepped a group of traveling dancers. It cost Sang Chip much rice and money before those traveling dancers would leave his courts. Even more money was needed to get rid of the priests who came out of the second gourd. They demanded thousands to rebuild a temple.

"Each opened gourd brought fresh demands on Sang Chip's cash chests. A funeral, whose mourners had to be paid. A band of singing girls, whose music and dancing and bright waving flags cost so much. Traveling performers. A clown who needed much money for a long journey. A group of officials wanting their share of his tax money. A band of mudang women, who threatened to bring sickness into his house instead of driving it out. All these pests sprang from the gourds to take this greedy man's money. Jugglers, fortune-tellers, and poets had to be paid. Finally, little was left. From the eleventh gourd stepped a great giant. He took the very last coin from Sang Chip.

Predict

What will Sang Chip's gourds contain?

▶ *Kimchi* [KIM-chee] is a spicy Korean dish made of cabbage or other pickled vegetables.

▶ The *mudang* [MOO-dang] are women who cure sick people.

"'At least we have the twelfth gourd,' Sang Chip's weeping wife cried. 'Surely we have been punished enough. Surely there will be something good inside this last one.'

"But when the carpenters sawed the last gourd in two, smoke and hot flames poured out. They destroyed every house, every stable, and every storehouse inside Sang Chip's walls. His money was gone. His houses were burned to the ground! Where could the selfish man go now to seek shelter?

"'We must ask help from my brother, Sang Hun,' he said to his wife.

"'But will he not turn us away from his gates, as you turned away his hungry child?' the woman asked.

"'I do not think so,' Sang Chip replied. 'Sang Hun has a heart as wide as the sky. He follows the ways of our father, who always gave with a big hand.'

"Sang Chip was right. His good younger brother opened his gates for them. He gave them tables of food. Just as we give a home to your unlucky uncle, Sang Hun helped his greedy brother. That was as it should be, my dragon. After all, there was plenty of room in the fine houses which the Bird King had given him."

Keys to Literature

The grandmother finishes her **story-within-a-story**. How does the story apply to Yong Tu's family?

Meet the Reteller

FRANCES CARPENTER *(1890–1972)*

Frances Carpenter grew up in Washington, D.C. Her father was a reporter there. Her father also wrote very popular books about the people and places of the world. When she was in her twenties, Frances traveled with him, taking photographs. Her first few books were cowritten with her father.

Later Carpenter continued to write on her own. She became known for her books of folktales. The books are full of stories from all over the world. Some of her tales are told by a loving grandmother. "The Good Brother's Reward" is one of these. Carpenter worked as a writer for almost 50 years, until her death in 1972.

Check Your Predictions

1. Look back at the answers you gave for the Predict questions. Would you change your answers? Explain.

Understand the Folktale

2. What good deed does Sang Hun, the good brother, do?

3. How does the bird reward the good brother?

4. What is the next event in the plot after the greedy brother hears about Sang Hun's good fortune?

5. How does the story-within-a-story end?

Think About the Folktale

6. Why does the greedy brother break a bird's leg?

7. Why does the grandmother tell her grandson the story of the two brothers?

8. How is Yong Tu's father like the good brother?

Extend Your Response

Think about what the brothers Sang Hun and Sang Chip might have been like when they were children. Write a short scene in which they discuss giving money to a beggar who comes to the house.

Keys to Literature

symbolism: using something to stand for something else

Example: The rat trap is a symbol of the world according to the peddler in "The Rat Trap."

external conflict: a struggle that a person has with another person, with society, or with nature

Example: The peddler's struggle to earn a living is an external conflict.

Did You Know?

Peddlers were once common in both Europe and America. Some walked from place to place, carrying the goods they sold on their backs. Others sold items from wagons or on horseback.

Words to Know

peddler	a person who sells things, often door to door
bait	something, often food, that attracts animals to a trap
anvil	an iron block on which hot pieces of metal are hammered into shapes
bellows	a machine operated by hand that makes a stream of air so a fire will burn hotter
clatter	a rattling noise
intruder	a person who does not belong in a place
shabby	old and worn
wretch	a person who is looked down on as worthless

Genre: Short Story

"The Rat Trap" is a short story. Read more about short stories on page 467 of the Genre Guide.

The Rat Trap

BY SELMA LAGERLÖF, *adapted*

READ TO FIND OUT...

How does a rat trap peddler get out of the trap he himself is caught in?

Once upon a time there was a **peddler** who went around selling wire rat traps. He made his traps from things he got by begging in stores and farms. But the business was not making much money. As a result, he had to beg and steal to keep body and soul together. Even so, his clothes were in rags. His cheeks were sunken, and hunger showed in his eyes.

This man had a sad and lonely life. One day, while he was walking, he thought about his rat traps. Suddenly he was struck by an idea. The whole world, he decided, was nothing but a big rat trap. It only existed to set **bait** for people. It offered riches and joys, a roof and food, heat and clothing. This is like the rat trap's offerings of cheese and pork. As soon as anyone touched the bait, the trap closed on him. Everything came to an end.

The world had never been very kind to him. It gave him unusual joy to think of it in this way.

Keys to Literature

The peddler thinks that a rat trap is a **symbol** of the way the world works. What does he mean when he says that good things in the world are like bait in a trap?

One dark evening as he walked along the road, he noticed a little gray cottage. He knocked on the door to ask shelter for the night. He was not refused. The owner, an old man without wife or child, was happy to see him. He wanted someone to talk to in his loneliness. Quickly he put the pot on the fire and gave his guest supper. Next he poured them both a cup of hot tea. Finally, he got out an old pack of cards. Together they played cards until bedtime.

The old man told his guest his secrets. The guest was told that in better times his host had rented a small farm from the Ramsjö Ironworks. There he had worked the land. Now he could no longer do such labor. It was his cow that supported him. The cow could give milk for the creamery every day. Last month he had received thirty kronor in payment.

▶ The krona is the money used in Sweden. Several krona are called kronor.

The guest must have been stunned by what happened next. The old man got up and went to the window. There he took down a leather pouch hanging on a nail by the window. From it he picked out three wrinkled ten-kronor bills. These he held up before the eyes of his guest. Then he stuffed them back into the pouch.

The next day both men got up. The old man was in a hurry to milk his cow. The other man felt he should not stay in bed since his host was up. They left the cottage at the same time. The old man locked the door. He put the key in his pocket. The man with the rat traps said good-bye and thank you. Then each man went his own way.

Predict

What do you think the peddler will do after he says goodbye?

Half an hour later the rat-trap peddler stood again before the old man's door. He did not try to get in, however. He only went up to the window. Then he smashed a pane and stuck in his hand. Grabbing the pouch, he took the money and shoved it in his pocket. Then he hung the leather pouch carefully back in its place and went away.

Walking along with the money in his pocket, he felt quite pleased. He knew that he could not take the public highway. He had to turn off the road into the woods. At first this caused him no problems. Later in the day, however, it became worse. The forest was big and confusing. The paths twisted back and forth so strangely. He walked and walked without coming out of the woods. Finally, he saw that he had only been walking around in circles. He remembered his thoughts

about the world and the rat trap. Now, his own turn had come. He had let himself be fooled by the bait. Now he had been caught. The whole forest closed in on him. It seemed like a tightly locked prison from which he could never escape.

It was late in December. Darkness was already settling over the forest. This added to the danger. It also added to his gloom and loss of hope. Finally, he saw no way out. He sank to the ground. He was very tired. He thought his last moment had come. As he laid his head on the ground, he heard a sound. It was a hard, regular thumping. There was no doubt as to what that was. He raised himself. "Those are the hammer strokes from an iron mill," he thought. "There must be people nearby." With his last bit of strength, he slowly stood up. He walked slowly toward the sound.

Keys to Literature

External conflict happens when a character struggles with something outside himself or herself. How does the forest present an external conflict for the peddler?

The Ramsjö Ironworks is now closed. At one time, however, it was a large plant. It had a huge melting pot, rolling mill, and forge.

On this winter evening just before Christmas, the master smith and his helper sat in the dark forge. They waited near the furnace for the pig iron in the fire to be ready to put on the **anvil**. Every now and then one man got up to stir the glowing mass with a long iron bar. Returning in a few minutes, he dripped with sweat. As was the custom, he wore nothing but a long shirt and a pair of wooden shoes.

There were always many sounds to be heard in the forge. The big **bellows** groaned. The burning coal cracked. The fire boy shoveled charcoal into the mouth of the furnace with a great deal of **clatter**. Outside the waterfall roared. At the same time, a sharp north wind whipped the rain against the roof.

It was probably because of these noises that the blacksmith did not see the man open the gate and enter the forge. When the blacksmith saw the man, he was standing close to the furnace.

Poor tramps often came there to warm themselves in front of the fire. The blacksmith glanced only casually at the **intruder**. He looked like most people of his type. He had a long beard. He was dirty and ragged. He had a bunch of rat traps hanging on his chest.

The rat-trap man asked if he might stay. The blacksmith nodded yes.

The tramp did not say anything else. He had not come there to talk. He wanted only to warm himself and sleep.

In those days the Ramsjö Ironworks was owned by a well-known ironmaster. It was his greatest desire to make good iron for his customers. He watched day and night to see that the work was done well. At this very moment he came into the forge on one of his nightly checks.

Naturally, the first thing he saw was the tramp. By then the tramp was sitting by the furnace. The ironmaster walked up to the tramp. He looked at the man closely. Then he tore off the man's floppy hat to get a better look at his face.

"But of course it is you, Nils Olof!" the ironmaster said. "How you do look!"

▶ Nils Olof
[NYELS O-lohf]

The man with the rat traps had never seen the ironmaster before. He did not even know his name. But he thought if the fine gentleman thought he was an old friend, he might give him a few kronor. He decided to pretend he knew the ironmaster.

"Yes, things have gone downhill with me," he said.

"You should not have left the regiment," said the ironmaster. "That was the mistake. If only I had still been in the service, it never would have happened. Well, now of course you will come home with me."

The tramp did not like this plan.

"No, I could not think of it!" he said, looking quite alarmed.

He thought of the thirty kronor. To go up to the manor house could be like throwing himself into the lion's den. He only wanted to sleep in the forge and then sneak away unnoticed.

The ironmaster believed that he felt uneasy because of his **shabby** clothing.

"Please don't think that I have such a fine home that you cannot be my guest," the ironmaster said. "Elizabeth is dead, as you may have heard. My boys are abroad. There is no one at home except my oldest daughter and me. We were just saying that it was too bad we didn't have company for Christmas. Now, come along with me. Help us make the Christmas food disappear a little faster."

Think About It
Why does the peddler pretend he knows the ironmaster?

But the stranger said no and no and again no. At last the ironmaster saw that he must give in.

"It looks as though Captain Nils Olof wants to stay with you," he said to the blacksmith. Then he turned away on his heel.

But the ironmaster laughed to himself as he went away. The blacksmith, who knew him, understood that he had not said his last word.

It was not more than half an hour before they heard the sound of a carriage. A new guest came in. This time it was not the ironmaster. He had sent his daughter. He seemingly hoped she might talk the tramp into coming to the house.

She entered followed by a servant. The servant carried a big fur coat on his arm. She was not at all pretty. She seemed modest and shy. The stranger had stretched himself out on the floor in front of the furnace. A piece of pig iron lay under his head. His hat was pulled down over his eyes. As soon as the young girl saw him, she went up and lifted his hat. The man was clearly used to sleeping with one eye open. He jumped up suddenly. He seemed to be quite frightened.

▶ Edla Willmansson
[EHD-lah wihl-mahns-sohn]

"My name is Edla Willmansson," said the young girl. "My father came home and said that you wanted to sleep here in the forge tonight. I asked if I might come and bring you home to us. I am so sorry, Captain, that you are having such a hard time."

She looked at him kindly. She noticed that the man was afraid. "Either he has stolen something or else he has escaped from jail," she thought. Then she added quickly, "You may be sure, Captain, that you will be allowed to leave as freely as you came. Only please stay with us over Christmas Eve."

She said this in such a friendly manner that the man must have felt he could trust her.

"I never thought that you would bother with me yourself, miss," he said. "I will come at once."

He accepted the coat from the servant. Throwing it over his rags, he followed the young lady out to the carriage. He did not give the surprised blacksmith so much as a glance.

But while he was riding up to the house, he had gloomy thoughts about what the future held.

"Why did I take that fellow's money?" he thought. "Now I am sitting in the trap and will never get out of it."

Keys to Literature

How is the money the peddler stole like the **symbol** of bait in the rat trap?

The next day was Christmas Eve. When the ironmaster arrived for breakfast, he was no doubt thinking happily of his old friend. How lucky it was to have run into him.

"First of all we must see to it that he gets a little flesh on his bones," he said.

"Then we must see that he gets something else to do. He should not run around the country selling rat traps."

His daughter was busy at the table. "It is odd that things have gone downhill with him as badly as that," said the daughter. "Last night there was nothing to show that he had once been an educated man."

"You must have patience, my little girl," said the father. "As soon as he gets clean and dressed, you will see something different. Last night he was, of course, ashamed. The tramp manners will fall away with the tramp clothes."

Just as he said this the door opened and the stranger came in. Yes, now he was truly clean and well dressed. The servant had bathed him, cut his hair, and shaved him. Moreover, he was dressed in fine clothes owned by the ironmaster. He wore a white shirt with a stiff collar and new shoes.

Even though his guest was now groomed, the ironmaster did not seem pleased. He looked at him with a frown. He had only seen the strange fellow in the dim light of the furnace. It was easy to understand how he might have made a mistake. Now with the stranger standing there in broad daylight, it was impossible to mistake him for his old friend.

"What does this mean?" the ironmaster thundered.

The stranger made no effort to carry on the disguise. He saw at once that all the glory had come to an end.

▶ The ironmaster's daughter has doubts that this is her father's old friend.

Think About It

Why does the ironmaster not seem pleased with the peddler?

"It is not my fault, sir," he said. "I never tried to be anything but a poor trader. I pleaded and begged to stay in the forge. But no harm has been done. At worst, I can put on my rags again and go away."

"Well," said the ironmaster, slowly. "It was not quite honest, either. You must admit that. I should not be surprised if the sheriff would like to know something of this matter."

The tramp took a step forward. He struck the table with his fist.

"Now, I am going to tell you, Mr. Ironmaster, how things are. This whole world is nothing but a big rat trap. All the good things that are offered you are nothing. They are just cheese rinds and bits of pork set out to drag a poor fellow into trouble. If the sheriff locks me up for this, then you, Mr. Ironmaster, must remember something. A day will come when you may want to get a big piece of pork. Then you too will get caught in the trap."

The ironmaster began to laugh.

"That was not so badly said, my good fellow. Perhaps we should let the sheriff alone on Christmas Eve. But now get out of here as fast as you can," the ironmaster said.

But as the man opened the door, the daughter spoke up. "I think he ought to stay with us today. I don't want him to go." With that she closed the door.

"What in the world are you doing?" said the father.

Think About It

Why does the ironmaster's daughter feel ashamed?

The daughter stood there feeling quite ashamed. She hardly knew what to answer. That morning she had felt so happy. She thought how homelike and Christmassy she was going to make things for the poor hungry **wretch**. She could not give up the idea all at once. That is why she spoke up for the tramp.

"I am thinking of this stranger here," said the young girl. "He walks and walks the whole year long. There is probably not a single place in the whole country where he feels at home. Wherever he turns, he is chased away. Always he is afraid of being arrested and questioned. I should like to have him enjoy a day of peace with us here. It would be just one day in the whole year."

The ironmaster mumbled something in his beard. He could not bring himself to say no.

"It was all a mistake, of course," she continued. "But I don't think we ought to send away someone we have asked to come here. We have promised him Christmas cheer."

"You talk worse than a preacher," said the ironmaster. "I only hope you won't be sorry about this."

The young girl took the stranger by the hand and led him to the table.

"Now sit down and eat," she said. She could see that her father had given in.

The man with the rat traps said not a word. He only sat down and helped himself to the food. Time after time he looked at the young girl who had spoken up for him. Why had she done it? What could the crazy idea be?

After that, Christmas Eve passed just as it always had. The stranger did not cause any trouble. He did nothing but sleep. The whole morning he lay on the sofa in a guest room and slept. At noon they woke him so he could have his share of the good Christmas food and drink. After that, he slept again. It seemed as though for many years he had not been able to sleep as quietly and safely.

In the evening, when the tree was lighted, they woke him again. He stood blinking as though the candlelight hurt him. After that, he disappeared again. Two hours later he was awakened once more. He then had to go down into the dining room to eat the Christmas supper.

As soon as they got up from the table, he went to each person and said thank you and good-night. When he came to the young girl, she told him that her father wished him to keep the suit he wore. It was to be a Christmas present—he did not have to return it. She

Think About It

Why do you think the peddler is so surprised and puzzled that Edla Willmansson has asked him to stay?

further told him if he wanted to spend next Christmas Eve with them, he would be welcomed back again.

The man with the rat traps did not answer. He only stared at the young girl in great amazement.

The next morning the ironmaster and his daughter got up to go to the early Christmas service. Their guest was still asleep. They did not disturb him.

At about ten o'clock, they drove back from church. The young girl sat and hung her head. She was more downcast than usual. At church she learned that one of the old farmers of the ironworks had been robbed by a man who sold rat traps.

Think About It

Why is Edla so sad after church?

"Yes, that was a fine fellow you let into the house," said her father. "I only wonder how many silver spoons are left in the cupboard."

The wagon had hardly stopped at the front steps when the ironmaster questioned the servant. He wanted to know if the stranger was still there. He added that he had heard at church that the man was a thief. The servant answered that the fellow had gone. He further stated that he had not taken anything with him. In fact, quite the opposite was true. He had left behind a little package, a Christmas present for Miss Willmansson.

Keys to Literature

How does the peddler attempt to escape the **symbolic** rat trap in his life?

The young girl opened the package. It was so badly wrapped that she saw at once what was inside. She gave a little cry of joy when she found a small rat trap. In it lay three wrinkled ten-kronor notes. But that was not all. In the rat trap lay also a letter written in large, uneven letters:

Honored and noble Miss:

   You have been so nice to me all day long, as if I was a captain. I want to be nice to you in return, as if I was a real captain. I do not want you to be shamed at Christmas by a thief. You can give back the money to the old man on the roadside. He has the money pouch hanging on the window as a bait for poor tramps.

   The rat trap is a Christmas present from a rat. This rat would have been caught in this world's rat trap if he had not been raised to captain. As a captain, he got the power to clear himself.

Written with friendship and high regard,

Captain Nils Olof

Meet the Author

SELMA LAGERLÖF *(1858–1940)*

Selma Lagerlöf grew up in southern Sweden. She was taught at home and spent much of her time alone as a child. Her grandmother filled her days with Swedish stories of fairies and magic.

Lagerlöf went to college to become a teacher. She taught school for ten years. While she was teaching, she began writing. Lagerlöf's writing shows her love of those childhood stories of fantasy and magic her grandmother told. She is best known for a children's book, *The Wonderful Adventures of Nils*. In 1909, Selma Lagerlöf became the first woman to win the Nobel Prize for literature.

Learn More About It

GENRE STUDY: SHORT STORIES AND NOVELS

Short stories and novels are two forms of fiction. They come from the writer's imagination. They both include characters and have a plot, or storyline. Some are realistic. They describe characters that could exist and events that could happen. Others are more fantastic. They probably could never happen.

Both novels and short stories usually contain a problem that needs to be solved. This problem is usually the center of the plot. A short story is usually several pages long. It often focuses on one theme or main idea.

A novel is usually more than 100 pages long. Because novels are longer, they may take place over a longer period of time than a short story. They may also have many more characters. In a novel, there may also be several subplots. These subplots often have their own problems or conflicts. Novels typically have more than one theme.

Check Your Predictions

1. Look back at the answers you gave for the Predict questions. Would you change your answers? Explain.

Understand the Story

2. What does the peddler think a rat trap is a symbol of? Why?

3. Why does the peddler travel through the forest instead of walking on the highway?

4. Why does the ironmaster invite a poor peddler into his home?

5. How does the peddler react when the ironmaster threatens to tell the sheriff about him?

Think About the Story

6. Name one reason why the peddler might want to go to the ironmaster's home and one reason why he does not want to go.

7. Why does the peddler sign his letter, "Captain Nils Olof"?

8. If you were the peddler, would you have left the money behind when you left the ironmaster's house? Why or why not?

Extend Your Response

Write a slogan that captures the message of this story. You might think about how the peddler changes from the beginning to the end of the story. What causes him to change?

BEFORE YOU READ
"The Story of Washing Horse Pond"

Keys to Literature

foreshadowing: hints about what might happen later in a story

> Example: The mention of the statue of Akui gives the reader a hint about what might happen to Akui later.

omniscient point of view: when the narrator knows what all the story characters do, say, and feel. An omniscient narrator uses *he*, *she*, and *they* to refer to the characters.

> Example: *All the neighbors came to say how sorry they were. They too were suffering.*

Did You Know?

This story is set in the Yunnan region of southern China. It's near Laos, Vietnam, and Burma. Dali is a city there, ringed with mountains. Many tourists visit Yunnan, which is an area famous for its beauty.

Words to Know

drought	a long time without rain
thrive	to grow; to be healthy
spring	a source of water flowing from the ground
withered	dried up
furiously	fiercely; intensely
parched	very dry
misery	great pain; suffering
priceless	of great worth

Genre: Folktale

"The Story of Washing Horse Pond" is a folktale. Read more about folktales on page 466 of the Genre Guide.

The Story of Washing Horse Pond

RETOLD BY HE LIYI, *adapted*

READ TO FIND OUT...

What does Akui's good deed cost him?

One of the most beautiful of Dali's nineteen peaks is called the Treasure Peak. There is a clean pond at the top of the peak. Pure water flows from it all year round. The pond is surrounded by trees and flowers, and is known as Washing Horse Pond. Next to the pond stands a large stone about the size of a man. People say that this stone is the statue of a brave young man called Akui. He lived a long time ago.

Once in Dali there was a terrible **drought**. For three whole years there had not been a single drop of rain. All the pools and ditches had dried up. Even huge Dali Lake had lost its fresh color and shrunk to a muddy hole. There were no more colorful flowers on the mountain slopes, and no birds sang. The crops wouldn't grow, and the cattle wouldn't **thrive**. All the beautiful mountains were sadly changed. People lived without hope.

Keys to Literature

The last two lines of this paragraph **foreshadow** what will happen to a young man named Akui. What story event might be foreshadowed here?

Keys to Literature

When a story is told from the **omniscient point of view**, the narrator explains what is happening to all the different characters. What clues show you that this story is written from the omniscient point of view?

Under one of those nineteen peaks was the village of Boluo. There lived a man by the name of Akui. His parents were old and weak. Because of the three-year drought, they could grow no food. Akui had to scrape out a living by looking for firewood in the hills. His parents just got older and weaker. A doctor was called, but there was nothing he could do. It was the drought. Many people could do nothing except wait to die. Akui's parents had no money to buy medicine or food. Very soon they died, one after the other. Akui was very sad.

All the neighbors came to say how sorry they were. They too were suffering. Some of the men talked of a **spring** that never failed. It was supposed to be somewhere at the top of the mountain peaks, but none of them knew where. Akui made up his mind to look for that spring. He took a hoe, a bow, some arrows, and some food. Then he set off for the peak above the village. The villagers watched him go. All their hopes and worries went with him.

For nine days and ten nights he climbed. He climbed over four huge peaks and four dry river beds, until he reached the top of the highest peak. It was a place called the Peak of Horses and Dragons. After his long journey, Akui was so tired that he fell asleep as soon as he lay down.

The day was just dawning when he awoke. As he looked around, all he could see was dry grass and **withered** trees. There was no water in the streams. There was no water anywhere. He searched all day but found nothing. That night he could not sleep. He just stared at the sky all night. Suddenly he saw something shining in the dark sky. It was way to the south. Then the shiny thing passed over his head and landed on another peak. Akui was amazed at the sight. He set out immediately for the other peak.

Dawn had come when Akui got there. Looking all around, he found everything just as dried up as everywhere else. Yet, there was one pine tree under a large rock. Its branches were green, and the needles were lush. Akui thought: Water! A tree lives on water. There must be water under the tree.

Lifting his hoe, he dug **furiously** until late that night. He dug until his hands were stained with blood, and his **parched** lips split. His throat was a burning fire. Still he found no trace of water.

That evening, to be safe from wild beasts, Akui climbed up the tree. He was so tired after digging all day that he soon fell asleep. At midnight he was awakened by a sudden flash of light. Looking up in the sky, he saw a number of winged horses flying to a large rock. The leading horse was as white as snow and larger than the rest. It stretched out its leg and struck the rock three times. The rock opened, just like a gate. Within the rock was a real pond of pure water.

Think About It

What details in this description of Akui show how much he wants to find water?

Predict

What will Akui do now that he has found the spring?

Think About It

Even as he drinks, Akui thinks of his fellow villagers. What does that tell you about Akui?

Think About It

Why does the God of Treasure Peak tell Akui about turning into a stone?

The flying horses drank and splashed. They didn't leave until day was about to break. The rock closed again behind them.

Akui jumped down from the tree and ran toward the rock. He hit it three times with his hoe. Slowly the stone gate opened. He went inside and found a lovely pool of rippling water. Grass and flowers grew on its banks. On a stone were carved the words "Washing Horse Pond."

Akui knelt to drink. The water tasted very cool. He was too excited to drink as much as he wished to. He was thinking of his fellow villagers. They were depending on him in their hour of need. They were suffering. So he started to dig a ditch right away.

In a wink, a stream of white smoke came out of the ground. In front of Akui stood a white-haired, old man, who said, "Young man, this water must not be touched. This is the only pond where the flying horses come to drink and swim. I am the God of this mountain peak, and this pond is in my care."

Akui told him all about the **misery** caused by the drought. He told him of the people's suffering. As he told the god about the death of his parents, he couldn't hold back the tears.

The God of Treasure Peak was very much moved by Akui's true story. He said, "Young fellow, let me tell you the truth. The one who frees the water of this magic pond will turn into a piece of rock. You are so young. Don't you think it a pity to become a stone? Go down and tell them to send up an old man instead. It is asking too much of you. It is more than enough for you to have found the water for everybody."

Akui paused for a while after hearing this. He replied, "My honored uncle, I thank you for your kindness. But there must be no delay. This water will save thousands of lives. I'd rather be stone than go back now. You needn't worry about me."

He began to dig again.

Soon Akui had dug out a trench, down which the pure water rushed. All along its path, the trees began to shoot green leaves and the birds sang. All the mountain flowers began to bloom.

Akui shouted for joy. He tried to walk out and watch the world come back to life, but alas! he couldn't find his feet. Looking down, he saw that his two feet had turned into a pair of stone feet. He tried to shout aloud, but his lungs were turned to stone. All his body was turning to stone. Akui knew now he could never return to his village; but he heard the water gurgling by. He knew it would go there for him. He was satisfied. He let his mouth set into a happy, loving, stone smile.

Keys to Literature

How does the **omniscient point of view** help readers understand what is happening in the story?

Think About It

Why does Akui smile while his feet are turning to stone?

The villagers were full of joy when the water from Washing Horse Pond reached them. The once dry land was turning green as the water passed. Everyone knew Akui must have found the water. They climbed up to the pond to look for him, but where had he gone? They couldn't find even Akui's shadow. They called and called at the tops of their voices, but nobody answered. Finally they saw the standing stone. The more they looked at it, the more it looked like Akui. A hoe was lying by, with mossy grass still sticking to it. From this more than anything, the people knew that Akui had become a stone.

From that time on, men and women from the villages near the mountain often came up to visit Akui. He was a hero who had given up his life for them. They made Washing Horse Pond a place of beauty, and it still is. Flowering shrubs are everywhere. The trees are thick and green, and the smell of flowers is delightful. It is said that the ancient kings of Dali used to spend their summer days by its banks. Even now, Akui stands stone still beside the **priceless** water.

Think About It

How did the villagers guess what had happened to Akui?

Meet the Author

HE LIYI *(Born 1930)*

He Liyi grew up in a village in southern China. More than anything, he wanted to teach English. He was a good student and went to a teachers' college. But the new government at that time was suspicious of educated people. Like many others, He Liyi was sent to a labor camp. When he returned home five years later, he had to work hard just to survive. He didn't get a teaching job again for almost 20 years.

He Liyi is best known for the book he wrote about his life. *Mr. China's Son* was published in 1993. It shows what life in China's villages was like in difficult times. These days, he owns a café in Dali. He enjoys helping people from around the world understand more about his country.

Check Your Prediction

1. Look back at the answer you gave for the Predict question. Would you change your answer? Explain.

Understand the Folktale

2. Why do Akui's parents die?

3. Why does Akui think there must be water near the pine tree?

4. What creatures help Akui find water?

5. Why does Akui refuse to take the advice of the God of Treasure Peak?

Think About the Folktale

6. The name of the first peak Akui climbs is the Peak of Horses and Dragons. What later event in the story does this foreshadow?

7. Why do the village people make sure Washing Horse Pond is a place of beauty today?

8. Why do you think the author uses the omniscient point of view in this story?

Extend Your Response

Imagine you are Akui. Write what you are thinking as you dig for water at the magic pond. You have just spoken with the God of Treasure Peak.

Learn More About It

POINT OF VIEW

The point of view of a story refers to who is telling the story. The most common points of view are first person, third person limited, and third person omniscient.

With first-person point of view, a narrator tells a story about himself or herself. The narrator uses the pronouns *I* and *we*. The narrator describes other characters, but does not know everything they think or do.

Apply and Connect

How might this story be different if it were told from the first-person point of view?

First-Person Point of View
I was enjoying the movie. But when I looked over at Kiko, I saw that she had fallen asleep.

In a story written in the third-person point of view, the narrator is not part of the story. The narrator uses the pronouns *he*, *she*, and *they*. There are two kinds of third person.

A narrator with a limited point of view can tell the thoughts and feelings of only one character.

Third-Person Limited Point of View
Justin was enjoying the movie. But when he looked over at Kiko, he saw that she had fallen asleep.

With omniscient point of view, the narrator knows all characters thoughts and feelings.

Third-Person Omniscient Point of View
Justin was enjoying the movie. But when he looked over at Kiki, he saw that she had fallen asleep. She was dreaming that she had just kicked a winning soccer goal.

Chapter 5 Review

Summaries

The Good Brother's Reward A grandmother tells a story about two brothers. One brother is poor but kind. The other brother is rich but greedy. After the poor brother helps an injured bird, he is rewarded with riches. The greedy brother hopes for the same reward. Instead, he loses his fine home. Fortunately, his good brother takes him in.

The Rat Trap A poor peddler sells rat traps. After stealing money, the peddler seeks shelter in an ironworks. The owner mistakes him for an old friend. He invites the peddler to spend Christmas with him. The ironmaster is angry when he learns his mistake, but his daughter has the peddler stay. At church they find out that the peddler has stolen money. They return home to find the peddler gone. He has left the stolen money with a note of thanks for their kindness.

The Story of Washing Horse Pond For three years a Chinese village has been without rain. The people suffer. A young man named Akui searches for a hidden spring. He finds the magic source of the water. Akui chooses to give his life so the village can have water.

huddled
intruder
misery
parched
shabby
sprouted

Vocabulary Review

Match each word in the box with its meaning. Write the word and its matching number on a separate sheet of paper.

1. began to grow
2. very dry
3. great pain; suffering
4. crowded closely
5. a person who does not belong in a place
6. old and worn

Chapter Quiz

Write your answers in one or two complete sentences.
Use a separate sheet of paper.

1. The Good Brother's Reward What happens when the son of the poor brother asks his uncle for food at the beginning of the story?

2. The Good Brother's Reward What does Sang Hun do when Sang Chip asks him for help at the end of the story-within-a-story?

3. The Rat Trap Why does the poor farmer invite the peddler into his house?

4. The Rat Trap Why does the ironmaster send his daughter to the forge?

5. The Story of Washing Horse Pond How does Akui find the hidden spring?

6. The Story of Washing Horse Pond What stands next to the pond today?

Critical Thinking

7. The Rat Trap Name two things about this story that show it is told in omniscient point of view.

8. The Story of Washing Horse Pond What kind of person is Akui? Give examples from the story to explain your answer.

Chapter Activity

Which character in these stories of good deeds would you most like to meet? Make a comic strip with word balloons. Show what you and the character might say to one another.

How are these friends enjoying themselves?

Chapter 6 Friendships

Learning Objectives

- Understand a story's theme.
- Explain what a fable is.
- Explain what a simile is.
- Identify the climax of a story.
- Understand the author's tone.
- Recognize details.
- Explain what a memoir is.
- Recognize concrete words.
- Understand onomatopoeia.

Preview Activity

Imagine you could create the perfect friend. What would he or she be like? Make a list of qualities. Then discuss your list with two classmates.

Theme Preview: Friendships

Feelings between friends are special. We open our hearts and our lives to our friends. We look to them for encouragement, advice, comfort, and support. We learn from them. The stories in this chapter are reminders of how precious a good friend is, especially in times of need.

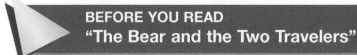

Keys to Literature

theme: the main idea of a story, novel, play, or poem

> Example: The theme of "The Bear and the Two Travelers" is
> "Never trust a friend who deserts you when you're in trouble."

Bears depend on
their sense of smell
because their eyes
and ears are small.
Most bears can climb
trees. All bears move
easily over rocks and
ice. Bears live in
caves. They go into
a deep sleep during
the winter.

Words to Know

bolted	ran away
snout	a long nose
deserts	abandons; leaves someone in need

Genre: Fable

"The Bear and the Two Travelers" is a fable. Read
more about fables on page 466 of the Genre Guide.

The Bear and the Two Travelers

BY AESOP, *retold*

Two boys were traveling on a narrow path through a dark wood. Suddenly an enormous bear rushed toward them. The boy who happened to be in front **bolted**. He dashed up the trail and climbed a tall tree.

The other boy saw that there was no escape. He threw himself facedown in the dirt. He closed his eyes and held very still, for he had heard that bears will not touch dead meat.

The powerful bear approached the boy. He pushed at him with his **snout**. He put his nose near the boy's ear and snuffled and sniffed. The boy held his breath. Finally, the bear shuffled off into the trees.

At that, the boy in the tree climbed down. He chuckled as the other boy dusted dirt off his clothes. "It looked as if that bear whispered in your ear!" he said. "What did he say?"

His companion glared at him. "He told me never to trust a friend who **deserts** you when you're in trouble!" he said.

READ TO FIND OUT...
What do two boys do when they run into a bear?

Predict

What will happen to the boy?

Keys to Literature

The **theme** is the main idea or lesson in a story. Some fables, such as this one, state the theme at the end.

Keys to Literature

fable: a short story that teaches a lesson. In fables, animals and other natural things act and talk like people.

> Example: In "The Pigeon and the Ant," the pigeon saves an ant's life.

Words to Know

blade	a single stem of a plant, especially grass
plank	a heavy, thick board
crossbow	a weapon similar to a bow and arrow

Genre: Fable

"The Pigeon and the Ant" is a fable. Read more about fables on page 466 of the Genre Guide.

The Pigeon and the Ant

BY JEAN DE LA FONTAINE, *adapted*

READ TO FIND OUT...

How does a tiny ant save a pigeon?

An ant leaned over the edge of the water. It leaned just a little too far. Suddenly, it lost its balance. The poor ant fell in.

A thirsty pigeon was getting a drink from the water. She saw the ant fall.

To the ant, the water was like a sea. The water was deep and wide. The ant struggled hard, but it began to sink.

Keys to Literature

Fables often feature animals who are like people. What human trait does the pigeon have?

The kind pigeon threw the ant a **blade** of grass. The ant used it as a **plank**. It crawled back to dry land. The ant was wet and tired. But it was safe. The pigeon had saved the ant's life.

Soon a man from the village walked by. His bare feet made no sound. He happened to have a **crossbow** in his hand.

Predict

How will the man use his crossbow?

He saw the pigeon, who is called the bird of Venus. He imagined the pigeon cooking in a pot. He thought of how good her meat would taste.

The pigeon never saw the man. But the ant did. Just as the man aimed his crossbow, the ant stung him in the heel.

The man jerked his head. Now the pigeon heard him. She flew up quickly. She was out of range of his crossbow. The man's supper was gone. Because of the ant, there would be no pigeon pie tonight!

Meet the Author

AESOP *(Lived around 600 B.C.)*

Very little is known about Aesop's life. He lived 2,400 years ago in Greece. He probably was a slave. Records of his life do exist, but they are full of tall tales. That makes it hard to tell what is truth and what is fiction. One thing is true—he was a wonderful storyteller. However, he probably didn't write all the fables that carry his name.

Meet the Author

JEAN DE LA FONTAINE *(1621–1695)*

Jean de la Fontaine lived among French royalty for much of his life. But his ideas were not always popular with the French government or church. Officials allowed his fables because they used animals instead of human characters to make his points. Many of the fables were sophisticated retellings of Aesop stories. They are still read widely in France today.

Check Your Predictions

1. Look back at the answers you gave for the Predict questions. Would you change your answers? Explain.

Understand the Fables

2. How does the boy trick the bear?

3. What does the boy do when the bear sniffs at him?

4. How does the pigeon help the ant?

5. How does the ant help the pigeon?

Think About the Fables

6. How does the boy feel about his friend who deserted him?

7. How do you know these stories are fables?

8. What lesson do both these fables teach about friendship?

Extend Your Response

Think about what makes a good friendship. Make a list of things friends do for each other. Then pick one and draw a comic strip to illustrate it.

Keys to Literature

simile: a comparison of two things using *like* or *as*

Example: *They were like four hungry cats about to pounce on a bird.*

climax: the high point of a story when the outcome is decided

Example: The climax of a story about a boxing match might be the moment when the hero tries to land a knock-out punch, just before the story ends.

Did You Know?

Sailing ships carried thousands of people from Asia to North America during the time of this story— the mid-1800s. Ships were often overcrowded. Travel was very uncomfortable. Sometimes it took weeks to make the trip. The ships usually docked in New York City or San Francisco.

Words to Know

warehouse	a place where food or other products are stored
apprentice	a person who works for an experienced worker to learn a skill
houseboy	a boy or man hired to do housework
mansion	a very large house
stingy	unwilling to spend money
scuffed	scratched or scraped
stale	not fresh; tasteless
tantrum	a display of bad temper or anger

Genre: Short Story

"The Friends of Kwan Ming" is a short story. Read more about short stories on page 467 of the Genre Guide.

The Friends of Kwan Ming

BY PAUL YEE, *adapted*

READ TO FIND OUT...
Why does Kwan Ming take the worst job that's available?

When his father died, Kwan Ming had to sell the house and his little rice field to pay for the burial. After the funeral, Kwan Ming looked around his village. He saw that he owned nothing—not even one roof tile. He had just enough money to buy a ticket on a ship to America. He had heard there were plenty of jobs there.

Kwan Ming told his mother, "I can start a new life in America. I will send money home."

The trip lasted six weeks. Kwan Ming sat in the bottom of the ship with hundreds of other Chinese. He became good friends with three men from nearby villages: Chew Lap, Tam Yim, and Wong Foon. Together the four men ate, told jokes, and shared their dreams for the future.

▶ Kwan Ming
  [KWAHN-mihng]

When they arrived in New York, everyone went off to different places to look for work. Kwan Ming hurried to the **warehouse** district, the train station, and the waterfront. But doors slammed in his face because he was Chinese. So he went to every store and laundry in Chinatown. But there were no jobs to be found anywhere. There were too many men looking for work in a country that was too young.

Every night, Kwan Ming went back to the inn where he was staying with his three friends. Like Kwan Ming, his friends had found no work. Every night the men ate their small bit of rice dotted with soy sauce. They talked about the places they had visited and the people they had met.

Every night, Kwan Ming worried more and more about his mother. He wondered how she was doing. His friends had worries, too.

One evening, Chew Lap said, "If I don't find work soon, I'm going back to China."

Tam Yim said, "What for, you fool? Things are worse there!"

Chew Lap said, "But at least I will be with my family!"

Wong Foon said, "Your family needs money for food more than they need your company. Don't forget that." Then there was a knock at the door. The innkeeper pushed his way into their tiny room.

The innkeeper said, "Good news! I have found a job for each of you!"

The men jumped to their feet.

The innkeeper said, "Three of the jobs are good, and they pay well. But the fourth job is, well...." The innkeeper coughed sadly.

Predict

Will Kwan Ming find a job? How?

Think About It

How do the men feel about their problem?

For the first time, the four men gave each other unfriendly looks. They were like four hungry cats about to pounce on a bird.

The innkeeper said, "The biggest bakery in Chinatown needs a worker. You'll always be warm next to the oven. Who will go?"

Kwan Ming said, "You go, Chew Lap. Your parents are sick. They need money for medicine."

The innkeeper said, "The finest tailor in Chinatown wants an **apprentice**. The man who takes this job will be able to throw away the rags he is wearing."

Kwan Ming said, "That's the job for you, Tam Yim. You have four little ones waiting for food in China."

The innkeeper said, "The best shoemaker in Chinatown needs a helper. He pays well. Who wants to cut leather and stitch boots?"

Kwan Ming said, "You go, Wong Foon. You said the roof of your house in China needs to be fixed. Better get new roof tiles before the rainy season starts."

The innkeeper shook his head and said, "The last job is for a **houseboy**. The boss owns the biggest **mansion** in town. But he is also the most **stingy** man around!"

Kwan Ming had no choice. He knew his mother needed money very badly. So off he went.

The boss was fatter than a cast-iron stove. He was as cruel as a blizzard at midnight. Kwan Ming's room was next to the furnace. Black soot and coal dust covered his pillow and blankets. It was hard to save money. For food, he had only leftovers.

Every day, Kwan Ming swept and washed every floor in the mansion. He moved the heavy oak tables. He rolled up the carpets. The house was huge. When Kwan Ming had finished cleaning the last room, the first one was dirty all over again.

Keys to Literature

This **simile** compares the men to hungry cats ready to pounce on a meal. It shows how eager they are to have work.

Think About It

Kwan Ming gives up the best jobs to his friends. What does this tell you about the kind of person he is?

Keys to Literature

What two things are compared in this **simile**?

One afternoon, Kwan Ming was mopping the front porch. His boss came running out in a hurry and slipped. He crashed down the stairs. Kwan Ming ran over to help. But the fat man turned on him.

The boss's neck turned purple as he screamed at Kwan Ming, "You turtle! You lazy oaf! You doorknob! You rock brain! You're fired!"

Kwan Ming said, "Please sir, give me another chance. I will work even harder if you let me stay."

The boss said, "Very well, Kwan Ming, I won't fire you. But I will have to punish you. You have ruined this suit. Because of you, I have **scuffed** my boots. You also made me miss my dinner."

The boss went on, "You have three days to find me the following things. Bring me a fine wool suit that will never tear. Bring me a pair of leather boots that will never wear out. Bring me forty loaves of bread that will never go **stale**. If you can't, you're fired. I will see that you never find another job!"

Kwan Ming ran off. What the boss wanted seemed impossible. Where would he ever find such things? He walked through the streets of Chinatown. He sat down on the wooden sidewalk.

Suddenly, he heard the familiar voices of his friends. Kwan Ming told them about the three things he had to bring to his boss.

Tam Yim said, "Don't worry! I'll make the wool suit you need."

Wong Foon said, "I'll make the boots."

Chew Lap said, "I'll make the bread."

Three days later, the friends brought the goods they had promised. The boss's eyes lit up when he saw them. He put on the suit. He was surprised at how well it fit. He sat down and tried on the boots. They slid onto his feet as if they had been buttered.

Keys to Literature

This is the **climax** of the story. The conflict between Kwan Ming and his boss is about to be solved.

Then the boss started eating the bread. It was so soft, so sweet, that he couldn't stop eating. He ate twelve loaves, then thirteen, then twenty.

The boss's stomach swelled like a circus tent. But his well-made suit and strong boots held him tight like a huge sausage. He shouted for help. He tried to stand up, but he couldn't. He kicked his feet like a baby having a **tantrum**.

Before anyone could do a thing, there was a great *Bang*!

Kwan Ming stared at the chair and blinked his eyes. There was nothing left of his boss.

He had exploded into a million little pieces.

Think About It

What do you think of the ending? Why?

Meet the Author

PAUL YEE *(Born 1956)*

Paul Yee was born and grew up in Canada. He studied history in college. He was very interested in his Chinese roots. Yee worked for the government studying archives and social policy. He organized festivals and education programs in the Chinese community. Yee used his experiences to write his first book.

Most of Yee's stories are about Chinese people in North America. *Tales from Gold Mountain* and *Ghost Train* are two of his best-known books. They are both about the hardships and strong spirits of early Chinese immigrants. Yee has won a number of awards for his writing.

"The Friends of Kwan Ming"

Check Your Predictions

1. Look back at the answers you gave for the Predict questions. Would you change your answers? Explain.

Understand the Story

2. Why do the four men leave their villages in China?

3. What is Kwan Ming's life like as a houseboy?

4. Why did Kwan Ming's boss want to fire him?

5. What happens in the climax of the story?

Think About the Story

6. Why did Kwan Ming's friends help him?

7. Identify one of the problems Kwan Ming has in this short story. How is it solved?

8. What two things are compared in this simile: "The boss's stomach swelled like a circus tent"? What does it mean?

Extend Your Response

Imagine you are applying for a job you found in the newspaper. Write a paragraph telling about your skills and how they will help you on the job.

Keys to Literature

tone: the feeling a writer shows toward his or her subject

> Example: *She had the best walk of any woman in France. She carried herself with much pride. It marked her as the queen.*

details: pieces of information that help to create a picture for the reader

> Example: *She had a long, narrow face. Her eyes were not large.*

Did You Know?

Marie Antoinette, a queen of France, came to a bad end. She was beheaded in 1793. When the French Revolution began, she was held as a prisoner in Paris. It was said she looked down on common people and told government secrets. The new French government ordered her death.

Words to Know

nobility	outstanding qualities; high moral character
splendor	grandness
satin	a smooth, shiny material
superior	better or more important than others
exhibit	present for viewing
rabble	a crowd of people who are hard to control

Genre: Memoir

Memoirs of Madame Vigée-Lebrun is a memoir. Read more about memoirs in the Learn More About It on page 190 or on page 466 of the Genre Guide.

from Memoirs of Madame Vigée-Lebrun

BY ÉLISABETH VIGÉE-LEBRUN, *adapted*

READ TO FIND OUT...
What is it like to work for a queen?

It was in the year 1779 that I painted the Queen, Marie Antoinette, for the first time. She was at the peak of her youth and beauty. She was tall and pleasantly built. Her arms were superb. Her hands, small and perfectly formed. Her feet, charming. She had the best walk of any woman in France. She carried herself with much pride. It marked her as the queen.

Keys to Literature

Tone is the feeling a writer shows about a subject. What is Madame Vigée-Lebrun's feeling about the Queen?

Marie Antoinette, Queen of France, with a Rose by Élisabeth Vigée-Lebrun (1873)

Madame Vigée-Lebrun painted this portrait of Marie Antoinette in Versailles, France.

Keys to Literature

The narrator includes many **details**, or pieces of information that help us picture the Queen. What are some of these details?

The Queen had both grace and **nobility**. Her features were not regular. She had a long, narrow face. Her eyes were not large. They were almost blue and at the same time merry and kind. Her nose was slender and pretty. Her mouth was not too large. The most striking thing about her face was the tone of her skin.

I have never seen skin so brilliant. I could never show the clearness of her skin as I wished. I had no colors to paint such freshness. Such fine shades were hers alone. I had never seen them in any other woman.

At the first sitting, the **splendor** of the Queen frightened me greatly. But Her Majesty spoke to me very pleasantly. I felt better. It was at that sitting that I began the picture showing her with a large basket. She wore a **satin** dress and held a rose. This portrait was for her brother, Emperor Joseph II. The Queen ordered two more copies. One was for the Empress of Russia, the other for her palace rooms.

I painted various pictures of the Queen. In one I did her wearing a pale red dress. She stood before a table arranging flowers in a vase. I liked to paint her in a plain gown without a wide skirt. She usually gave these portraits to friends or foreign officials. One shows her wearing a straw hat and a plain cotton dress. When this work was viewed, cruel people remarked that the Queen had been painted in her underclothes. Even so, the portraits were very successful.

Keys to Literature

The author uses a respectful **tone** toward the Queen. What words show that tone?

I was fortunate to be a friend of the Queen. She heard I had a fair voice. After that, we rarely had a sitting without singing. The Queen was very fond of music. But she did not sing very well.

Marie Antoinette was wonderful to talk with. She never missed a chance to praise others. The kindness she showed to me has been one of my sweetest memories.

One day I missed the time she had given me for a sitting. I had suddenly become ill. The next day I hurried to Versailles to offer my excuses. The Queen was not expecting me. Her horses had been harnessed for a drive. Her carriage was the first thing I saw in the palace yard. Even so, I went to speak with the officials on duty. One received me with a stiff, **superior** manner. Then he bellowed at me in a loud voice, "It was yesterday, madame, that Her Majesty expected you." Then he added, "I am sure she is going out driving. I am also very sure she will give you no sitting today!" I replied that I had only come to set another day. With that, he went to the Queen. She at once had me brought to her room. She had just finished dressing. In her hand she held a book while she listened to her daughter say her lessons. My heart was beating wildly, for I knew I was wrong. But the Queen looked up and said most kindly, "I was waiting for you yesterday. What happened?"

"I am sorry, Your Majesty," I replied. "I was so ill that I was unable to obey your commands. I came to receive more now. Then I will leave without delay."

"No, no! Do not go!" exclaimed the Queen. "I do not want you to have made your journey for nothing!" She canceled her carriage and gave me a sitting. In my confusion, I eagerly opened my box. I was so excited I spilled my brushes on the floor. I stooped down to pick them up. "Never mind, never mind," said the Queen. In spite of all I said, she picked them all up herself.

The Queen overlooked nothing to teach her children the polite manner which made her so beloved to all. I once saw her make her little daughter dine with a country girl. The Queen saw to it that the little visitor was served first. She told her daughter, "You must do the honors."

▶ Versailles is a city in France. It is famous for the palace and gardens built during the rule of King Louis XIV.

Think About It

The Queen picks up the author's brushes. What does this show about the kind of person the Queen is?

This painting shows Marie Antoinette and her children at Versailles.
It was well-known that the Queen was a dedicated and loving mother.

Marie Antoinette of Lorraine-Habsburg, Queen of France, with her children by Elisabeth Vigée-Lebrun (1789)

The last sitting I had with Her Majesty was at Trianon. I did her hair for a large picture of her with her children. After doing the Queen's hair, I did separate paintings of the children. Then I busied myself with my large picture. I gave it great importance and had it ready to **exhibit** in 1788. The frame, which had been sent ahead, caused many hateful remarks. "That's how the money goes," the people said.

At last I sent my picture. However, I could not find the courage to follow it. I was afraid it would be badly received. In fact, I became quite ill with fright. I shut myself in my room. There I prayed for the success of my "Royal Family." Suddenly my brother and a group of friends burst in. They told me my picture had received the highest praise. After the exhibit, the King had the picture moved to the palace. A minister presented me to the King. Louis XVI kindly agreed to talk to me at length. He told me he was very pleased. Then, looking at my work, he added, "I know nothing about painting, but you make me like it."

The picture was placed in one of the rooms in the palace. The Queen passed it going to and from mass. After the death of her son early in 1789, the picture reminded her of her painful loss. She could not go through the room without tears. The Queen ordered the picture taken away. With her usual thoughtfulness, she told me of her reasons for removing the picture. It is because of the Queen's tender feelings that my picture was saved. The common **rabble** who soon came to the palace would have destroyed it.

Predict

How do you think the painting will be received? Why?

▶ At this time in France, a revolution against the wealthy ruling class was forming. A mob later stormed the palace.

Meet the Author

MADAME ÉLISABETH VIGÉE-LEBRUN *(1755–1842)*

Madame Vigée-Lebrun was known as an artist, not a writer. She became one of the most successful women painters of her time. She painted many portraits. Her subjects were often queens and kings. When the French Revolution began, she was forced to leave the country. Afterward, she was able to return to France.

In 1835, Madame Vigée-Lebrun published her memoirs. They give us a glimpse into the lives of the wealthy people of her time. Her paintings are in museums today. Several are in the Metropolitan Museum of Art in New York City.

Self Portrait in a Straw Hat by Élisabeth Vigée-Lebrun (1782)

Learn More About It

GENRE STUDY: AUTOBIOGRAPHY AND MEMOIR

Autobiographies and memoirs are types of nonfiction. Nonfiction deals with real people, places, and events. In each, the author describes real things that happened to him or her and people he or she knows. Some autobiographies and memoirs are written by people who are famous. Other times they are written by people who have had unusual lives. Still others are written by people whose lives are quite normal.

Sometimes the terms autobiography and memoir are used to mean the same thing. However, autobiographies usually deal with a person's whole life. Usually the author is looking back on his or her life. Memoirs often deal with parts of a person's life or specific events. They also may describe the author's relationship with someone else as *Memoirs of Madame Vigée-Lebrun* does.

Check Your Prediction

1. Look back at the answer you gave for the Predict question. Would you change your answer? Explain.

Understand the Memoir

2. Why does Madame Vigée-Lebrun visit the Queen?

3. What detail of the Queen's appearance does Madame Vigée-Lebrun find most striking?

4. In what order are the events in this memoir presented?

5. How does Madame Vigée-Lebrun feel about the Queen?

Think About the Memoir

6. What does the story about Madame Vigée-Lebrun missing an appointment show about the Queen?

7. How would you describe the relationship between the Queen and the artist?

8. What tone does the author take toward the Queen in the last paragraph? How can you tell?

Extend Your Response

Imagine you are Madame Vigée-Lebrun. The French Revolution has begun. The Queen is being held prisoner in Paris. Write a letter to the Queen telling her how you feel. The tone of your letter should match how you feel about the Queen. Include a heading, a body, and a closing.

Keys to Literature

onomatopoeia: the use of words that imitate sounds

Example: *It's so cold that when you walk it crackles.*

concrete words: words that describe things that the reader can see, hear, feel, smell, or taste

Example: *Fox* is a concrete word.

Did You Know?

Earth is part of a galaxy called the Milky Way. People on Earth see it as a band of light across the night sky. Ancient people believed the band of light was a river of milk or a road to the heavens.

Words to Know

milky	like milk in color or form
crackles	makes a crisp snapping sound

Genre: Poetry

"Things I Forgot Today" is a poem. Read more about poetry on page 467 of the Genre Guide.

Things I Forgot Today

BY MARTHA B. MALAVANSKY

I sat across from her
She talked of little things
like the fox she had fed today
She said it had been around
5   for some time

"Did you see the stars tonight
I whistled to see
if they would dance
They were **milky**

10   "Did you hear the snow
It's so cold
that when you walk
it **crackles**"

READ TO FIND OUT...

Why does the speaker add "fox feeding" to her to-do list?

Think About It

Who is talking here?

Keys to Literature

The word crackles is an example of **onomatopoeia**. What else makes that sound?

The Fox Hunt by Winslow Homer (1893)

Keys to Literature

What **concrete words** does the speaker use to describe what she did?

15   I didn't see the stars
    hear the snow
    feed a fox
    I fed my kids
    washed dishes
    typed reports
20   did my homework

    My days are full
    but let me write these in
    fox feeding
    star watching
25   and walking

Meet the Author

MARTHA B. MALAVANSKY *(Born 1958)*

Martha Malavansky was born on St. George Island, Alaska. She is an Aleut-Inupiaq Eskimo. Malavansky graduated from high school when she was just sixteen. She studied science and business at the University of Alaska. She has worked for the City of St. George and for traditional Eskimo groups.

Malavansky has seen the effect of the modern world on village life in Alaska. There have been many changes in St. George. Malavansky says her poetry reflects the changes she sees. She hopes her people will maintain their culture in modern times.

Understand the Poem

1. How does the speaker's friend spend her day?

2. What does the speaker's friend want the stars to do?

3. How does the speaker spend her day?

4. Choose one word from the poem. What do you know about how the item looks, sounds, feels, smells, or tastes?

Think About the Poem

5. What does the speaker mean when she says, "let me write these in"?

6. What do the other woman's choices tell about who she is?

7. What does the speaker learn from her friend?

8. Do you think the speaker's tasks are more important than the "little things" her friend does? Why?

Extend Your Response

Write about your day, a recent event, or a trip you took. Use **onomatopoeia**, such as my alarm clock *buzzed*, the bus *honked*, or the leaves *crunched*, in your description.

Summaries

The Bear and the Two Travelers In this fable, two boys come upon a bear. One boy gets away, but the other is forced to play dead.

The Pigeon and the Ant A pigeon saves an ant from drowning. Later, the ant returns the favor by saving the pigeon from a hunter.

The Friends of Kwan Ming Kwan Ming leaves China for America to make money to support his family. On the ship, he meets three friends. After some time in America, they learn about four jobs. Kwan Ming takes the worst job. When his boss gives him some difficult tasks, Kwan Ming's friends help him.

Memoirs of Madame Vigée-Lebrun The author shares her experiences painting portraits of Queen Marie Antoinette. She shares details about the Queen's beauty and kindness.

Things I Forgot Today The speaker in the poem tells about her full days. Her friend also and reminds the speaker that it is also important to do simple things.

exhibit
mansion
snout
crackles
stingy

Vocabulary Review

Match each word in the box to its meaning. Write the word and its matching number on a separate sheet of paper.

1. present for viewing
2. a long nose
3. makes a crisp snapping sound
4. unwilling to spend money
5. a very large house

Chapter Quiz

Answer the following questions in one or two complete sentences. Use a separate sheet of paper.

1. The Bear and the Two Travelers How does each boy react to the bear?

2. The Pigeon and the Ant Why does the ant sting the hunter?

3. The Friends of Kwan Ming How does Kwan Ming get the suit, boots, and bread his boss demands?

4. Memoirs of Madame Vigée-Lebrun How does the author feel during her first sitting with the Queen?

5. Memoirs of Madame Vigée-Lebrun Why does the Queen have the family portrait removed from the palace?

6. Things I Forgot Today What does the speaker in the poem forget?

Critical Thinking

7. The Friends of Kwan Ming What is the theme of this story?

8. Memoirs of Madame Vigée-Lebrun Why do you think the painter was so worried that people wouldn't like her last painting of the Queen?

Chapter Activity

Choose a character from one of the selections in this chapter. Write a paragraph about the person using an admiring or respectful tone. Then rewrite the description. Use a critical or judging tone.

Unit 3 **Review**

On a separate sheet of paper, write the letter that best completes each sentence below.

1. In "The Good Brother's Reward," the greedy brother hopes to gain riches by
   A. setting his house on fire.
   B. injuring a small bird.
   C. helping his younger brother.
   D. rebuilding a temple.

2. The peddler in "The Rat Trap" feels that he is caught in a trap because
   A. he is a rat trap peddler.
   B. he stole money.
   C. Nils Olaf thinks he is a captain.
   D. Edla Willmansson invites him home.

3. In "The Story of Washing Horse Pond," Akui
   A. cannot drink the water.
   B. angers the God of Treasure Peak.
   C. is turned into a flying horse.
   D. saves the village.

4. In "The Bear and the Two Travelers," one friend climbs a tree and the other
   A. fights the bear.
   B. digs a hole.
   C. hides behind a rock.
   D. plays dead.

5. In *Memoirs of Madame Vigée-Lebrun*, Madame Vigée-Lebrun says that the Queen was
   A. a good singer.
   B. often upset.
   C. easy to talk to.
   D. impolite.

6. In "Things I Forgot Today," the speaker's friend reminds her to
   A. wash dishes.
   B. appreciate life.
   C. write a to-do list.
   D. keep busy.

Making Connections
On a separate sheet of paper, write your answers to the following questions.

7. Describe an external or internal conflict of one of the characters in this unit.

8. Which selection in this unit did you like best? Explain why.

Writing an Essay
Which friendship in this unit do you think is the strongest or most meaningful? Explain why. Give examples from the selection.

Unit Four

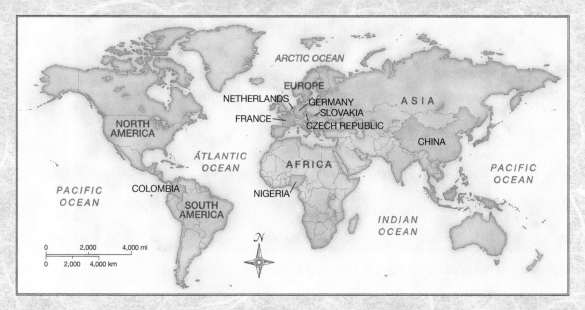

Poor Man's Cotton (1944) by Hale A. Woodruff

How are these people working together as a community?

Chapter 7

Community

Learning Objectives

- Recognize character traits.
- Understand dialogue.
- Find sensory details.
- Recognize and understand plot.
- Understand character clues.
- Recognize irony.
- Identify the speaker of a poem.

Preview Activity

Who makes up your community? Make a list of the people who are most important in your life. They can be teachers, neighbors, family, or friends. Compare lists with a classmate. How are your communities the same? How are they different?

Theme Preview: Community

Our community is where we belong. It is made up of our families, friends, and neighbors. These are the people we depend on and who depend on us. Each relationship helps us define who we are and what we can become. In this chapter, you will read about people whose lives change because of their relationships or their communities.

Keys to Literature

character traits: qualities that a person has, such as bravery or honesty

Example: In this story, Manka's main character trait is cleverness.

dialogue: a conversation between characters in a story or play; words that characters actually say

Example: *"What is the matter, husband?" his wife asked. "It's the new mayor...."*

Did You Know?

Cleverness is a prized quality in many folktales. As in this story, clever characters are often poor people. In animal stories, the clever characters are often coyotes, spiders, or rabbits.

Words to Know

dishonest	not honest; likely to cheat or lie
swiftest	fastest
cottage	a small house in the country
sneering	curling the upper lip in an unpleasant way
meddle	to get involved with another person's business
quarrel	an argument
judgment	a decision

Genre: Folktale

"Clever Manka" is a folktale. Read more about folktales on page 466 of the Genre Guide.

Clever Manka

RETOLD BY PARKER FILMORE, *adapted*

READ TO FIND OUT...
What effect does Manka's cleverness have on a young mayor?

There was once a rich farmer who was greedy and **dishonest**. He always cheated his poor neighbors. One neighbor, a simple shepherd, was to receive a cow for work he had done for this farmer. When the payment was due, however, the farmer would not give up the cow. The shepherd took the matter to the mayor. The mayor, a young man with little experience, listened to both sides. After some thought, he said, "I will not decide this case. Instead, I will give you both a riddle. The man who gives the best answer will have the cow. Do you agree?"

Keys to Literature

Character traits are the qualities a person has. What character traits does the farmer have?

The farmer and the shepherd agreed. Then the mayor said, "Well, then, here is my riddle: What is the **swiftest** thing in the world? What is the sweetest thing? What is the richest? Think about your answers and bring them to me at this time tomorrow."

The farmer went home angry.

"What kind of mayor is this young man!" he growled. "If he had let me keep the cow, I'd have sent him a basket of pears. But now I'm in danger of losing my cow. I can't think of any answer to his foolish riddle."

"What is the matter, husband?" his wife asked.

"It's the new mayor. The old one would have given me the cow without delay. This young man decides the case by asking riddles."

Then he told his wife the riddle. She cheered him quickly by saying she knew the answers at once.

"Why husband," she said, "our gray mare must be the swiftest thing in the world. You know nothing passes us on the road. As for the sweetest, did you ever taste honey sweeter than ours? I'm also sure there is nothing richer than our chest of gold coins. You have been saving them for forty years."

The farmer was thrilled.

"You're right, wife, you're right! That cow stays with us!"

The shepherd arrived home. He was very sad. He had a clever daughter named Manka. She met him at the door of his **cottage** and asked, "What is it, father? What did the mayor say?"

The shepherd sighed.

"I am afraid I've lost the cow. The mayor gave us a riddle, and I know I shall never guess it," the shepherd said.

Think About It

Why do you think the farmer is so angry?

Keys to Literature

Which two characters are speaking this **dialogue**?

"Perhaps I can help you," Manka said. "What is it?"

The shepherd told her the riddle. The next day as he left to see the mayor, Manka told him how to answer the riddle.

When he reached the mayor's house, the farmer was already there. He was rubbing his hands. He was extremely happy.

The mayor again stated the riddle. First he asked the farmer for his answers.

The farmer cleared his throat and with a superior look began, "The swiftest thing in the world? Why, my dear sir, that's my gray mare, of course. No other horse ever passes us on the road. The sweetest? Honey from my beehives, to be sure. The richest? What can be richer than my chest of gold coins!"

The farmer pulled his shoulders back and gave them a **sneering**, satisfied smile.

Predict

Will the farmer's answers to the riddle be correct? Why?

"H'mm," said the young mayor. Then he asked, "What answers does the shepherd give?"

The shepherd bowed politely and said, "The swiftest thing in the world is thought. Thought can run any distance in the blink of an eye. The sweetest thing of all is sleep. When a person is tired and sad, what can be sweeter? The richest thing is the earth, for out of the earth come all the riches of the world."

"Good!" the mayor cried. "Good! The cow goes to the shepherd!"

Later the mayor said to the shepherd, "Tell me now, who gave you those answers? I'm sure they never came from your head."

At first the shepherd tried not to tell. But when the mayor pressed him, he confessed. The answers came from his daughter, Manka. The mayor, who decided to test Manka's cleverness again, sent for ten eggs. He

Think About It

Why do you think the mayor wants to test Manka's cleverness again?

gave the eggs to the shepherd and said, "Take these eggs to Manka. Tell her to have them hatched by tomorrow and to bring me the chicks."

When the shepherd got home, he gave Manka the mayor's message. Manka laughed and said, "Take a handful of seeds and go right back to the mayor. Say to him, 'My daughter sends you these seeds. She says that if you plant them, grow them, and have them harvested by tomorrow, she'll bring you the ten chicks. You can feed them the ripe grain.'"

When the mayor heard this, he laughed heartily.

Keys to Literature

Who is speaking in this **dialogue**?

"That's a clever girl of yours," he told the shepherd. "If she is as lovely as she is clever, I think I'd like to marry her. Tell her to come to see me. However, she must come neither by day nor by night, neither riding nor walking, neither dressed nor undressed."

When Manka received this message, she waited until the next dawn. Night was not yet gone and day had not arrived. Then she wrapped herself in a fish net and threw one leg over a goat's back, keeping one foot on the ground. In this manner she went off to the mayor's house.

Now I ask you: did she go dressed? No, she wasn't dressed. A fish net isn't clothing. Did she go undressed? Of course not, for wasn't she covered with a fish net? Did she walk to the mayor's? No, she didn't walk, for she went with one leg over a goat. Then did she ride? Of course she didn't ride, for wasn't she walking on one foot?

When she reached the mayor's house she called out, "Here I am, Mr. Mayor. I have come neither by day nor by night, neither riding nor walking, neither dressed nor undressed."

The young mayor was delighted with Manka's
cleverness and lovely appearance. He asked to marry
her at once, and in a short time they were married.

▶ A *mare* is a female horse. A *colt* is a young male horse.

"But you must know this, my dear Manka," he said. "You are not to use your cleverness against me. I won't have you **meddle** in my cases. In fact, if ever you advise anyone who comes to me, I will turn you out of my house. I will send you home to your father."

All went well for a time. Manka was busy with her housework. She was careful not to meddle in any of the mayor's cases.

Then one day two farmers came to the mayor with a **quarrel**. One of the farmers owned a mare that had given birth to a colt in the marketplace. The colt had run under the wagon of the other farmer. The owner of the wagon, therefore, claimed the colt was his.

The mayor was thinking of something else when the case was being presented. He said carelessly, "The man who found the colt under his wagon is, of course, the owner of the colt."

As the owner of the mare was leaving the mayor's house, he met Manka. He stopped to tell her about the case. Manka was ashamed of her husband for making such a foolish **judgment**. She said to the farmer, "Come back this afternoon with a fishing net and stretch it across the dusty road. When the mayor sees you, he will come out and ask you what you are doing. Say to him that you're catching fish. He will ask you how you expect to catch fish on a dusty road. Tell him it's just as easy for you to catch fish in a dusty road as it is for a wagon to give birth to a colt. Then he will see the unfairness of his judgment and have the colt returned to you. But remember one thing: you mustn't let him find out that it was I who told you to do this."

That afternoon the mayor happened to look out the window and saw a man stretching a fish net across the dusty road. He went out to him and asked, "What are you doing?"

"Fishing," the man answered.

"Fishing in a dusty road? Are you mad?" the mayor asked.

▶ *Mad* means insane.

"Well," the man said, "it's as easy for me to catch fish in a dusty road as it is for a wagon to give birth to a colt."

Then the mayor saw that this was the man who owned the mare. The mayor had to admit that what the man said was true.

"Of course, the colt belongs to your mare and must be returned to you. But tell me," he said, "who put you up to this? You did not think of it yourself."

The farmer did not want to tell, but the mayor questioned him until he found out that Manka was at the bottom of it. This made him very angry. He went into the house and called his wife.

"Manka," he said, "did you forget what I told you would happen if you meddled in any of my cases? Home you go this very day. I don't care to hear any excuses. The matter is settled. You may take with you the one thing you like best in the house. I won't have people saying that I treated you badly."

Manka made no complaint.

"Very well, my dear husband, I shall do as you say. I shall go home to my father's cottage. I will take with me the one thing I like best in your house. But don't make me go until after supper. We have been very happy together, and I should like to eat one last meal with you. Let us have no more words but be kind to each other as we've always been. Then we will part as friends."

The mayor agreed to this, and Manka prepared a fine supper. She made all the dishes her husband loved. The mayor wished Manka good health, then sat down. The supper was so good that he ate and ate and ate.

Predict

What will Manka choose to take with her to her father's house?

Think About It

Why does Manka make such a fine meal for her husband?

Keys to Literature

Why does the author have the mayor roar his line of **dialogue**?

The more he ate, the more tired he became until he fell sound asleep in his chair. Then without waking him, Manka had him carried to the wagon that was waiting to take her home.

The next morning, when the mayor opened his eyes, he found himself in the shepherd's cottage.

"What does this mean?" he roared out.

"Nothing, dear husband, nothing!" Manka said. "You know you told me I might take the one thing I liked best in your house. So I took you! That's all."

For a moment, the mayor rubbed his eyes in shock. Then he laughed loud and heartily at how clever Manka was.

"Manka," he said, "you're too clever for me. Come on, my dear, let's go home."

So, they climbed back into the wagon and drove home.

The mayor never again scolded his wife. But whenever a very difficult case came up, he always said, "I think we had better ask my wife. You know she's a very clever woman."

Check Your Predictions

1. Look back at the answers you gave for the Predict questions. Would you change your answers? Explain.

Understand the Folktale

2. How would you describe the community in this story?

3. What tool does the mayor use to decide the dispute between the farmer and the shepherd?

4. Why does the mayor decide to send Manka back to her father's house?

5. Why does Manka take the mayor to her father's house?

Think About the Folktale

6. What does the dialogue between Manka and the owner of the colt show about Manka?

7. Why doesn't Manka complain when her husband says he's going to send her back to her father's house?

8. The mayor laughs and invites Manka back home when he sees she's tricked him. What does that tell you about him?

Extend Your Response

Imagine you are making a movie of "Clever Manka." Draw several panels that show the most important scenes in the film. Below each drawing, write what is happening.

Keys to Literature

sensory details: details that show how something looks, sounds, smells, tastes, or feels

> Example: *Loose clothes puffed about their thin bodies.*

plot: the action of a story or play. Most stories have a problem and, at the end, a solution.

> Example: Two friends are running against each other for class president. They campaign, the election is held, and one wins.

Did You Know?

Some communities still have a market day, when farmers bring their goods to town to be sold. It is more than just a chance to shop. Market day is also the time when neighbors and friends meet to chat and find out the latest news in the community.

Words to Know

thrifty	not wasteful; careful with spending
harness	the leather straps and metal pieces used to connect a horse to a plow or wagon
grudge	bad feeling toward someone who is supposed to have done something wrong
solemnly	very seriously
squabbled	argued noisily
innocence	freedom from guilt
oaths	promises to speak the truth

Genre: Short Story

"A Piece of String" is a short story. Read more about short stories on page 467 of the Genre Guide.

A Piece of String

BY GUY DE MAUPASSANT, *adapted*

READ TO FIND OUT...
How does a piece of string cause a man's death?

Along all the roads around Goderville, peasants and their wives were walking toward the village. It was market day. The men moved with slow steps. Their whole bodies bent forward at each movement of their long, twisted legs. Their legs were twisted from the hard work of pulling heavy plows and using heavy tools. Loose clothes puffed about their thin bodies. Each man looked like a balloon ready to fly away. From each, a head, two arms, and two feet stuck out.

▶ A *peasant* is a poor farmer.

Some led a cow or calf by a rope. The wives walked behind whipping the animal with a branch to hurry it along. They carried large baskets on their arms. From some baskets, chickens and ducks poked out their heads. The wives walked more quickly and with a livelier step than their husbands. Their lean, straight frames were wrapped in thin shawls pinned in the front. Their heads were wrapped in white cloths, then held in place by caps.

Keys to Literature

A **sensory detail** shows how something looks, sounds, smells, tastes, or feels. What sounds are described in the next paragraph?

In the public square of Goderville, there was a crowd of people and animals mixed together. The horns of cattle and the hats of the peasants rose above the crowd. Loud, sharp voices could be heard. Sometimes the rough sound of a countryman's laugh or the moo of a cow could be heard above all the noise. Everything carried the odor of the dirt, hay, and sweat of men and animals.

Maître Hauchecome [MEH-truh OSH-kum] of Breaute [BROHT] *Maître* is a title, like Mister.

Malandain [Mah-LAN-dahn]

Keys to Literature

Plot is the action in a story. The plot begins when Hauchecome picks up the string.

Maître Hauchecome of Breaute had just arrived in Goderville. He was walking toward the public square when he noted a little piece of string on the ground. Being a **thrifty** man, he thought that everything useful should be picked up. He bent painfully to pick it up. He suffered from rheumatism. He took the bit of thin string from the ground and rolled it carefully. As he did this, he saw Maître Malandain, looking at him from his doorway. Malandain was the **harness**-maker. The two men were angry at each other over a business deal. Both were good at holding a **grudge**. Maître Hauchecome was ashamed to be seen picking up a string out of the dirt. He therefore quickly hid his "find" in his pocket. For a time, he pretended to be looking for something on the ground that he could not find. Then he continued his slow, painful trip to the square.

There he was soon lost in the dealings of the noisy crowd. Peasants came and went, troubled and always in fear of being cheated. During the bargaining, they watched for tricks or flaws in the goods. The women placed their great baskets on the ground. They lay terrified chickens and ducks on the ground, their legs tied together. They listened to offers and gave their prices. Suddenly agreeing to a price, they might shout: "All right, I'll give it to you for that."

Then little by little, the square emptied. At Jourdain's, the great room was soon filled with people eating. The flames from the huge fireplace warmed the backs of the diners. Over the fire, chickens, pigeons, and legs of lamb turned slowly. The smell of roast meat and gravy rose from the hearth, making everybody's spirits rise and their mouths water. The wealthier farmers ate at Maître Jourdain's. He was a tavern keeper and horse dealer. He was a man who had money.

▶ Jourdain's [zhoor-DAHNZ] is a tavern, a place where food and drinks are served.

Plates of food and jugs of yellow cider were passed and emptied. Everyone talked of what he bought or sold, of crops, or of the weather. Suddenly, a drum beat sounded outside the inn. Most of the diners rose and ran to the door or the windows. Their mouths were full, and napkins were still in their hands.

Keys to Literature

What **sensory details** tell about the scene at the tavern?

After the town crier stopped his drum-beating, he called out slowly: "Let it be known that there was lost this morning a black leather purse. This purse held five hundred francs and some business papers. The finder is asked to return it to Maître Houlbreque or to the mayor's office. There will be twenty francs reward."

Then the town crier went away. His drum and voice were heard again in the distance. Then the talk turned to Maître Houlbreque's chances of finding or not finding his purse. As the meal ended, the chief of police came to the door.

He asked, "Is Maître Hauchecome here?"

Maître Hauchecome answered, "Here I am."

The officer replied, "Maître Hauchecome, will you kindly come with me to the mayor's office? The mayor would like to talk to you."

The peasant was surprised and shaken. He rose painfully to his feet. The first steps after a rest were especially painful. Then he moved forward saying, "Here I am, here I am."

The mayor was waiting for him in his armchair. He was a large, serious man who spoke **solemnly**. "Maître Hauchecome," he said, "you were seen this morning picking up Maître Houlbreque's purse."

Maître Hauchecome was stunned. He looked at the mayor, terrified by his words. Why was he being blamed?

"Me? Me? Me pick up the purse?"

"Yes, you, yourself."

"On my word, I never saw it."

"But you were seen."

"I was seen, me? Who says he saw me?"

"Maître Malandain, the harness-maker."

The old man remembered and understood. His face became red with anger.

"Ah, he saw me pick up this string." He reached in his pocket and drew out the little piece of string.

But the mayor shook his head with doubt.

"Maître Malandain is an honest man. You want me to believe he thought a string was a purse?"

The peasant was furious. "It is God's truth, Maître Mayor! I swear by my soul!"

Predict

What will happen when Maître Hauchecome goes to the mayor's office?

Keys to Literature

Many **plots** center on a problem. What problem do you see forming here?

The mayor went on. "You picked up the purse and stood looking for a long while in the mud to see if any piece of money had fallen out."

The good old man choked with fear and rage. "How anyone can tell—how anyone can tell—such lies. Lies to ruin my good name! How can anyone—"

It was no use. Nobody believed him. Maître Malandain arrived and repeated the charge. The two men **squabbled** for an hour. Maître Hauchecome asked to be searched. Nothing was found on him.

Finally, the mayor, very much puzzled, let Maître Hauchecome leave.

Think About It

Why do you think the people in the village do not believe him?

The news had spread. As he left the mayor's office, the old man was surrounded and questioned. He retold the story of the string. No one believed him. They laughed at him.

He stopped his friends, endlessly telling his story. He turned his pockets inside out to prove he had nothing. Still no one believed him. He grew angry and hot at not being believed.

Night came. He must leave. He started on his way with three neighbors. He pointed to the place where he had found the bit of string. All along the road, he spoke of his adventure. In the evening, he walked around his own village of Breaute. He told the people of Breaute his story. Again, no one believed him. It made him ill all night.

The next day, a hired man from Ymanville returned the purse and its contents to Maître Houlbreque. He claimed he found the purse in the road. Not knowing how to read, he took it to his employer, Maître Breton.

The news spread through the town. Maître Hauchecome soon heard it and was filled with joy.

"What hurt me so much was not the thing itself, as the lying. Nothing is so shameful as being ruined by a lie."

Hauchecome talked of his adventure all day long. He told it on the highway to people who passed by. He told people in shops and people coming out of church the following Sunday. He stopped strangers to tell them about it. He was calm now, but something still bothered him. He didn't know what exactly it was, though. People appeared to be joking while they listened. They did not seem to believe him. He thought that they were making comments about him behind his back.

Predict

What do you think will happen next?

Think About It

What still bothers Maître Hauchecome?

On Tuesday of the next week, he went to the market at Goderville. His only reason was the need he felt to discuss his story.

Malandain was standing at his door. He began laughing when he saw the old man pass.

Then he spoke to a farmer from Crequetot, but the farmer would not let him finish. He poked the old man's stomach and said: "You big rascal." Then he turned his back on him.

Maître Hauchecome was confused. He had no idea why he was being called a big rascal.

At Jourdain's, he began to explain his story. A horse dealer called to him. "Come, come, that's an old trick. I know all about your piece of string!"

Hauchecome stammered, "But the purse was found."

Another man said, "Shut up, papa. One man finds, and another man returns. At any rate, you are mixed up in it."

Think About It

Why do you think people still don't believe him?

The peasant stood choking. He understood. They thought he had a partner who returned the purse. He tried to explain. All the table began to laugh. He could not finish his dinner. He left to the sound of people laughing.

At home he felt ashamed and upset. It was impossible to prove he did not find the purse since he was known to be quite clever. The thought that people did not believe him hurt him deeply.

Then he began telling his story again and again. Each time the story got longer. New reasons were added. More solemn **oaths** and stronger protests were made. His whole mind was given to the story of the string. Yet the more he explained, the less he was believed.

"Those are lies," they said behind his back.

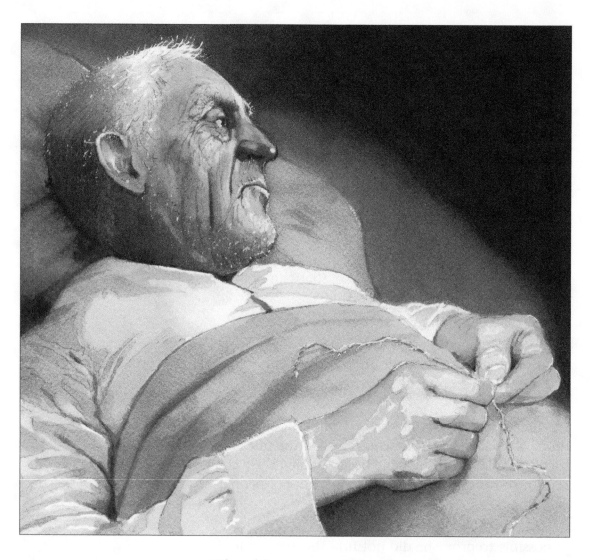

Think About It

Why does Maître Hauchecome's mind weaken?

The old man wore himself out over it and wasted away before their eyes. Some made him tell about the string for their amusement. His mind, touched deeply, began to weaken.

Toward the end of December, he took to his bed.

He died in the first days of January. Until his death, he claimed his **innocence** and said again and again:

"A piece of string. A piece of string—look—here it is, M'sieu' Mayor."

Meet the Author

GUY DE MAUPASSANT *(1850–1893)*

Guy de Maupassant (moh-puh-SAHNT) grew up in a comfortable middle-class family. He was studying law when his family lost their money and he was forced to quit school. He became an office clerk to make a living. To keep from being bored, de Maupassant began to write stories. Soon, he was part of the writing world of Paris.

Once de Maupassant began writing, he did not stop. He wrote almost 300 stories and 200 newspaper articles, as well as nine books. He is known for his honest, sometimes grim, view of life. The public loved his work. Writing made him rich and he died a wealthy man.

Check Your Predictions

1. Look back at the answers you gave for the Predict questions. Would you change your answers? Explain.

Understand the Story

2. Why does Maître Hauchecome hide the string he picks up?

3. Give two details that describe Jourdain's tavern.

4. Who told the police that Maître Hauchecome had stolen the purse?

5. What does Maître Hauchecome do to try to make people believe he did not take the purse?

Think About the Story

6. Why do the people of Maître Hauchecome's village make fun of him?

7. What is the problem in the story's plot?

8. Why does Maître Hauchecome's health fail?

Extend Your Response

Write a short scene from this story in the form of a play. You might choose Maître Hauchecome's meeting with the mayor or another interesting scene.

Learn More About It

PEASANT LIFE IN NINETEENTH-CENTURY FRANCE

The life of a French peasant in the 1800s was often difficult. Peasants made their living by farming. They worked hard in the fields for long hours each day. They kept some of their harvest for themselves. But they also sold goods in the village on market day. The goods might have been vegetables, milk, or livestock, such as chickens. They might also have traded with other peasants for items their families needed.

The Woman at the Well by Jean-Francois Millet

Market day was not only a day for business. During those times, there were few entertainments. On market day, people from the village and the nearby farms would catch up on the latest news. They might have discussed what was happening in the village or on nearby farms. Villages were like family. The villages were often small. Most people knew each other. They stuck together in hard times. However, people often did not trust strangers or people from other villages.

Apply and Connect

How might the villagers' distrust of strangers have affected Maître Hauchecome?

Keys to Literature

character clues: the thoughts, actions, and words in a story that help you understand what a character is like

> Example: *She began to see herself as the honored wife of the headmaster. She would be the queen of the school.*

irony: a result that is the opposite of what is expected; it is often unfortunate.

> Example: In a famous story, a man sells his watch to have enough money to buy his wife a comb. However, his wife sells her hair to buy her husband a watch chain.

Did You Know?

Britain once ruled Nigeria. Some of the "modern ways" in this story may be based on British ways. Nigerians fought the British for independence. The "modern ways" of the British were one reason for conflict.

Words to Know

headmaster	a school principal
proper	correct
hobble	walk with a limp
shrine	a place where people pay respect to a god
pagan	having to do with ancient religion
ancestors	the family or group a person comes from
sacrifices	offerings of valued objects
misplaced	wrongly given importance

Genre: Short Story

"Dead Men's Path" is a short story. Read more about short stories on page 467 of the Genre Guide.

*D*ead Men's Path

BY CHINUA ACHEBE, *adapted*

Michael Obi's hopes came true much sooner than he thought. He was appointed **headmaster** of Ndume Central School in January 1949. It had always been a backward school. For this reason those in charge decided to send a young, eager man to run it. Obi took the job with great excitement. He had many wonderful ideas. This was the chance to put them to work. He had had a **proper** education which earned him the title "master teacher." This set him apart from the other headmasters. He spoke out often against the narrow views of the older, less-educated ones.

"We shall make a good job of it, don't you think?" he asked his young wife when they heard the news.

"We shall do our best," she replied. "We shall have such beautiful gardens. Everything will be modern and delightful...." They had been married two years. In that time, she had become completely taken by her husband's passion for "modern ways." Like him, she mocked "these old useless teachers." They would be better off as traders in the market. She began to see herself as the honored wife of the headmaster. She would be the queen of the school.

The wives of the other teachers would envy her. She would set the style in everything.... Then, suddenly, she thought there might not be other wives. Torn between hope and fear, she anxiously asked her husband.

"All our teachers are young and unmarried," he said happily. For once, his wife did not share his feelings. "It's a good thing," he went on.

"Why?" his wife asked.

READ TO FIND OUT...
What is the "dead men's path"?

▶ Ndume [n-DOO-muh]

▶ Michael Obi speaks out often against the "narrow views" of the older teachers. This tells you he thinks he is better than they.

Keys to Literature

Mrs. Obi wants to set the style in everything. What does this **character clue** tell you about her?

"Why? They will give all their time and energy to the school," her husband answered.

Nancy was sad. She was not sure about the new school. But this lasted only a few minutes. Her personal bad luck could not blind her. This was her husband's great chance. She looked at him as he sat folded up in a chair. His back was bent, and he looked weak. But he sometimes surprised people with sudden bursts of energy. Now his strength seemed to be resting behind his deep-set eyes. They gave him a rare, piercing power. He was only twenty-six, but looked thirty or more. On the whole, he was fairly handsome.

"A penny for your thoughts, Mike," said Nancy after a while. She sounded like the women's magazines she read.

Predict

Will the headmaster and his wife get along with the people at the new school?

"I was thinking about the grand opportunity we have. At last we can show these people how a school should be run."

Ndume School was backward in every way. Mr. Obi put his whole life into the work. His wife did too. He had two aims. First, the teaching had to be of the highest quality. Second, the school grounds were to become a place of beauty. Nancy's dream gardens came to life with the rains. Beautiful flowers and hedges of bright red and yellow set the school gardens apart from the untended neighborhood plants.

One evening Obi was admiring his work. He was horrified to see an old woman from the village **hobble** across the school grounds. She went right through a flower-bed and some hedges. On going there he found the faint signs of an old path. It went from the village across the school grounds. This little-used path ended in the bushes on the other side of the school.

Think About It

What problem is developing here? Why?

"It amazes me," said Obi to a teacher who had been there three years. "You allowed the villagers to use this path. It is simply beyond belief." He shook his head.

"The path," said the teacher, "seems to be very important to them. It's hardly used, but it connects the village **shrine** with their place of burial."

"What has that got to do with the school?" asked the headmaster.

"Well, I don't know," said the other teacher with a shrug of the shoulders. "But I remember there was a big quarrel some time ago. It happened when we tried to close the path."

"That was some time ago. But it will not be used now," said Obi as he walked away. "What will the Government Officer think? He comes to inspect the school next week. The villagers might, for all I know, decide to do something else. Perhaps they will use a schoolroom for a **pagan** ritual during the inspection."

Heavy sticks were planted across the path at two places. Some were placed where the path entered the school grounds. The others were placed where it left the grounds. Both were wrapped with barbed wire.

Three days later the village priest called on the headmaster. The priest was an old man and walked with a slight stoop. In his hand he carried a thick walking stick. He often tapped it on the floor to mark the importance of what he said.

"I have heard," he said after a few pleasant words, "that our ancient path has been closed...."

"Yes," replied Mr. Obi. "We cannot let people make a road of our school grounds."

"Look here, my son," said the priest bringing down his stick. "This path was here before you were born. It was here before your father was born. The whole life of the village depends on it. Our dead depart by it and our **ancestors** visit us by it. But most important, it is the path of children coming in to be born...."

Mr. Obi listened with a satisfied smile on his face.

Think About It

What are the differences between Mr. Obi and the village priest?

"The whole purpose of our school is to erase such beliefs," he said at last. "Dead men do not need paths. The whole idea is ridiculous. Our duty is to teach your children to laugh at such ideas."

"What you say may be true," replied the priest. "But we follow the ways of our fathers. If you open the path, we shall have no quarrel. What I always say is: let the hawk perch and let the eagle perch." He rose to go.

Think About It

"Let the hawk perch and let the eagle perch" is a proverb. What do you think the proverb means?

"I am sorry," said the young headmaster. "But the school grounds cannot be a highway. It is against our rules. I suggest you build another path around our grounds. We can even get our boys to help you build it. I don't think your ancestors will find the extra distance a hardship."

"I have no more words to say," said the old priest, already outside.

Two days later a young woman in the village died giving birth. A wise man was immediately called. He ordered heavy **sacrifices** to satisfy the ancestors angered by the fence.

Keys to Literature

The things the schoolmaster does in order to try to obtain a good report from the inspector are things that lead to the bad report. This is an example of **irony**.

Obi woke up the next morning among the ruins of his work. The beautiful hedges were torn up. Not only near the path but all around the school, flowers were trampled to death. One of the school buildings had also been pulled down.... That day the inspector came to see the school and wrote a nasty report on the appearance of the school grounds. More serious, however, was his damaging report on the war between the school and the village. A war, he said, that was caused in part by the **misplaced** eagerness of the new headmaster.

Meet the Author

CHINUA ACHEBE *(Born 1930)*

Chinua Achebe was born in southeastern Nigeria in 1930. He was the fifth of six children. He grew up in a small village, in a simple house with dirt floors. Achebe's love of studying English soon led people in the village to call him "Dictionary." He left home at a young age to attend school. After college, he worked in radio broadcasting. He also worked for Nigeria's independence from Britain. For much of his working life, he has been a professor and writer.

His first book, *Things Fall Apart*, was published in 1958. It tells the story of how Europeans changed African culture. That clash of cultures is the subject of much of Achebe's work. He has written more than a dozen books and received many awards for his stories about African life.

Check Your Predictions

1. Look back at the answers you gave for the Predict questions. Would you change your answers? Explain.

Understand the Story

2. What are Mr. Obi's plans for the school?

3. Why is the path important to the villagers?

4. Why do the villagers destroy the grounds of the school?

Think About the Story

5. Mr. Obi thinks the villagers should change their ways. What does this tell you about him?

6. What could Mr. Obi have done to prevent the school grounds from being ruined?

7. What is the irony of the ending of this story?

8. What is the message of this story about community?

Extend Your Response

The school grounds have been ruined and the inspector has written his report. Pretend you are Mrs. Obi, writing home to her family. Explain, from her point of view, what has happened and why.

Keys to Literature

speaker of the poem: the one who is describing or telling about something in the poem

> Example: The speaker of the poem often uses pronouns, such as *I* and *we*.

During the Tang Dynasty in China, when Po Chü-i was writing, poets were huge celebrities. During that time (618–907), the government gave poets high honors and good jobs. Many think that the poems written during this time are the best in Chinese history.

Words to Know

bamboos	tropical plants with hollow woody stems
cypress	a kind of evergreen tree
perished	died
homespun	loosely woven homemade cloth
brambles	prickly bushes
thatched	covered with straw, grass, or leaves

Genre: Poem

"Bitter Cold, Living in the Village" is a poem. Read more about poetry on page 467 of the Genre Guide.

Bitter Cold, Living in the Village

BY PO CHÜ-I

READ TO FIND OUT...
What lesson can a bitter winter teach?

In the twelfth month of this Eighth Year,
On the fifth day, a heavy snow fell.
Bamboos and **cypress** all **perished** from the freeze.
How much worse for people without warm clothes!

5 As I looked around the village,
Of ten families, eight or nine were in need.
The north wind was sharper than the sword,
And **homespun** cloth could hardly cover one's body.
Only **brambles** were burnt for firewood,
10 And sadly people sat at night to wait for dawn.

Keys to Literature

The **speaker of the poem** is remembering a very cold winter. How does the speaker refer to himself?

Streams and Hills Under Fresh Snow

Think About It

How can you tell the
speaker is richer than
others in the village?

From this I know that when winter is harsh,
The farmers suffer most.
Looking at myself, during these days—
How I'd shut tight the gate of my thatched hall,
15 Cover myself with fur, wool, and silk,
Sitting or lying down, I had ample warmth.
I was lucky to be spared cold or hunger,

Neither did I have to labor in the field.
Thinking of that, how can I not feel ashamed?
20 I ask myself what kind of man am I.

Meet the Author

Portrait of Po Chü-i by anonymous

PO CHÜ-I *(772–846)*

When he was just five years old, Po Chü-i
began writing poems. Throughout his life, he
never stopped writing. He made his living as a
government official, though. He began his career
in the palace library. By the time he retired, he had
been a governor and a mayor. When Po Chü-i was
alive, poetry was popular in China. He was one of
the best-loved poets.

In Po Chü-i's time, much Chinese poetry
was written for the rulers. It had little to do with
ordinary people. However, Po Chü-i thought
poetry should be direct and simple. He wanted
to reach everyone with his poetry. He wrote
poetry about problems in society he wanted to
change. Even today, his clear, graceful style wins
him many readers.

Understand the Poem

1. What event is the speaker of this poem remembering?

2. How can you tell the villagers are poor?

3. What do the villagers do to survive the cold winter?

4. How is the life of the speaker different from the lives of the other villagers?

5. Who suffers most when winter is harsh?

Think About the Poem

6. What do we know about the speaker of the poem?

7. Why does the speaker feel ashamed?

8. What is this poem's message about community?

Extend Your Response

Chinese poetry was often illustrated and written in beautiful handwriting, or calligraphy. Draw a picture that captures the feeling of this poem. Or rewrite the poem in your best and most interesting handwriting.

Summaries

Clever Manka The new mayor decides a court case by asking a riddle. The winner admits that his answers came from his daughter, Manka. The mayor and Manka marry, but her cleverness gets her into trouble— and then out of trouble again.

A Piece of String Maître Hauchecome picks up a piece of string while visiting another village. Maître Malandain sees him picking up something, and he says the old man has stolen a purse. Although Maître Hauchecome shows the piece of string, no one believes he is innocent.

Dead Men's Path Young Mr. Obi is the new headmaster of a village school. To keep the school grounds neat, he closes a path that is important to the villagers. The priest explains how important the path is. However, Mr. Obi does not listen, with sad results.

Bitter Cold, Living in the Village The speaker recalls a bitter winter when many poor people struggled to survive. The speaker was warm and dry and could have helped his neighbors. He is ashamed that he did not.

ancestors
brambles
dishonest
grudge

Vocabulary Review

Complete each sentence with a word from the box. Use a separate sheet of paper.

1. During the hike, he tore his clothes on some _____.
2. We knew we couldn't trust her, because she'd been _____ in the past.
3. My great-grandparents, like my other _____, came from Italy.
4. My sister had hurt my feelings, but I tried not to hold a _____ against her.

Chapter Quiz

**Write your answers in one or two complete sentences.
Use a separate sheet of paper.**

1. Clever Manka How does the mayor find out about Manka?

2. Clever Manka Why does Manka ask the owner of the colt not
    to tell her husband that she has helped him?

3. A Piece of String Why does Maître Hauchecome pick up
    the string?

4. A Piece of String What is the relationship between Maître
    Hauchecome and Maître Malandain?

5. Dead Men's Path What does the title of this story refer to?

6. Bitter Cold, Living in the Village How does the speaker of the
    poem spend the winter?

Critical Thinking

7. Dead Men's Path How might the plot of this story be
    different if Mr. Obi were more respectful?

8. Bitter Cold, Living in the Village Do you think the speaker of
    the poem will change his way of life? Explain your answer.

Chapter Activity

Choose one of the stories in this chapter. Change one
event in the plot. Then rewrite the story to show what
would happen.

The Life of Harriet Tubman, #10 (1940) by Jacob Lawrence © 2005 Gwendolyn Knight Lawrence/Artists Rights Society (ARS), New York

What does the picture of Harriet Tubman say about courage?

Learning Objectives

- Recognize figurative language and metaphors.
- Understand a writer's tone.
- Understand how colloquial language is used.
- Identify similes and how they are used.
- Recognize realism as a style of writing.

Preview Activity

Think about a time when you showed great courage. What did you fear? How did you overcome your fear? Share your story with a partner.

Theme Preview: Courage

Courage comes in many forms. It takes courage to overcome fear. It takes courage to make decisions. It also takes courage to write or create art or music. In this chapter, the characters face extraordinary difficulties. But they stay true to themselves and exhibit great courage in some of the worst situations possible.

Keys to Literature

figurative language: words that describe something by comparing it to something else; similes and metaphors are types of figurative language.

> Example: *Anne's eyes were like saucers.*

metaphor: a comparison of two things that does not use *like* or *as*

> Example: *Margot and I were two allies against the strength of the German beast.*

Did You Know?

Thousands of Jewish people fled from Europe during World War II. Some others, like the Frank family, went into hiding. Adolf Hitler, the leader of Nazi [NAHT-see] Germany, wanted to wipe out all Jewish people in Europe. His army killed millions of people, both Jewish and non-Jewish. Memorials worldwide honor these people.

Words to Know

brigade	a group of people organized for a purpose
lodger	a person who rents a room
reassure	make a person feel comfortable or confident

Genre: Autobiography

Anne Frank Remembered: The Story of the Woman Who Helped to Hide the Frank Family is an autobiography. Read more about autobiographies on page 466 of the Genre Guide.

from Anne Frank Remembered: The Story of the Woman Who Helped to Hide the Frank Family

READ TO FIND OUT...
How do Miep Gies show courage in hiding the Frank family?

BY MIEP GIES (with ALISON LESLIE GOLD), *adapted*

During World War II, Jewish people who went into hiding often had helpers. These non-Jewish people brought them food and other necessary items. Miep Gies once worked for Anne Frank's father, Otto. Miep and her husband, Henk, helped hide the Frank family, Mr. and Mrs. Van Daan and their son Peter, and a dentist named Dussel. They lived in Amsterdam. For more than two years, Miep scraped together enough food to feed all eight people. The following is Miep's account of the day the Franks went into hiding.

The back of the building in which Anne and her family hid from the Germans during World War II.

▶ Herman Van Daan works for Mr. Frank. He later goes into hiding with the Franks.

It was the first Sunday in July. The night was warm. Henk and I had eaten our dinner. Suddenly, the doorbell rang.

A ringing doorbell could mean trouble. We became very nervous. Our eyes darted to one another. Quickly, Henk went to the door. I followed him. There stood Herman Van Daan. He was very upset.

Van Daan said, "Please come right away. Margot Frank just got a postcard. She is being ordered to report for a forced labor **brigade**. The Franks cannot let this happen. They have decided to go into hiding right away. Can you come right now? Can you take a few things they'll need?"

Henk said, "We will come."

We put on our raincoats. We could not be seen carrying bags and packages. It would be too dangerous. We could hide many things under our baggy old raincoats. It might seem odd to be wearing raincoats on a dry night in summer, but it was better than carrying bags.

Henk and I left with Mr. Van Daan. When Mr. Frank had told me the plan for his family to go into hiding, I told Henk about it. Henk and I did not need to talk it over. He said right away he would help the Frank family as much as he could. But Henk and I didn't know the Franks would go into hiding this soon.

Van Daan said, "The Franks are having a hard time. There is so much to do, and so little time. Also, their **lodger** keeps hanging around, so it is very difficult to get anything done."

As we walked to the Franks' apartment, I worried for them. I thought of the postcard Margot had received. Now the Germans were sending sixteen-year-old girls into forced labor. This was a new horror for the Jews. How many young girls like Margot had gotten such a postcard? What if they had no father like Mr. Frank?

What if they had no place to hide? Those girls must be horribly afraid tonight. I had to force myself not to run to the Franks' apartment.

When we got to the Franks' apartment, we spoke little. There was a feeling of near-panic in the air. I could see that they had much to do, and many things to prepare. It was all too terrible. Mrs. Frank handed us piles of things. They felt like children's clothes and shoes. I was so nervous and scared I didn't look at what she was giving me.

I hid the bunches of things under my coat, in my pockets, under Henk's coat, in his pockets. The plan was I would take these things to the hiding place some time after the Franks had moved in.

Our coats were bursting. Henk and I went back to our place. We quickly unloaded what we had under our coats. We put it all under our bed. When our coats were empty again, we hurried back to the Franks' apartment for another load.

We had to keep everything secret from the Franks' lodger. Everyone tried to seem normal. We did not run. We did not raise our voices. The Franks handed us more things. Mrs. Frank put things in bundles. She sorted through things quickly. She gave them to us and again we took and took. Her hair was falling from her tight bun into her eyes. Anne came in. She brought too many things. Mrs. Frank told her to take them back. Anne's eyes were like saucers. They were a mixture of excitement and terrible fear.

Henk and I took as much as we could and quickly left.

The next day was Monday. I woke to the sound of rain. We had planned what to do the night before. I rode my bicycle to the Franks' apartment. Margot's bike was standing outside. She had been ordered to hand it in, but she had not done so.

Think About It
Why don't they raise their voices at the Franks' house?

Keys to Literature

The **figurative language** here helps describe Anne's eyes. What are Anne's eyes compared to?

▶ The Nazis ordered all Jewish people to turn in their bicycles in June of 1942.

Margot came out the apartment door. Mr. and Mrs. Frank were inside. Anne hung back inside the doorway. Her eyes were wide.

I could tell that Margot was wearing layers of clothing. Mr. and Mrs. Frank looked at me. Their eyes pierced mine.

The Nazi soldiers were called the "Green Police" because of the color of their uniforms.

I tried to **reassure** them. I said, "Don't worry. The rain is very heavy. Even the Green Police won't want to go out in it." Mr. Frank looked up and down the street. He said to Margot and me, "Go. Anne and Edith and I will come later in the morning. Go now."

Margot and I pushed our bicycles onto the street. Quickly, we pedaled away, but not too fast. We wanted to look like two everyday working girls on their way to work on a Monday morning.

The Nazis required all Jewish people to wear yellow stars. That way the Nazis could single them out.

Not one Green Policeman was out in the rain. I took the big crowded streets. All the way, Margot and I did not speak. We knew that from the moment we had gotten on our bicycles, we had become criminals. There we were, a Christian and a Jew. She was a Jew without a yellow star, riding an illegal bicycle. This Jew was ordered to report for a forced-labor brigade. She had been about to leave for some unknown place in Hitler's Germany. Margot's face showed no fear. She showed nothing of what she was feeling inside. Suddenly, Margot and I were two allies against the strength of the German beast.

Keys to Literature

This **metaphor** describes the Nazi German government. What is it compared to?

We arrived at the office building and carried our bicycles into the storeroom. All at once I could see that Margot was about to crumble.

I took Margot's arm and led her past Mr. Frank's office. Then we went up the stairway to the hiding place. By now it was time for the office to open. I was afraid that people would be coming to work, but I kept silent.

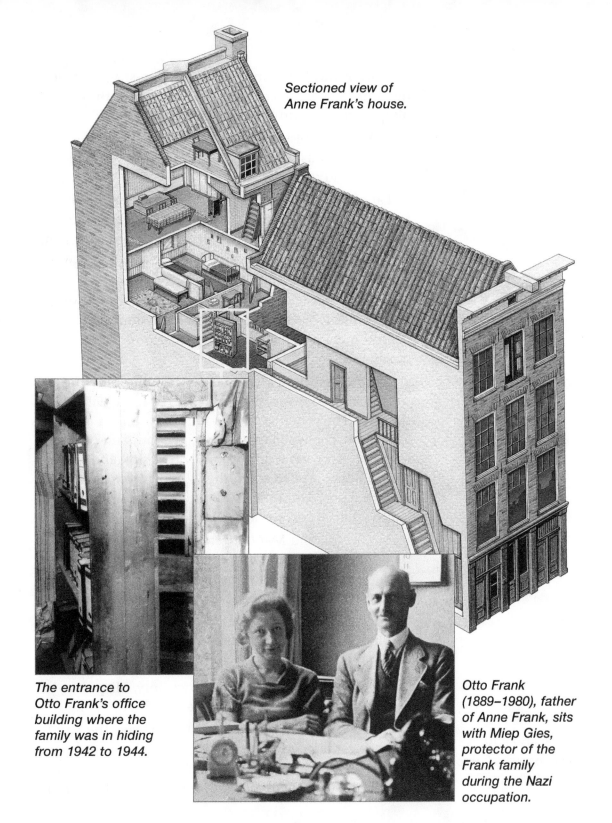

Sectioned view of Anne Frank's house.

The entrance to Otto Frank's office building where the family was in hiding from 1942 to 1944.

Otto Frank (1889–1980), father of Anne Frank, sits with Miep Gies, protector of the Frank family during the Nazi occupation.

Margot was like someone stunned, in shock. I held her arm to give her courage. Still, we said nothing. She disappeared behind the door to the hiding place. I went to the front office and sat down at my desk.

My heart was thumping. I wondered how I could get my mind onto my work.

Later that morning, the moment I had been waiting for finally came. I heard Mr. and Mrs. Frank and Anne coming through the office door. I quickly joined them. I hurried them through the office and up the stairway to the door of the hiding place.

In the afternoon, when no one was around, I went to the hiding place myself. I closed the door tight behind me. I had never been there before. Sacks and boxes and things were piled everywhere.

Think About It
What details describe the Franks' hiding place?

On the first floor were two very small rooms and a toilet. One room was shaped like a rectangle with a window. The other room was long and thin. It also had a window. The wallpaper was old, yellow, and peeling. Upstairs there was a large room with a sink and stove and cabinets. In this room the windows were covered with curtains. Then there was another stairway. This led to an attic and storage area.

Mrs. Frank and Margot were like lost people. The blood seemed drained from them. Anne and her father were trying to do something with all the boxes and sacks. They were pushing, carrying, clearing. I asked Mrs. Frank, "What can I do?"

Mrs. Frank shook her head.

I said, "Let me bring you some food?"

She gave in to me. "A few things only, Miep. Maybe some bread, a little butter. Maybe milk?"

Think About It
What do you think Miep Gies is feeling here?

The situation upset me. I wanted to leave the family alone together. I couldn't begin to imagine what they must be feeling. They had walked away from everything they owned in the world. They left behind their home, a lifetime of possessions they had gathered, Anne's little cat, Moortje, keepsakes from the past, and friends.

They had simply closed the door of their lives. They had disappeared from Amsterdam. Mrs. Frank's face said it all. Quickly, I left them.

Meet the Author

MIEP GIES *(Born 1909)*

Miep Gies was born in Vienna, Austria. During World War I, many children, including Gies, did not have enough to eat. A family from Holland adopted Gies. As a young woman, Gies worked for Otto Frank. She became close to his family. When Nazi Germany invaded Holland in 1940, she helped the Franks and others hide from the Germans. She brought food and supplies to them every day. When the Nazi police raided the hiding place, Gies tried to convince them to spare her friends. It didn't work.

After the raid, Gies saved photographs, papers, and Anne Frank's diary. She returned the diary to Otto Frank after the war. Anne's famous diary was read by millions of people. Years later, Gies wrote *Anne Frank Remembered*. She traveled around the United States talking about her book.

Check Your Prediction

1. Look back at the answer you gave for the Predict question. Would you change your answer? Explain.

Understand the Autobiography

2. Why is Miep Gies surprised when Van Daan tells her the Franks need her help?

3. Why do the Franks need to go into hiding right away?

4. How do the Gieses hide the belongings that they are taking from the Franks' house?

5. Where is the Franks' hiding place?

Think About the Autobiography

6. Why is the metaphor "the German beast" a good description of the Nazi government at that time?

7. What is the comparison "Mrs. Frank and Margot were like lost people" an example of?

8. What kind of person is Miep Gies? How do you know?

Extend Your Response

Imagine that you have the chance to interview Miep Gies. Write six questions you would ask her. Then write what you think her answers would be.

Learn More About It

WORLD WAR II AND THE HOLOCAUST

Almost every major power in the world fought in World War II. The war had many causes. Mostly, it occurred because several governments wanted more power. Japan, Germany, and Italy all sought to control more territory and people. Other European countries and the United States took action against them. The war began on September 1, 1939. On this day, Hitler, the dictator of Germany, invaded Poland. After almost six years of fighting on several continents, the war ended with surrenders by Germany and Japan in 1945.

Jewish families being forced from their homes in Poland by Nazi soldiers.

World War II was devastating to many nations. More than 55 million people died. Of these, almost 6 million Jewish men, women, and children died in the Holocaust. The Holocaust was a mass killing of Jewish people in Europe. Like Anne Frank, many Jews were sent to concentration camps. At these camps, people were forced to do dangerous and difficult work. They were given little or nothing to eat. Many died. At some, Jews were put to death in gas chambers.

More than 250,000 people survived the Holocaust. Today, some continue to tell their stories. Others work to improve human rights. Memorials worldwide honor those who survived and those who died in the Holocaust.

Apply and Connect

How do reading Anne Frank's diary and Miep Gies' autobiography help us understand the Holocaust?

Keys to Literature

tone: the feeling a writer shows toward his or her subject

> Example: Anne Frank's diary has a frustrated, but hopeful tone.

colloquial language: everyday language people use when talking to friends

> Example: *Just had another big blow-up with Mother.*

Did You Know?

For thousands of years, people around the world have written down their feelings and thoughts in diaries. Writing in a diary or journal can help people deal with the world's challenges.

Words to Know

mischief	action that bothers or annoys others
failings	faults or weaknesses
reserves	extra supplies
forbid	order not to do something

Genre: Diary

The Diary of a Young Girl is Anne Frank's published diary. Read more about diaries on page 466 of the Genre Guide.

from The Diary of a Young Girl

BY ANNE FRANK, *adapted*

On June 12, 1942, Anne Frank celebrated her 13th birthday. She received a diary from her father. She named the diary "Kitty." A little less than a month later, Anne's family went into hiding. Anne told all her feelings, fears, and thoughts to her diary.

On August 4, 1944, the Green Police arrested Anne Frank and the seven other people in hiding. Someone had given their hiding place away to the Nazis. Sometime in March of 1945, Anne and her sister died at Bergen-Belsen, one of Hitler's work camps in Germany. Otto Frank was the only one of the eight who survived. Miep Gies had collected Anne's writings from the hiding place after the arrest. She gave the diaries and papers to Mr. Frank on the day they learned that Anne was not coming back.

READ TO FIND OUT...

How are the experiences of a teenager in hiding similiar to those of teenagers everywhere?

Keys to Literature

Anne expresses her feelings about the people in her life and her studies. These feelings make up the **tone** of her writing.

The living room and kitchen of the Anne Frank house.

Monday, 21 September, 1942

Dear Kitty,

I can't stand Mrs. Van Daan. I get nothing but blow-ups from her. She thinks I talk too much. Now she's making up excuses to get out of washing the pans when it's her turn.

I'm busy with Daddy working out his family tree. As we go along, he tells me a little about everyone. It's most interesting. Mr. Koophuis brings a few special books for me every other week.

School time has begun again. My favorite subject is history. We brought a lot of school books and supplies with us. I'm working hard at my French. Peter sighs and groans over his English.

The adults were talking about me. They decided that I wasn't completely stupid after all. Of course, that made me work extra hard the next day.

I was just writing something about Mrs. Van Daan when in she came. Slap! I closed the book. She wanted to take a peek anyway, but I wouldn't let her. It gave me quite a shock!

Sunday, 27 September, 1942

Dear Kitty,

Just had another big blow-up with Mother. We just don't get along these days. It's not going too well between Margot and me, either. We usually don't yell much in our family, but lately Margot and Mother are getting on my nerves.

The Van Daans love to talk about other people's children. Margot doesn't mind; she is such a goody-goody. I, however, seem to have enough **mischief** in

Think About It

Why do you think the Van Daans care how Anne behaves?

Think About It

The Franks have been hiding for about three months. What might cause them to get on each other's nerves?

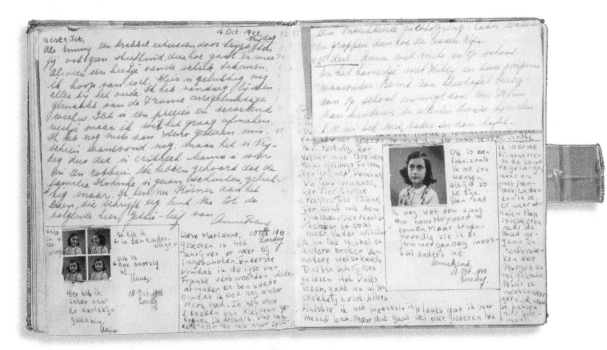

Anne Frank's diary, written in October 1942.

Family portrait of the Franks.

Anne Frank with Dopy the dog.

me for two. The Van Daans think I'm spoiled. They are always quick to let Mother and Daddy know it. My parents always defend me. But they do tell me I shouldn't talk so much or poke my nose into everything. If Daddy weren't so sweet, I'd be afraid I was a disappointment to them.

Monday, 28 September, 1942

Dear Kitty,

Why do grown-ups quarrel so much, and over the stupidest things? I used to think it was only children who had quarrels. Of course grown-ups call them "discussions." I suppose I should get used to it. But I can't, not as long as nearly every discussion is about me! Nothing about me is right. They talk about the way I look, my character, my manners. I'm just supposed to take it and keep quiet. But I can't! I'll show them! Maybe they'll keep their mouths shut when I start educating them. I am amazed at their awful manners and especially by Mrs. Van Daan's stupidity.

Kitty, if only you knew how angry they make me! I shall just explode one day!

Keys to Literature

What does the **colloquial language** "explode one day" mean?

Tuesday, 7 November, 1942

Dear Kitty,

Mother is in a bad mood. That always means problems for me. Is it just chance that she and Daddy never scold Margot and always dump on me for everything? Just last evening I picked up a book Margot had been reading. When Margot came back into the room, she had this look. She asked for "her" book back. Just because I wanted to look at it a little

Think About It

Why does Anne feel that her parents are unfair?

while longer, she got angry. Then Mother jumped in. "Give the book to Margot; she was reading it," she said. Then Daddy came in. He didn't even know what it was about, but he took Margot's side. I put the book down and left the room. They thought I was angry, but it was only that my feelings were hurt.

I knew Mother would stick up for Margot. She always takes her side. I'm so used to it that I don't care any more. I love them, but only because they are my mother and sister.

With Daddy, it's different. He's the one I look up to. He doesn't notice that he treats Margot differently from me. I have always been second-best. I have always had to pay double for anything I did wrong. First, I am scolded and then my feelings get hurt. I won't take it any more. I want something from Daddy that he is not able to give me.

I'm not jealous of Margot. It's only that I long for Daddy's real love. I don't want him to love me just as his child, but as Anne, myself.

Only through Daddy can I feel the least bit of family feeling. He doesn't like it when I talk about Mother's **failings**. He doesn't want to hear about it. Just the same, I find her failings harder to take than anything else. I don't like always having to call attention to how mean and sloppy she is. But I just can't keep it all to myself. I wish I could only see Mother's good side. But it doesn't work. Neither she nor Daddy understands this empty space in my life. I wonder if parents can ever make their children happy.

Sometimes I think that God wants to test me. I must become good on my own, with no one to be an example for me. Then later on it will make me stronger. From whom but myself will I get comfort? I need comforting. My faults are too great. I know this, and every day I try to make myself better.

Think About It

Why does Anne think that God is testing her?

Think About It

What is Anne's tone like when writing to her diary, "Kitty"?

The way they treat me changes so much. One day they think I'm grown up. The next day I hear that Anne is just a silly little goat. She doesn't know anything. I'm not a baby any more. I'm not to be laughed at. I have my own plans and ideas, even though I can't put them into words yet. I'm tired of having no one who understands me. That is why in the end I always come back to my diary, because Kitty is always patient. I'll promise her that I'll be strong. I'll find my own way through it all, without crying. I only wish I could sometimes hear a kind word from someone who loves me.

▶ June 12, 1943, was Anne's 14th birthday.

Tuesday, 15 June, 1943

Dear Kitty,

Daddy wrote me a sweet poem for my birthday. I got some lovely things. One was a fat book on my favorite subject—the myths of Greece and Rome. There were also a lot of sweets. Everyone broke into their last **reserves**. As the youngest of our family in hiding, I am more honored than I deserve.

We must hand in our radio next month. Koophuis has a small, secret one at home that he will let us use. It is a shame to have to hand in our big one, but one can't take any chances of getting caught. The radio has been our source of courage. It helps us say, "Chin up. Better times will come."

Sunday, 11 July, 1943

Dear Kitty,

We are back on the "upbringing" theme again. I really am trying to be helpful and polite. It is very hard to be on such good behavior with people you can't stand. But I really do see that I get along better by pretending a little.

Margot and I have been studying shorthand. Now I have to let it go a bit. I need more time for my other subjects, and I am also having trouble with my eyes.

I have needed glasses for a long time. (Yuck, I would look like an owl!) Yesterday Mother talked about sending me to the eye doctor with Mrs. Koophuis. Imagine it! Going outside on the street! But I don't think it will happen. Now that the British have landed in Sicily, Daddy is hoping for a "quick finish."

Elli gives Margot and me a lot of office work. It makes us both feel very useful, and it is a big help to her. We take special care to do a good job.

> Elli works in the office downstairs. She leaves work for the girls to do at night.

Miep is just like a pack mule. Almost every day she finds some vegetables for us. She brings them on her bicycle. We long for Saturdays, when our books come. It's just like getting a present. People outside don't know what books mean to us. Reading, learning, and the radio are our fun.

Friday, 5 May, 1944

Dear Kitty,

Daddy is not happy with me. He thought that after our talk on Sunday I wouldn't go upstairs every evening. He is making it very hard for me. I will talk to him today. This is roughly what I want to say:

"I believe, Daddy, that you are not happy with me. I suppose you want me to be just as a 14-year-old should be. But that's where you're wrong.

"Since we came here, I have not had an easy time. If you knew how unhappy I felt, how lonely, you would understand that I want to be with Peter!

> Anne and Peter Van Daan have become good friends.

Predict

Do you think Anne will say this to her father? Why or why not?

"I am now able to live on my own, without Mother's help or yours. You can laugh at me and not believe me, but that can't hurt me. I am only telling you this because I thought that otherwise you might think I was being sneaky. I don't have to explain what I do to anyone but myself.

"When I had problems, none of you helped me. You only scolded me about being so loud and foolish. I acted that way only so that I wouldn't be hurting all the time. Now the battle is over. I have won! I am free. I don't need a mother any more. This battle has made me strong.

Keys to Literature

Anne's **tone** has changed. How is it different?

"And now I will go my own way. You must not see me as 14, for all these troubles have made me older. I will not be sorry for what I do. I will act as I think I must. Either **forbid** me to go upstairs, or trust me. Then leave me in peace!"

Sunday, 7 May, 1944

Dear Kitty,

Daddy and I had a long talk yesterday. I cried a lot, and he joined in. On Friday I wrote what I explained to you in a letter. I put it in his pocket before supper. Margot told me that he was very upset for the rest of the evening. (I was upstairs doing the dishes.)

Yesterday he told me that I had done him a great wrong. "You, Anne, who have received such love from your parents, can you say we have not helped you? We have always been ready to help you. We have always defended you. How can you talk of feeling no responsibility to us? Maybe you didn't mean it that way, but that is what you wrote."

Think About It

Why is Anne's father upset by her note?

Oh, this is the worst thing I have ever done! I was only showing off. I was just trying to appear big so that he would respect me. Certainly I have had problems. But to accuse Daddy, who has done so much for me—no, that was too low for words.

It's right that my pride has been shaken. I was becoming much too taken up with myself again. The way Daddy has forgiven me makes me feel ashamed of myself. No, Anne, you still have much to learn.

I want to start over with him. That can't be hard, now that I have Peter. With him to help me, I can and will!

Think About It

How has Anne's talk with her father changed Anne?

Anne Frank's last diary entry, August 1, 1944, made three days before she and her family were discovered by the Nazis.

Meet the Author

ANNE FRANK *(1929–1945)*

Anne Frank was born in Frankfurt, Germany. A few years later, the Nazis took over the country. The Franks were not welcome because they were Jewish. They moved to Holland. Anne enjoyed a happy childhood until the Nazis invaded Holland, too. They began sending Jewish people to labor camps. Anne's family went into hiding. They lived in hidden rooms in Mr. Frank's office building. After two years of hiding, the police discovered the group. Anne died of a fever in a camp in Germany.

After World War II, Anne's father published her diary. It was a huge success. People were amazed by Anne's cheerfulness and hope during such a dangerous time. Anne wrote, "I still believe that people are really good at heart." Anne's diary was printed in many languages. Plays and films are based on her story. Millions of people have read Anne's diary.

Check Your Prediction

1. Look back at the answer you gave for the Predict question. Would you change your answer? Explain.

Understand the Diary

2. Why does Anne complain about Mrs. Van Daan?

3. How does Anne feel about her mother?

4. Why does Anne write her father a note?

Think About the Diary

5. Why do you think Anne calls her diary "Kitty"?

6. Why do you think Margot and Anne enjoy doing office work?

7. What is the tone of Anne's note to her father?

8. Do you think Anne is courageous? Why or why not?

Extend Your Response

Imagine that you were forced into hiding as Anne Frank was. What books and belongings would you want? Make a list of six items. Next to each tell why you would want it.

Keys to Literature

simile: a comparison of two things using the word *like* or *as*

> Example: *Since an early hour the old church bells, sounding like the braying of a donkey, have been tolling.*

realism: a style of writing in which people and events are presented the way they actually are in life

> Example: *She tosses away a large tomato that the soldier's boots squashed.*

Words to Know

criticized	blamed; found fault with
escorting	taking someone from place to place
recruits	people who have just joined the military
condemnation	strong disapproval
congregation	a group of people who attend a church
hemp	a strong, fibrous plant
mannequin	a model of the human form
imitate	try to be like
exile	a person forced to leave a country

Genre: Novel

   The Honorable Prison is a novel. Read more about novels on page 467 of the Genre Guide.

from The Honorable Prison

BY LYLL BECERRA DE JENKINS, *adapted*

*Marta's father is a newspaper editor who has **criticized** the government in his paper. Because of this, Marta, her parents, and her brother Ricardo have been imprisoned in a house on a hill overlooking a small town. They are guarded by soldiers. In this passage, Marta and Ricardo are allowed to go to the weekly market for the first time to buy food and supplies.*

The pueblo, which was like a ghost town yesterday, is filled with townspeople and campesinos this morning. Since an early hour the old church bells, sounding like the braying of a donkey, have been tolling. There is also the music of harmonicas and the off-pitch singing of the campesinos. *¡Fiesta!* is the one word that comes clear.

▶ *Campesinos* are farmers.

Fruits and greens, pottery and chicken, are spread all over the pavement. From the window the plaza looks like a gigantic, colorful blanket.

▶ A *fiesta* is a celebration or party.

My mother gives us a long list. Besides the food for the week, we also must buy blankets and straw mats to cover the dampness of the brick floors. We also need cooking pots and ant insecticide.

Keys to Literature

Similes use *like* or *as* to compare two things. Authors use similes to describe things. What is being compared in a simile here?

"My name is Polo Beltrán," our **escorting** soldier comes in saying. He skips the military salute and the clicking of boots. He is short and stocky with a stonelike face. He is no different from the soldiers we saw everywhere in the city. "Raw **recruits** from the countryside or from the city slums," Papa often explains about the soldiers. "Some find pleasure in carrying guns and torturing and killing. Others obey like robots and are helpless victims of the dictatorship."

To which group does this Polo belong? I wonder. But my brother and I can't hide our high spirits as we leave the house and walk downhill.

We are eager to be part of the festive mood of the market. Ricardo doesn't stop talking. "Are there dishes ready to eat at the market?" he wants to know. "No? What about a bakery? No bakery either?" Well, he will find the biggest banana in the plaza, he says.

There is a twitch of a smile on Polo's face. He looks at us out of the corner of his eye. One moment he seems friendly. The next, he frowns. Straightening his shoulders, he changes his step to a marching gait to show us that he is *la autoridad*.

"Where do you come from, Polo?" Ricardo asks.

The soldier does not answer for a moment. Then he says, "From around here." His almond-shaped eyes look ahead toward the mountains in the distance, behind the church tower.

We find ourselves inside the plaza, moving with the crowd. "We must move fast!" Polo says. "One hour, that's what Captain Paredes orders. Then I have to report to him, and he…"

"He what?" I ask.

"One hour," the soldier repeats.

Everybody turns to stare at us. "Look, *los hijos del prisionero … nero … ero … ero*" (the prisoner's children). The whisper follows us around the square.

The campesinos chant their goods, calling "Sweet little oranges … little red tomatoes … fresh little eggs!"

First we buy two large baskets. Ricardo takes one, I the other. We go separate ways, Ricardo already eating the banana he had promised himself.

Trying to catch up with us, Polo steps over the tomatoes and eggs, the fruits and pottery. The peasants,

▶ *La autoridad* means "the person in charge."

Keys to Literature

Polo seems to think something bad will happen if they're not back in an hour. The threatening details are part of the **realism** in this story. Realism shows things as they are in real life.

not the soldier, apologize, calling him "my lieutenant."
"*Perdón, mi teniente*," an old campesina repeats. She
tosses away a large tomato that the soldier's boots
squashed. Ricardo and I exchange a glance. We must
keep close to each other and to the soldier.

    Near the church a group of local men in city suits
interrupt their conversation. They glare at us with
something more than curiosity: with **condemnation**
of our father. My brother and I are experts at
recognizing the pursed lips and flaring nostrils.
It's the same expression we saw in our teachers and
neighbors in the city.

▶ *Perdón, mi teniente*
means, "Excuse me,
lieutenant."

I pretend not to notice and call a loud "Good morning!" The men half bow and glance away.

The village boys dart their little hands to their temples in the military fashion. They shout, "*¡Buenos días, Señor Alcalde, viva mi General!*"

Like an echo, our soldier and other voices around us repeat it. "Good morning, Mr. Mayor, long live our General!"

"*¡Buenos días! ¡Buenos días!*" a bony man with glasses in the center of the gathering answers. He lifts his hand in the manner of a priest blessing his **congregation**.

Someone is tipping his hat, calling a clear, friendly "Good morning" to Ricardo and me. It's a young man standing by himself on the other side of the church. He is about twenty-five. His pale complexion makes his dark eyes intense.

"Let's keep an eye on the campesinos, Ricardo. Maybe we'll see one of Papa's friends."

My father has fought for peasants' rights in his newspaper. Often he has been criticized, even by his close friends, for his repeated editorials exposing the landowners' abuse of the campesinos. Ever since I can remember, there have been campesinos visiting our house, thanking my father for some favor. They would bring fruits, eggs, goat cheese wrapped in banana leaves, and dry herbs to make tea for my father's cough.

He would tell them about new experiments he had read about in a farmers' magazine that would improve their harvest of corn and other crops.

Often Papa would invite Ricardo and me to visit his peasant friends' huts in nearby villages. I was bored by the campesinos' rambling stories about sickness and poverty and the ghosts they saw everywhere. I had to

Think About It

The government is run by the military. Why is everyone so eager to show support of the General?

fight my distaste to eat *mazamorra*, a dark, thick corn soup. They always served it in gourd bowls, their thumbs in the dish.

"I am a campesino, Marta," Papa would tell me. "Your grandfather lived in a hut and wore **hemp** sandals." And his eyes glistened with an emotion I could not share at those moments, surrounded by the toothless and rotten-toothed smiles of my father's campesinos.

Away from them, I was able to see in my mind a hut set against a hill. There would be the fragrance of eucalyptus and a neat little man with a poncho and hemp sandals, my grandfather. He would smile at me with all his white teeth. "I am a campesino, Marta" sounded romantic in the city.

Now Ricardo and I search for a familiar face. But with their dark ponchos and battered hats, the campesinos around us all look alike. I pat the heads of the runny-nosed children. We compliment their goods. We do not haggle. But they are tight-lipped, counting our change hurriedly, trying to get rid of us. Their eyes dart toward the spot where the mayor and his friends are standing. As we say good-bye, the murmur goes on, "... *prisionero, los hijos del prisionero*."

"Time to go home!" the soldier announces, looking at the loaded baskets. He's carrying the folded straw mats, a kettle, and a can of insecticide.

"I forgot something. It's very important, Polo. I will take only a minute!" Ricardo says.

Both turn back. I move toward the little street that leads to the paved road and up to our hill inside the fort.

The friendly young man who greeted us earlier is now standing nearby, smoking and looking bored. His

Keys to Literature

What examples of **realism** show what the campesinos are like?

Think About It

Why do the sellers in the market want to get rid of Marta and Ricardo quickly?

rather formal black suit and tie give him the look of a handsome **mannequin**. As he sees me he takes one step forward, coming perhaps to help me with the heavy basket. Then he stops abruptly. Glancing at his wristwatch, he pretends he has not seen me. The mayor and his friends are approaching.

Ricardo comes home after a short while. He is wearing a man-sized poncho, the same gray as Papa's.

"He wants to **imitate** Miguel in everything!" Mama comments, smiling. But I suspect that the poncho has another purpose.

"What are you hiding under the poncho, Ricardo?"

Ignoring my question, he walks away.

He shares his secret with my father. They laugh and whisper. At one point my brother, his back to me, thrusts his arms forward. Papa's hands move quickly, and there is more laughter and hissing between them. It's obvious that they're taking turns concealing under their ponchos what Ricardo bought at the market at the last moment.

Predict

Will Ricardo show what is under the poncho? What is he hiding?

I discover Papa's and Ricardo's secret. It's a chicken with red, shiny feathers that my brother calls Perico.

"Don't tell Mama, please, Marta. She wouldn't allow me to keep him."

At noon, Mother and I take turns bathing. Papa and Ricardo keep watch outside the outdoor bathroom. The soldiers sometimes climb the hill and appear in our yard unexpectedly.

Ricardo plays hopscotch. His chicken follows, oddly never moving far from Ricardo. The animal's beady eyes look around as if studying the surroundings.

"See, Marta? The chicken is a perfect addition to our family," my father says. "He's as distrustful of this place as we are. Why, Perico even whispers his cackling."

Indeed, the chicken keeps up a continual but low clucking. In the midst of following my brother, Perico lifts one leg and leans his head as if to catch an unusual sound. Mostly he does this when Mama opens the squeaky door of the bathroom, alerting the three of us to throw a towel over the chicken.

Think About It

In what ways is Perico like the family?

On Sundays, Papa does not type. After church, he waits for us in the front yard with a book.

He is cheerful, or rather he makes an effort to appear cheerful. "We must start," he says, pointing to the three chairs around the hammock. Sunday is English-lesson day. He opens the book, *Cortizos' Easy Guide to Learning English.* "We don't need a teacher," he repeats every Sunday. "You see the text has a system. It guarantees a perfect pronunciation. "'Welcome, Meester González, you arr in a free country now.'" (A Mr. González, no doubt a political **exile**, is the subject of the conversation lessons.) "'Speek with no fear, Meester González!'"

Think About It

Why do you think the family is learning English?

Think About It

Why doesn't Papa's silliness make the family laugh any more?

▶ *Margarita* is Mama's first name.

He acts out the lessons as he moves about the yard. He bows grandly in front of Mama. He pulls his reading glasses down his nose. Skipping from one spot to another, he asks questions of Ricardo and me. But his clowning, which used to make us laugh, brings only forced smiles from my brother and me. And Mama says, "Be still, Miguel, or you will have a fit of coughing."

He pretends not to notice our long faces, which even Mama doesn't bother to cover up on Sundays. Sundays are the beginning of another hopelessly long week.

"It's your turn, Margarita!"

"Please, Miguel, leave me out of this. I'm too old to learn English."

"Come, dear. Speek with no fear, Señora Margarita!"

Mama sighs. She repeats with a pronunciation that sounds better than his and that he corrects. "Again, speek, speek, see?"

He points at things in the yard. We name them in English.

"Weeds."

"Wall."

"Ashes."

He gives the most attention, though, to Señor González's speeches. He repeats them over and over. "Welcome ... you arr in a free country now!"

Today, as soon as the lesson is finished, Ricardo disappears into his room. After a moment, Mama calls, "Ricardo, will you come out of that room with your silly chicken!"

I turn to Papa, now relaxing in the hammock. "Does Mama know about Perico?"

"Of course I know. The three of you seem to believe that I'm blind, deaf, and dumb. Who do you suppose has been cleaning the chicken droppings that are everywhere?"

Ricardo is at the door of his room. He clutches his pet, glancing at Mama. "You don't mind my having Perico? I'll clean up after him. I promise, Mama."

"You must find a place for the animal besides your room. And no more whistling, Ricardo. I'd rather hear the chicken's clucking."

We laugh.

Predict

What will Mama do next?

"Well, the mystery is over," Papa says. "We'll have to think of something else, Ricardo. Your mother is too clever!"

"Mama, I want to show you the tricks I've taught Perico," Ricardo says. He puts the chicken on the ground. Then he dashes to his room to get the sticks and fences he has made for his chicken's act.

Mama sighs.

Papa chuckles.

Because of being constantly in hiding, the chicken moves slowly. He looks so serious, it's funny.

Papa gets up from the hammock.

"Welcome, Perico, you arr in a free country now!" He bows.

Think About It

Is the chicken "in a free country now"? Why or why not?

Meet the Author

LYLL BECERRA DE JENKINS *(1925–1997)*

Lyll Becerra de Jenkins grew up in San Gil, Colombia. Her father was a judge and a writer. Jenkins didn't see why her father cared so much about politics. Then she moved to the United States. She realized that many people in Colombia were treated unfairly. Suddenly she understood her father's concerns. Jenkins began writing stories about politics and human rights.

Magazines and newspapers printed Jenkins's short stories. One of the stories became her first novel, *The Honorable Prison*. Jenkins won the Scott O'Dell Award for Historical Fiction for the book. She continued to write about social issues. Jenkins hoped that her work would encourage young people to learn more about politics.

Check Your Predictions

1. Look back at the answers you gave for the Predict questions. Would you change your answers? Explain.

Understand the Story

2. Why does a soldier go with Marta and Ricardo to the marketplace?

3. What do people in the market whisper about Marta and Ricardo?

4. Why does Marta want to keep an eye on the campesinos?

5. What does Ricardo buy secretly in the market?

Think About the Story

6. What does Marta's father mean when he says some soldiers "obey like robots"?

7. How does Marta know that the men in city suits disapprove of her father's actions?

8. How does Marta feel about the campesinos that her father champions?

Extend Your Response

What do you think about a newspaper editor being put under house arrest for his articles? Imagine you are a reader of Marta's father's newspaper. Write a letter to the new editor about it.

Summaries

Anne Frank Remembered: The Story of the Woman Who Helped to Hide the Frank Family A woman helps a Jewish family named Frank during World War II. The young woman tells how she helps on the day the family must go into hiding.

The Diary of a Young Girl Anne Frank, a 14-year-old Jewish girl, has been forced into hiding. She shares her thoughts and feelings in her diary, which she calls "Kitty."

The Honorable Prison Marta's family is being held in prison in a house in a small town. For the first time, Marta and her brother, Ricardo, are allowed to go to the market. However, they are escorted by a soldier, and people in the town want nothing to do with them. There, Ricardo secretly buys a pet chicken. Later, his mother surprises everyone by allowing him to keep it.

criticized
lodger
imitate
forbid
reassure
mischief

Vocabulary Review

Complete each sentence with a word from the box. Use a separate sheet of paper.

1. I watched the boys _____ a soldier by marching back and forth.

2. Fans _____ the athlete for his poor sportsmanship.

3. I needed my friend to _____ me that my hair looked okay.

4. We saw that the cat had done some _____ ; yarn was everywhere.

5. The noisy _____ disturbed everyone else in the house.

6. "I _____ you to go to the party," my mother said.

Chapter Quiz

Write your answers in one or two complete sentences.
Use a separate sheet of paper.

1. Anne Frank Remembered: The Story of the Woman Who Helped to Hide the Frank Family What does the postcard Margot receives say?

2. Anne Frank Remembered: The Story of the Woman Who Helped to Hide the Frank Family How do Miep and Henk help carry the Franks' belongings?

3. The Diary of a Young Girl Why does Anne feel frustrated with her parents?

4. The Diary of a Young Girl How does Anne feel at the end of the selection?

5. The Honorable Prison What cause has Marta's father been fighting for?

6. The Honorable Prison How does Marta show her courage in this story?

Critical Thinking

7. The Diary of a Young Girl How are Anne's problems like those of other teenagers?

8. The Honorable Prison Why doesn't the friendly young man in the plaza help Marta carry her basket?

Chapter Activity

Imagine that Marta from *The Honorable Prison* could communicate with Anne Frank. Have Marta write a letter to Anne.

Unit 4 **Review**

On a separate sheet of paper, write the letter that best completes each sentence below.

1. In "Clever Manka," the thing in the house Manka likes best is
   A. making dinner.
   B. her horse.
   C. her husband.
   D. being clever.

2. In "A Piece of String," Maître Hauchecome picks up the piece of string because he
   A. wants to hide the fact that he stole a purse.
   B. thinks that everything useful should be picked up.
   C. sees Maître Malandain and does not want to talk to him.
   D. hates litter.

3. In "Dead Men's Path," Mr. Obi closes the path because he
   A. knows that it is not used.
   B. feels that it is dangerous.
   C. dislikes the villagers' ways.
   D. wants to build a building.

4. The speaker of "Bitter Cold, Living in the Village" feels
   A. tired.
   B. ashamed.
   C. pleased.
   D. proud.

5. In *Anne Frank Remembered* Miep Gies helped the Franks hide in
   A. the Van Daans' apartment.
   B. Otto Frank's office building.
   C. Miep and Henk Gies' home.
   D. a school basement.

6. In *The Honorable Prison*, Ricardo uses his poncho to hide a
   A. typewriter.
   B. banana.
   C. chicken.
   D. basket.

Making Connections

On a separate sheet of paper, write your answers to the following questions.

7. Both Anne Frank and the characters in *The Honorable Prison* were forced to leave their lives behind. Compare and contrast how these young people made the best of their situations.

8. Which selection in this unit do you think had the best descriptions and details? Explain why.

Writing an Essay
Choose two selections in this unit. Compare and contrast their themes.

Unit Five

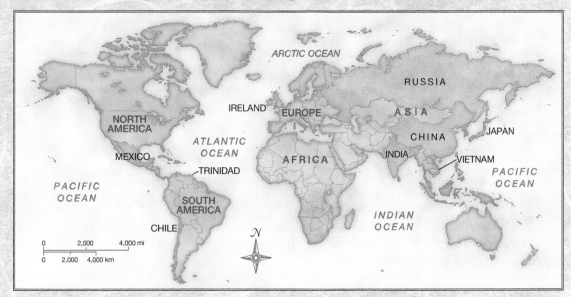

Tiger in a Tropical Storm (Surprise!) by Henri Rousseau (1844–1910)

How is this tiger affected by its environment? How are people affected by animals in their environments?

Learning Objectives

- Recognize imagery.
- Recognize free verse.
- Explain what the form of a poem is.
- Recognize dialogue in a story.
- Identify the turning point in a story.

Theme Preview: Animals

Animals play a huge part in human lives. Animals give us food and help us do work. They entertain us and keep us company. They can affect our lives in powerful ways. They can amaze us. In this chapter, you will read about some special animals.

Keys to Literature

imagery: colorful words that appeal to the senses

Example: *Their colour was amber and honey, was on fire.*

free verse: poetry that is not written in a regular pattern; the words do not rhyme.

Example: "Horses" does not have a regular pattern. The words don't rhyme.

Did You Know?

After World War II, Germany was divided into two countries. The Berlin Wall divided the city into two parts. Today Germany is one country again. When this poem was written, Berlin was still divided.

Words to Know

deserted	empty; left behind
arena	an open space used for sports or events
scarcely	hardly
disgruntled	unhappy; irritated
intense	very strong or deep
beckoning	calling
unwitting	innocent; unaware
obliterated	erased; forgotten

Genre: Poetry

"Horses" is a poem. Read more about poetry on page 467 of the Genre Guide.

Horses

BY PABLO NERUDA

From the window I saw the horses.

I was in Berlin, in winter. The light
was without light, the sky skyless.

The air white like a moistened loaf.

5   From my window, I could see a **deserted arena**,
a circle bitten out by the teeth of winter.

All at once, led out by a single man,
ten horses were stepping, stepping into the snow.

Scarcely had they rippled into existence
10 like flame, than they filled the whole world of my eyes,
empty till now. Faultless, flaming,
they stepped like ten gods on broad, clean hoofs,
their manes recalling a dream of salt spray.

READ TO FIND OUT...
How do ten horses bring life to a dark winter day?

Think About It
What do you think the deserted arena is?

Keys to Literature
What **imagery**, or colorful words, does the speaker use to describe the horses?

The Small Yellow Horses by Franz Marc

Keys to Literature

Free verse does not have a regular pattern or rhyme. Notice that the words in this poem do not rhyme.

Their rumps were globes, were oranges.

15 Their colour was amber and honey, was on fire.

Their necks were towers
carved from the stone of pride,
and in their furious eyes, sheer energy
showed itself, a prisoner inside them.

20 And there, in the silence, at the mid-
point of the day, in a dirty, **disgruntled** winter,
the horses' **intense** presence was blood,
was rhythm, was the **beckoning** of light of all being.

I saw, I saw, and seeing, I came to life.
25 There was the **unwitting** fountain, the dance of gold, the sky,
the fire that sprang to life in beautiful things.

I have **obliterated** that gloomy Berlin winter.

I shall not forget the light from these horses.

Think About It

How are the speaker's feelings about the horses different from his feelings about winter?

$\mathcal{M}$eet the $\mathcal{A}$uthor

PABLO NERUDA (1904–1973)

Pablo Neruda was born in Chile. As a young man, he moved to the city of Santiago to write. There he became active in politics. He worked as a diplomat for Chile. He also wrote poetry all his life. He was forced to leave Chile for several years because he criticized the president. He returned home when politics in Chile changed. He was nominated for president, but helped a friend get elected instead.

Neruda wrote poetry about a variety of topics. Some were political, others humorous. Still others were about love or about loneliness. Neruda's writing earned him the Nobel Prize for literature in 1971.

Understand the Poem

1. What does the speaker see from his window?

2. How does the speaker describe the winter in Berlin?

3. How does the speaker describe the horses?

4. What effect do the horses have upon the speaker?

Think About the Poem

5. What do you think "the air white like a moistened loaf" means?

6. What senses does the speaker appeal to in the poem? Give examples.

7. Why do you think the speaker says he "shall not forget the light from these horses"? Explain your answer.

8. Is free verse a good form for this poem? Explain why or why not.

Extend Your Response

Think about a time you saw something that had a powerful effect on you. How did you feel? Write a poem in free verse about your experience. Have a class poetry reading to share your poems.

Keys to Literature

form: the structure of a poem. A poem can be open form (free verse) or closed form.

> Example: "Eight Puppies" in its English translation has an open form. In Spanish, it has a closed form where some of the lines rhyme.

Did You Know?

At birth, puppies are blind and deaf. They stay very close to their mother. After about two weeks, they begin to see, hear, and explore their environment.

Words to Know

deluge	flood
azaleas	bushes with bright flowers
rasping	scratchy, harsh
riddled	filled with
hallowed	holy

Genre: Poetry

"Eight Puppies" is a poem. Read more about poetry on page 467 of the Genre Guide.

*E*ight Puppies

BY GABRIELA MISTRAL

READ TO FIND OUT...

What do eight puppies make the speaker wish for?

Between the thirteenth and fifteenth day
the puppies opened their eyes.
Suddenly they saw the world,
anxious with terror and joy.
5 They saw the belly of their mother,
saw the door of their house,
saw a **deluge** of light,
saw flowering **azaleas**.

They saw more, they saw all,
10 the red, the black, the ash.
Scrambling up, pawing and clawing
more lively than squirrels,
they saw the eyes of their mother,
heard my **rasping** cry and my laugh.

Keys to Literature

The **form** of this poem is open form. There is no regular pattern or rhyme. A closed form poem usually rhymes or has a rhythm. In the original Spanish version, this poem is in closed form.

Tumbling Retriever Puppies by Frederico Olaria

15 And I wished I were born with them.
   Could it not be so another time?
   To leap from a clump of banana plants
   one morning of wonders—
   a dog, a coyote, a deer;
20 to gaze with wide pupils,
   to run, to stop, to run, to fall,
   to whimper and whine and jump with joy,
   riddled with sun and with barking,
   a **hallowed** child of God, his secret, divine servant.

Think About It

What does the poet
mean by "child of God"?

Meet the Author

GABRIELA MISTRAL *(1889–1957)*

Gabriela Mistral was born Lucila Godoy Alcayaga in Chile. She took the pen name Gabriela Mistral after two of her favorite poets. At the early age of 15, Mistral began teaching. As an adult, she traveled to Mexico, the United States, Puerto Rico, and Europe. In these places, she taught and studied how others taught. She also served as consul for Chile in Europe and the United States.

Mistral became well-known as a poet in 1914. In that year, she won a Chilean poetry prize. Later she became the first Latin American to receive the Nobel Prize for literature. Mistral's poems often deal with deep feelings and emotions. Her poetry has been translated into many languages.

Understand the Poem

1. What happens to the puppies between the thirteenth and fifteenth day?

2. How do the puppies feel when they open their eyes?

3. What do the puppies see when they open their eyes?

4. How do the puppies react to being able to see?

Think About the Poem

5. Why might the puppies feel both terror and joy when they open their eyes?

6. Why does the speaker wish to be born with the puppies?

7. Why do you think the speaker asks "Could it not be so another time"?

8. What form is this poem? How might a different form change the poem?

Extend Your Response

This poem was originally written in closed form. Almost every other line rhymed. Write a few lines about puppies, making sure that the last word of every other line rhymes. If you know Spanish, you may also want to research and read the original.

Keys to Literature

dialogue: a conversation between characters in a story or play; words that characters actually say

Example: *"You knew?" she asked.*
But Martin said, "No, I didn't know."

turning point: the event in a story that leads to a solution to the problem

Example: When Julia hears someone unwind a fishing reel, she decides to save the trout.

Did You Know

Fish use gills to breathe in the water. They usually die out of water because their gills dry out. However, some fish that live in waters that often dry up can live out of water. They can hold water in their gills so they don't dry out.

Words to Know

sneer	an expression that shows dislike
panting	breathing rapidly in short gasps
reel	a spool attached to a fishing rod used for winding and storing the fishing line
scuttling	running in a hurry
slimy	slippery, wet, and smooth
lashed	moved suddenly or violently
ooze	soft mud at the edge of a body of water
superior	better or more important than others

Genre: Short Story

"The Trout" is a short story. Read more about short stories on page 467 of the Genre Guide.

The Trout

BY SEAN O'FAOLAIN, *adapted*

READ TO FIND OUT...
Can a trout survive in a shallow well?

One of the first places Julia went was The Dark Walk. It is a very old, tree-lined walk. It rose like a large, dark tunnel with smooth, strong branches. Underfoot the tough brown leaves never crackle.

Julia raced right into it. For the first few yards, she could still remember the sun behind her. Then she felt the end of the day fading around her. It made her scream with pleasure. She would race to the light at the far end of the walk. The end was always just a little too long in coming. So, she always came out gasping, laughing, clasping her hands, and drinking in the sun. When she was warmed by the light, she would turn around. For a moment she would think about doing it again.

Think About It
What does "drinking in the sun" mean?

This year she had the added joy of showing her game to her small brother. She could terrify him as well as herself. For him the fear lasted longer because his legs were so short. She had gone out the far end while he was still screaming and racing.

When they had done this many times, they came back to the house. There they could tell everybody about their game. They began to argue.

"Cry baby!" Julia said to her brother.

"You were afraid yourself, so there!" he shot back.

"I won't take you anymore," she threatened.

"You're a big pig," her brother said.

"I hate you," she shouted back.

Tears were threatening to fall. Then someone said, "Did you see the well?"

Julia held up her long lovely neck. Julia was suspicious. How could there be a well in The Dark Walk? She knew the Walk. She had visited it year after year. With a **sneer** she said, "Nonsense."

Keys to Literature
Notice the **dialogue** between Julia and her brother. What does the dialogue tell you about their relationship?

But she went back to The Dark Walk. She acted as if she were going somewhere else. Once there she found a hole scooped in the rock at the side of the walk. It was choked with damp leaves. It took her a while to uncover the hole. At the back of this small hole there was about a quart of water. In the water she suddenly saw a trout breathing heavily. She rushed for Stephen and dragged him to see it. They were both so excited that they were no longer afraid of the darkness as they hunched over the hole. There they saw the fish **panting** in his tiny prison. His silver stomach went up and down like an engine.

Nobody knew how the trout got there. Even old Martin in the kitchen garden laughed. He would not believe that it was there. At least he pretended not to believe, until she made him come down and see. Kneeling and pushing back his ragged cap, he looked in.

"You're right. How did that fella get there?" Martin asked.

Julia stared at him. There was doubt in her eyes.

"You knew?" she asked.

Think About It

Do you think Martin is being honest? Why or why not?

But Martin said, "No, I didn't know." He reached down to lift it out. Julia stopped him. If she had found it, then it was her trout.

Her mother suggested that a bird had carried the egg. Her father thought a small stream might have carried it down there as a baby. It may have happened in the winter when it was safe. But in the summer the water began to dry up. She said, "I see."

Think About It

Does Julia agree with her parents' explanations? How can you tell?

She went back to look again and think about it alone. Her brother stayed behind. He wanted to hear the whole story of the trout. He was not really interested in the story his mummy began to make up for him. She began her story with, "So one day Daddy Trout and Mummy Trout.... " When he retold the story to his sister, she said, "Pooh."

It troubled her that the trout was always in the same place. He had no room to turn. All the time the silver belly went up and down. Otherwise he never moved. She wondered what he ate. Between visits to Joey Pony and the boat and a cool bath, she thought of his hunger. She brought him down bits of dough. Once she brought a worm. The trout never gave the least thought to the food. He just went on panting. Hunched over him she thought how all the winter, he had been in there. All day, all night, he floated around alone in The Dark Walk. She was still thinking of it as she lay in bed.

It was late June, the longest days of the year. The sun had sat still for a week, burning up the world. Although it was after ten o'clock, it was still bright and still hot. She lay on her back under a single sheet,

Predict

What do you think will happen to the trout?

trying to keep cool. She could see the half moon through the trees. Before they went to bed her mummy had told Stephen the story of the trout again. She, in her bed, however, had purposely turned her back to them and read a book. But she had kept one ear turned to the story.

"So, in the end, this naughty fish who would not stay at home got bigger and bigger and bigger. The water got smaller and smaller.... "

With great passion, she cried, "Mummy, don't make it a horrible old story that teaches us some lesson!"

Her mummy had brought in a fairy godmother then. The fairy godmother sent lots of rain and filled the hole. A stream poured out of the hole. The trout floated down to the river. Staring at the moon, she knew that there are no such things as godmothers. She also knew that down in The Dark Walk the trout was panting like an engine. She heard somebody unwind a fishing **reel**. Would the beasts fish him out?

She sat up. Stephen was a hot lump of sleep, lazy thing. She leaped up and looked out the window. Somehow she did not feel as lively now that she saw the dim mountains and the black trees. The land seemed to breathe as she heard a dog bark. Quietly she lifted the pitcher of water and climbed out the window. **Scuttling** along the cool gravel, she reached the open mouth of the tunnel. Her night clothes were very short so that when she splashed water, it wet her ankles. She gazed into the tunnel. Something alive rustled inside there. She raced in. She cried aloud, "Oh, gosh, I can't find it." Then at last she did. Kneeling down in the damp she put her hand into the **slimy** hole. When the body **lashed** out, they were both mad with fright. But she gripped him. She shoved him into the pitcher. With her teeth ground, she raced out of the tunnel and down the steep paths to the river's edge.

Think About It

Why do you think Julia is upset with her mother?

Keys to Literature

The **turning point** leads to a solution to the problem. What is happening here?

Predict

Are you surprised that Julia snuck out of her house? What do you think she will do next?

All the time she could feel him lashing his tail against the side of the pitcher. She was afraid he would jump right out. The gravel cut her feet until she came to the cool **ooze** of the river bank. She poured the water out. She watched the fish until he plopped. For a second he could be seen in the water. She hoped he was not dizzy. Then all she saw was the glimmer of the moon in the silent-flowing river.

She scuttled up the hill, climbed through the window, plonked down the pitcher, and flew through the air like a bird into bed. The dog barked. She hugged herself and giggled. Like a river of joy, her holiday spread before her.

In the morning Stephen rushed to her, shouting that "he" was gone. He wanted to know "where" and "how." Lifting her nose in the air, she said in a **superior** voice, "Fairy godmother, I suppose?" She strolled away patting the palms of her hands.

Think About It
Do you think Julia will ever tell anyone about what she did? Why or why not?

Meet the Author

SEAN O'FAOLAIN *(1900–1991)*

Sean O'Faolain was born John Whelan in County Cork, Ireland. When he was a teenager he became very interested in Irish culture and politics. Because of this Irish pride, he changed his name to Sean O'Faolain, a Gaelic, or Irish, name. He also joined an Irish political group.

Irish pride also had an effect on his choice of career. As a short story writer he told the stories of the Irish lower and middle classes. He also wrote biographies and travel essays. O'Faolain once said, "As I see it … [a good story] is like a child's kite—a small wonder, a brief, bright moment."

Check Your Predictions

1. Look back at the answers you gave for the Predict questions. Would you change your answers? Explain.

Understand the Story

2. What changes Julia's fear of The Dark Walk?

3. What does Julia say that tells you what she thinks of her parents' ideas about the trout?

4. What finally convinces Julia to save the trout?

5. Why do you think Julia lets the trout go?

Think About the Story

6. Which character had the best idea about how the trout ended up in the well?

7. How did Julia feel when Stephen asked her what happened to the trout?

8. Could this story really happen? Explain your answer.

Extend Your Response

Write a news article about how the trout ended up in the well. Include information about *who*, *what*, *where*, *when*, *why,* and *how*. Create a sensational headline for your article.

Chapter 9 Review

Summaries

Horses The speaker recalls a dark winter day in Berlin. He describes how he saw ten beautiful, fiery horses walking in the snow. He explains that he will never forget them.

Eight Puppies The speaker watches eight puppies open their eyes and explore their world. She wishes she could be born with them and be able to experience life as they do.

The Trout Julia and her brother often play a game running through a dark, tree-lined walk. One day, they discover a trout trapped in a small well. Everyone wonders how it got there. Late one night, Julia secretly frees the trout.

---

deserted

intense

deluge

panting

superior

Vocabulary Review

Complete each sentence with a word from the box. Use a separate sheet of paper.

1. The _____ swept away the fence and filled the garden with water.

2. We were all _____ as we climbed to the top of the hill.

3. The park was _____ ; no one wanted to stay out in the rain.

4. Jake, a _____ tennis player, has won many matches.

5. Learning Italian took many hours of _____ study.

Chapter Quiz

**Write your answers in one or two complete sentences.
Use a separate sheet of paper.**

1. Horses How does the speaker feel about winter
   in Berlin?

2. Horses What imagery does the speaker use to describe the
   horses?

3. Eight Puppies What are the puppies doing for the first time?

4. Eight Puppies Why does the speaker wish to be like
   the puppies?

5. The Trout Where does Julia find the trout?

6. The Trout What happens to the trout?

Critical Thinking

7. Eight Puppies What other title could you give this poem?
   Explain your choice.

8. The Trout If Julia had not saved the trout, who do you
   think would have fished him out? Why?

Chapter Activity

Suppose you are a writer for an encyclopedia of amazing facts. Write an
entry for the encyclopedia about a special animal. Choose one of the
animals in this chapter or research another amazing animal. Make a list of
special characteristics. Use the list to write your entry.

Landscape with Rising Sun by Vincent van Gogh (1853–1890)

How do you think this artist feels about nature? Why?

Chapter 10 ▷ Nature

Learning Objectives

- Recognize and understand imagery.
- Understand what haiku is.
- Identify atmosphere.
- Define alliteration.
- Identify stanzas.
- Understand personification.

Preview Activity

What is your favorite season? Write a short paragraph describing your favorite season and explaining why you like it so much.

Theme Preview: Nature

Nature can have a powerful effect on people. It can cause great joy or terrible fear. It can be both a friend and an enemy. The poems in this chapter celebrate nature and explore our varied relationships with it.

Keys to Literature

imagery: colorful words that appeal to the senses

> **Example:** *On a withered branch / a crow has settled— / autumn nightfall.*

Did You Know?

Basho wrote a book of rules for haiku. He defined the form (the number of syllables per line) and described the kinds of imagery a poet could use in the poems.

Words to Know

withered	dried up, shriveled
captured	caught
remains	stays behind
collide	crash or bump into

Genre: Haiku

These poems are a specific kind of poetry called haiku. Read more about haiku in the Learn More About It on page 305 or on page 466 of the Genre Guide.

Four Haiku

BY BASHO, JOSO, CHIYO, AND SHIKI

Autumn

On a **withered** branch
   a crow has settled—
      autumn nightfall.

                —*Basho*

Winter

Mountains and plains,
   all are **captured** by the snow—
      nothing **remains**.

                —*Joso*

View of Mount Haruna Under the Snow by Ando Hiroshige

READ TO FIND OUT...
How do four poets describe the four seasons?

Think About It
How does the description in the first line show that it is autumn?

Keys to Literature

Imagery is the use of colorful words that appeal to our senses. What images here help you see the winter landscape?

After a Long Winter

After a long winter, giving
    each other nothing, we **collide**
      with blossoms in our hands.

                          —*Chiyo*

Heat

The summer river:
    although there is a bridge, my horse
      goes through the water.

                          —*Shiki*

Think About It

Why does the horse go through the water instead of using the bridge?

Fuji from Kogane-Ga-Hara, Shimosa by Ando Hiroshige

Meet the Authors

BASHO *(1644–1694)*, **JOSO** *(1661–1704)*,
CHIYO *(1703–1775)*, and **SHIKI** *(1867–1902)*

Matsuo Basho is known as one of the greatest haiku poets. He lived in Japan during the seventeenth century. Around 1680, he became known as a haiku master. People praised the scenes of nature he created in such poems as "Autumn." Basho also began a school where he taught many students to write haiku in his style.

Basho's best students were called "The Ten Philosophers." They, too, became respected poets. Joso was one of these students. He carried on Basho's tradition.

Chiyo wrote during the eighteenth century. She began writing haiku when she was seven. She studied under two of Basho's students. Chiyo is thought to be one of the greatest female haiku masters of her time.

Shiki wrote about 100 years later. Initially, he thought he wanted to have a career as a politician. While in school, though, he discovered his love of literature. He tried to reform haiku. He wanted the poems to present "sketches from life."

Matsuo Basho, by Anonymous

Understand the Poems

1. In "Autumn," what description captures the feeling of the season?

2. What is captured by the snow in "Winter"?

3. What do the blossoms in "After a Long Winter" symbolize?

4. In "Heat," what does the speaker's horse go through?

Think About the Poems

5. What description in "Autumn" helps indicate that it is nightfall?

6. How do the kinds of images used in "Winter" and "Heat" differ?

7. If these haiku were in the original Japanese, what pattern would they have?

8. Do you think these haiku capture the feelings of the seasons? Why or why not?

Extend Your Response

Choose an image to capture in a haiku of your own. It can be something from nature or any other image that strikes you. When you write your haiku, use five syllables in the first line, seven syllables in the second, and five in the last. You might include an illustration or a photograph with your haiku.

Learn More About It

GENRE STUDY: HAIKU

Haiku is a specific form of Japanese poetry. It always has three lines. It does not rhyme, but it does have a pattern. The pattern is in the number of syllables per line. The first and last lines have five syllables. The second line has seven syllables. However, Japanese haiku translated into English, like those in this chapter, will not always have this pattern. Recent haiku written in English also do not always follow the syllable rule.

Haiku often describe natural images, especially the seasons. These images can also be symbols for challenges or joys in life. The haiku has been popular in Japan for over 300 years. Basho is known as one of its most important poets. In the United States and Europe, the haiku has grown in popularity during the past 100 years.

Since the Crescent Moon I Have Been Waiting for Tonight (1891), by Yoshitoshi

An illustration of one of Basho's haiku. The haiku is in the top right corner.

Apply and Connect

Why do you think haiku has become more popular in the past 100 years? What is interesting or appealing about this form?

Keys to Literature

atmosphere: the general mood of a piece of literature

> Example: Words like *serene* and *lazy* create a relaxed atmosphere.

Words to Know

bounds	jumps forward quickly
dense	thick or crowded
water chestnuts	plants found in watery marshes of Asia and Africa
lucid	clear
serene	calm and peaceful
loaf	pass the time doing little

Genre: Poetry

"Green Creek" is a poem. Read more about poetry on page 467 of the Genre Guide.

Green Creek

BY WANG WEI

To find the meadows by Yellow Flower River
you must follow Green Creek
as it turns endlessly in the mountains
in just a hundred miles.
5 Water **bounds** noisily over the rocks.
Color softens in the **dense** pines.
Weeds and **water chestnuts** are drifting.
Lucid water mirrors the reeds.

My heart has always been **serene** and lazy
10 like peaceful Green Creek.
Why not **loaf** on a large flat rock,
dangling my fishhook here forever?

READ TO FIND OUT...
What does the speaker compare his heart to?

Think About It
What does the speaker of the poem mean when he says Green Creek "turns endlessly ... in just a hundred miles"?

Keys to Literature
The **atmosphere**, or mood of the piece of literature, is relaxed and serene. What words create this atmosphere?

Landscape by Cai Jia

Meet the Author

WANG WEI *(698–759)*

Wang Wei was a Chinese poet, musician, painter, and statesman. He lived in China during the Tang Dynasty (618–907). This was a period of great artistic and cultural growth. From an early age, Wang Wei showed his many talents. In 721, he received high honors in the civil service exam. He rose quickly within the government.

Although Wang Wei was quite famous as a painter, none of his art remains today. From records, we know that he was known for landscapes, especially snowy landscapes. Much of his poetry survives, though. In his poetry, he also focused on natural scenes. His descriptions of water and landscapes capture the sights, sounds, and feelings of the natural world.

Understand the Poem

1. Where is Green Creek?

2. To what senses does the following line appeal:
"Water bounds noisily over the rocks"?

3. What comparison does the speaker make in
lines 9–10?

4. How are these two things similar?

Think About the Poem

5. How does the atmosphere shift during the poem?

6. The speaker starts out by giving directions to
the meadows by Yellow Flower River. Why do
you think the speaker never finishes giving
the directions?

7. Would you like to spend time at Green Creek?
Why or why not?

8. Wang Wei was also a painter. Do you think this
affected how he wrote poetry? Why or why not?

Extend Your Response

What kind of person do you think the speaker is?
Write a few interview questions for the speaker of the
poem. Then use the information in the poem to infer
the kinds of answers the speaker would likely give.

Keys to Literature

alliteration: repeating the same consonant sound

> Example: <u>f</u>orever the <u>f</u>ragrance

stanza: a group of lines in a poem set apart from other groups of lines

> Example: The first four lines of "The Cedar Chest" are its first stanza.

Did You Know?

Cedar trees have been used for thousands of years. The wood is strong and lasts a long time. It also has a pleasant smell, which keeps away moths. Because of this, it is often used in chests and closets.

Words to Know

felled	cut down
fragrance	a sweet or pleasing smell
torso	trunk
severed	separated, broken apart
routines	regular ways or patterns of doing things

Genre: Poetry

"The Cedar Chest" is a poem. Read more about poetry on page 467 of the Genre Guide.

The Cedar Chest

BY ROSARIO CASTELLANOS

The ax that **felled**
forever the **fragrance**
and the tree taken
with its **torso severed.**

5 Now here you are, under a roof,
in the corner of a bedroom
and guests take you for granted
and you, you seem to accept it and to keep still.

Don't sell away your memory
10 to sad **routines** and to time.

Do not forget the woods
or the wind or the birds.

READ TO FIND OUT...
What are a cedar chest's memories?

Keys to Literature

The *f* sound is repeated in *felled / forever the fragrance*. What other **alliteration** occurs in this stanza?

Stanzas in poems are like paragraphs in prose. The beginning of a new stanza is marked by a space before it.

Meet the Author

ROSARIO CASTELLANOS (1925–1974)

Rosario Castellanos was born in Mexico City and grew up in Southern Mexico. Her father owned coffee and sugar plantations. At college, she studied sociology and literature and later became a literature professor. However, she was also interested in politics. This led to her becoming Mexico's ambassador to Israel in 1971.

Castellanos wrote poetry, fiction, plays, and nonfiction. However, it was her novel *The Nine Guardians* that began her rise to fame. Her novels, poetry, and essays often deal with women's issues and the problems facing Mexico's native Indian population.

Understand the Poem

1. How many stanzas make up the poem?

2. What event does the speaker describe in the first stanza?

3. What alliteration is used in the fourth stanza?

4. What does the speaker want the cedar chest to remember?

Think About the Poem

5. How does the speaker personify the cedar chest in the following line: "you seem to accept it and to keep still"?

6. The first two stanzas of the poem tell about the chest's past and present. What do the remaining stanzas do?

7. How do you think the speaker feels about the cedar chest?

8. Do you think the speaker of the poem offers good advice to the cedar chest? Why or why not?

Extend Your Response

Illustrate each stanza of the poem. Be creative in your illustration, using any form of art you like. You might make a collage of magazine clippings. You might want to draw or paint pictures. Be sure to capture the feeling of the poem in your illustrations.

Keys to Literature

personification: giving human characteristics to something that is not human

> Example: *Day came in / on an old brown bus / with two friends.*

Words to Know

prodded	moved to action
glimpse	a fleeting look or glance

Genre: Poetry

"Morning" is a poem. Read more about poetry on page 467 of the Genre Guide.

$\mathcal{M}$orning

BY DIONNE BRAND

Day came in
on an old brown bus
with two friends.
She crept down
5 an empty street
bending over
to sweep the thin dawn away.
With her broom,
she drew red streaks
10 in the corners
of the dusty sky
and finding a rooster still asleep,
prodded him into song.
A fisherman,
15 not far from the shore,
lifted his eyes,
saw her coming,
and yawned.
The bus rolled by,
20 and the two friends caught
a **glimpse** of blue
as day swung around a corner
to where the sea met a road.
The sky blinked,
25 woke up,
and might have changed its mind,
but day had come.

READ TO FIND OUT...
How does day sweep
the dawn away?

Keys to Literature

The first three lines of
the poem **personify** day
by saying day rode in a
bus with two friends.
How is day personified
in the next four lines?

▶ A rooster's song is
a sign of daybreak or
early morning.

Meet the Author

DIONNE BRAND *(Born 1953)*

Dionne Brand was born in Trinidad. She moved to Canada in 1970 to attend college. Since then she has taught English literature and creative writing. She has also been politically active. She has worked to help women of African descent and immigrants in Canada.

Brand's writing includes nonfiction, fiction, and poetry. Brand has said that she prefers writing poetry. However, her first two novels, *Another Place, Not Here* and *At the Full and Change of the Moon* have won her great respect as a novelist. Brand's writing often reflects her interest in Caribbean women's issues.

Learn More About It

THE CARIBBEAN

The islands of the Caribbean Sea are located between Florida and South America. Some islands are independent countries. Other islands are controlled by other nations, such as France and the United States. The islands of the Caribbean are very different from each other. For

Martinique (1887) by Paul Gauguin

hundreds of years, three separate groups of native people lived on these islands. Starting in the 1500s, different European nations took control. These nations shaped the islands' cultures. Enslaved people from Africa were also put to work on some islands. Today, people of African descent are the majority on some islands, such as Haiti and Jamaica.

Understand the Poem

1. How does day arrive in the poem?

2. How is the sky personified in lines 24–26?

3. How does the fisherman react to the arrival of day?

4. What do the two friends see from the bus?

Think About the Poem

5. How is day personified?

6. How does the arrival of day affect the fisherman and the two friends differently?

7. Why do you think the sky "might have changed its mind"?

8. What kind of character is day?

Extend Your Response

Draw a poster representing the arrival of day. Use specific images from the poem to include in your poster. You might choose one specific image and use the lines from the poem as a caption.

Chapter 10 Review

Summaries

Four Haiku Each of the four haiku presents a different season. These create strong images using few words.

Green Creek The speaker shares his thoughts about Green Creek. He uses these thoughts to examine the things that are important to him.

The Cedar Chest The speaker describes the death of a cedar tree. Then, she describes its new life as a cedar chest. She encourages the cedar chest not to forget its life as a tree.

Morning Day comes in on a bus at dawn and brings life and light to the earth and the sky.

fragrance

lucid

prodded

serene

severed

withered

Vocabulary Review

Complete each sentence with a word from the box. Use a separate sheet of paper.

1. He _____ me with his elbow to get me to wake up.

2. The fruit on the vine _____ because there was no rain.

3. The afternoon was completely still and _____.

4. The phone line was accidentally _____ by the falling tree.

5. The _____ lake glowed in the setting sun.

6. The _____ of the roses filled the garden.

Chapter Quiz

**Write your answers in one or two complete sentences.
Use a separate sheet of paper.**

1. Four Haiku How does the poet show the season in "After a Long Winter"?

2. Four Haiku Why does the horse cross through the river in "Heat"?

3. Green Creek How is the speaker's heart like Green Creek?

4. The Cedar Chest What does the speaker tell the cedar chest to do?

5. Morning How is day personified in this poem?

Critical Thinking

6. The Cedar Chest What lesson do you think the poet wants us to learn from what happened to the cedar tree?

7. Morning If day really were a person, how would you describe her?

Chapter Activity

Write a free verse poem about something in nature that you have enjoyed. Be sure to describe it in detail and tell how it made you feel.

How do the boy and his grandfather feel about each other?

Chapter 11 > Family

Learning Objectives

- Recognize the turning point in a story.
- Identify the theme of a story.
- Identify and understand idioms.
- Define free verse.
- Recognize comparison.

Preview Activity

Think of an important event that happened to you in childhood. Write it as a first-person memory. Then share it with a classmate.

Theme Preview: Family

Family often plays a huge role in people's lives. Family members share childhoods. They share habits and tastes. They may also share hair colors or nose shapes. Most of all, they share lives. These writings are about those shared lives and memories.

Keys to Literature

turning point: the event in a story that leads to a solution to the problem

> Example: In a mystery story, finding the fingerprint that leads to the thief might be the turning point.

theme: the main idea of a story, novel, play, or poem

> Example: The theme of the fable "The Tortoise and the Hare" is that sometimes it is better to be slow and steady than fast and careless.

Did You Know?

Tolstoy is one of the most loved Russian authors. However, he did not make up this story. It comes from the tradition of Russian folktales. Tolstoy wanted to honor the oral literature of Russian farmers and country people by writing it down.

Words to Know

scolded	told someone angrily what he or she did wrong
ashamed	feeling guilty or sorry for something done wrong

Genre: Folktale

"The Old Grandfather and His Little Grandson" is a folktale. Read more about folktales on page 466 of the Genre Guide.

The Old Grandfather and His Little Grandson

RETOLD BY LEO TOLSTOY, *adapted*

READ TO FIND OUT...
What important lesson does a small child teach his parents?

The grandfather had become very old. His legs would not carry him. His eyes could not see and his ears could not hear. He had no teeth. Sometimes when he ate, bits of food dropped out of his mouth. His son and his son's wife no longer let him eat with them at the table. He had to eat his meals in the corner near the stove.

One day they gave the grandfather his food in a bowl. He tried to move the bowl closer. It fell to the floor and broke. His daughter-in-law **scolded** him. She told him that he spoiled everything in the house and broke their dishes. She said that from now on, he would get his food in a wooden dish. The old man sighed and said nothing.

Predict

Look at the title of this folktale. How do you think the grandson will be important in the story?

A few days later, the old man's son and his wife were in their hut, resting. They watched their little boy playing on the floor. He was making something out of small pieces of wood. His father said, "What are you making, Misha?"

The little grandson said, "I'm making a wooden bucket. When you and Mamma get old, I'll feed you out of this wooden dish."

The young man and his wife looked at each other. Tears filled their eyes. They were **ashamed** they had treated the old grandfather so badly. From that day on, they let the old man eat at the table with them, and they took better care of him.

Meet the Author

LEO TOLSTOY (1828–1910)

Leo Tolstoy was born into a rich family. They had an estate near the city of Moscow. He grew up there, studying with teachers brought to his home. He studied at universities for several years, but returned home before he earned a degree. Then, Tolstoy left home to join the Russian Army.

Tolstoy began writing while in the army. He soon became a rising star in literature. He returned to the estate to set up a school for the farmers' children. He kept writing, and is still celebrated for his novels. He is also famous for the length of his masterpiece, *War and Peace*. It is more than 1,400 pages long.

Check Your Prediction

1. Look back at the answer you gave for the Predict question. Would you change your answer? Explain.

Understand the Folktale

2. Describe the grandfather. Use details to tell about him.

3. Why is the grandfather eating in the corner?

4. Why does the grandfather's daughter-in-law tell him he will now eat from a wooden dish?

5. Why do tears fill the eyes of the young man and his wife?

Think About the Folktale

6. Why do the young man and his wife treat the old grandfather so badly?

7. Why is the boy's making the bowl the turning point?

8. What do the parents learn from their son?

Extend Your Response
Imagine this story ends just before the last sentence. Write a new ending. Tell what happens in the house a month later.

Keys to Literature

idiom: a phrase or expression that has a different meaning from what the individual words usually mean

> Example: *My heart sank* means "I was suddenly sad or worried."

Did You Know?

Women are said to have played a large role in the Vietnamese army during the first century A.D. Phung Thi Chinh was a famous warrior in the Vietnamese army in A.D. 42. Two leaders of the army were also women, Trung Trac and Trung Nhi.

Words to Know

soy	a salty, thin brown sauce made from soybeans
flexible	easy to bend
merit	cause, earn
penalty	punishment
worthy	having value or honor
dowry	money or belongings that a bride brings to her new husband
sacred	holy
dikes	dams
savage	cruel, wild, unkind
shriveled	wrinkled, sometimes from being in water
shrine	a place where people pay respect to a god

Genre: Autobiography

When Heaven and Earth Changed Places is an autobiography. Read more about autobiographies on page 466 of the Genre Guide.

from When Heaven and Earth Changed Places

BY LE LY HAYSLIP, *adapted*

READ TO FIND OUT...
How does a famous warrior set an example for a young Vietnamese girl?

My father had a solid build for a Vietnamese man. This meant he probably had come from a family of well-fed, noble people. Many people said he had the body of a natural warrior. He was a year younger and an inch shorter than my mother. Still, he was just as good-looking. His face was round and his skin was brown as **soy** from working outdoors all his life. He took life easy and seldom hurried. Seldom, too, did he say no to a request from his children or his neighbors. Although he was relaxed, he was a hard worker. Even on holidays, he was always fixing things or taking care of our house and animals. He would not wait to be asked for help if he saw someone in trouble. Likewise, he also said what he thought. Like most honest men,

Predict

Look at the title. What do you think the selection will be about?

though, he knew when to keep silent. Because of his honesty and his feelings for others, he understood life deeply. Perhaps that is why he was so calm.

As a parent, my father was less strict than our mother. We sometimes ran to him for help when she was angry. Most of the time it didn't work. He would just rub our heads as we were dragged off to be spanked. The village saying went: "A naughty child learns more from a whipping stick than a sweet stick." We children were never quite sure about that. Still, we agreed the whipping stick was a powerful teacher. When he just had to punish us himself, he didn't waste time. Without a word, he would find a long, **flexible** bamboo stick. Then he would let us have it behind our thighs. It stung, but he could have whipped us harder. I think seeing the pain in his face hurt more than feeling his half-hearted blows. Because of that, we seldom did anything to **merit** a father's spanking. That was the highest **penalty** in our family. Violence in any form bothered him. For this reason, I think, he grew old before his time.

Once, when I was the only child at home, my mother went to Da Nang to visit Uncle Nhu. My father had to take care of me. I woke up from my nap in the empty house. I began to cry for my mother. My father came in from the yard and comforted me. Still, I was cranky and kept on crying. Finally, he gave me a rice cookie to shut me up. Needless to say, this was an approach my mother never used.

The next afternoon I woke up again. Though I was not feeling cranky, I thought a rice cookie would be nice. I cried a fake cry. My father came running in.

"What's this?" he asked with a worried face. "Little Bay Ly doesn't want a cookie?"

I was confused.

> ▶ *Da Nang* is a city in Vietnam.

Keys to Literature

An **idiom** has a different meaning than the individual words that make it up. *To shut up* means to keep from talking.

> ▶ *Little Bay Ly* is the nickname Le Ly's father gives her.

"Look under your pillow," he said with a smile.

I twisted around. Then I saw that, while I was sleeping, he had placed a rice cookie under my pillow. We both laughed. He picked me up like a sack of rice and carried me outside. All the while I gobbled the cookie.

In the yard, he plunked me down. He told me stories. After that, he got some scraps of wood and showed me how to make things. We made a doorstop for my mother and a toy duck for me. This was unheard of—a father doing these things with a daughter! My mother would teach me about cooking and cleaning. She would tell stories about brides. My father showed me the mystery of hammers. He explained the ways of our people.

He had much knowledge about the Vietnamese. His knowledge reached back to the Chinese Wars in ancient times. I learned about one of my distant ancestors, a woman named Phung Thi Chinh. She led Vietnamese fighters against the Han. In one battle, she was about to have a baby. She was surrounded by Chinese. Even so, she delivered the baby and tied it to her back. Then she cut her way to safety, waving a sword in each hand. I was amazed at this warrior's bravery. I was proud to be of her family. Even more, I was amazed by my father's pride in her great deeds. He believed that I was **worthy** of her example. "Follow in her footsteps," he said. Only later would I learn what he truly meant.

▶ Phung Thi Chinh
[fung teye chihn]

Keys to Literature

Follow in her footsteps is an **idiom**. What does it mean?

Never again did I cry after my nap. Phung Thi women were too strong for that. Besides, I was my father's daughter, and we had many things to do together.

On the eve of my mother's return, my father cooked a feast. He made roast duck. When we sat down to eat it, I felt guilty. My feelings showed on my face. He asked why I acted so sad.

"You've killed one of mother's ducks," I said. "One of the fat kind she sells at the market. She says the money buys gold. She saves this for her daughters' weddings. Without gold for a **dowry**, I will never marry."

My father looked properly moved at first. Then he brightened. "Well, Bay Ly," he said, "if you can't get married, you will just have to stay at home with me!"

I clapped my hands at the happy possibility.

My father cut into the rich, juicy bird. He said, "Even so, let's not tell your mother about the duck, okay?"

I giggled and swore to keep the secret.

The next day I took some water out to him in the fields. My mother was due home any time. I used every chance to step outside and watch for her. My father stopped working and drank gratefully. Then he took my hand and led me to the top of a nearby hill. It had a good view. I could see the village and the land beyond it, almost to the ocean. I thought he was going to show me my mother coming back. In fact, he had something else in mind.

He said, "Bay Ly, you see all this here? This is the Vietnam we have been talking about. You know that a country is more than dirt, rivers, and forests, don't you?"

I said, "Yes, I understand." We had learned in school that one's country is as **sacred** as a father's grave.

Think About It

Vietnam has a history of being taken over by other countries. How does this affect how the Vietnamese feel about their country?

"Good. You know, some of these lands are battlefields. Your brothers and cousins are fighting there. They may never come back. Even your sisters have all left home looking for a better life. You are the only one left in my house. If the enemy comes back, you must be both a daughter and a son. I told you how the Chinese used to rule our land. People in this village had to risk their lives diving in the ocean. They took the risk just to find pearls for the Chinese emperor's gown. They had to risk tigers and snakes in the jungle

Vietnamese forced by the French to build and repair bunkers.

just to find herbs for his table. For this they got a bowl of rice and another day of life. That is why Phung Thi Chinh fought so hard to rid us of the Chinese. When the French came, it was the same old story. Your mother and I were taken to Da Nang. We had to build a runway for their airplanes. We worked from sunup to well after dark. If we stopped to rest, a Moroccan would whip us. Our reward was a bowl of rice and another day of life. Freedom is never a gift, Bay Ly. It must be won and won again. Do you understand?"

I said that I did.

"Good." He moved his finger from the brown **dikes**. Finally he pointed to our house near the village. "This land here belongs to me. Do you know how I got it?"

I thought a moment, trying to remember my mother's stories. Then I said honestly, "I can't remember."

He squeezed me lovingly. "I got it from your mother."

Morocco, like Vietnam, was a colony of France. The French used Moroccans to fight on their side in Vietnam's war for independence from France.

"What? That can't be true!" I said. Everyone in the family knew my mother was poor and my father's family was wealthy. Her parents were dead. She had to work like a slave for her mother-in-law to prove herself worthy. Such women don't have land to give away.

"It's true." My father's smile widened. "When I was a young man, my parents needed someone to look after their lands. They had to be very careful about whom they chose as wives for their three sons. In the village, your mother was known as the hardest worker of all. She raised herself and her brothers without parents. At the same time, I noticed a beautiful woman working in the fields. Then my mother said she was going to talk to the matchmaker about this hard-working village girl she'd heard about. My heart sank. I was attracted to this mysterious, tall woman I had seen in the rice paddies. Imagine my surprise when I learned the girl my mother heard about and the woman I admired were the same.

"Well, we were married, and my mother tested your mother harshly. She had to cook and clean and know everything about children. She had to be able to manage several farms and know when and how to take the extra crops to the market. Of course, she was testing her other daughters-in-law as well. When my parents died, they divided their many farms among their sons. You know what? They gave your mother and me the biggest share. They knew we would take care of it best. That's why I say the land came from her. Because in fact it did."

I suddenly missed my mother very much. I looked down the road to the south, hoping to see her. My father noticed my sad face.

"Hey." He poked me in the ribs. "Are you getting hungry for lunch?"

▶ In traditional Vietnam, as in some other societies, marriages are sometimes arranged by matchmakers.

"No. I want to learn how to take care of the farm. What happens if the soldiers come back? What did you and Mother do when the soldiers came?" I asked my father.

My father squatted on the dusty hilltop. He wiped the sweat from his face. "The first thing I did was to tell myself that it was my duty to survive. I had to take care of my family and my farm. That is a tricky job in a war. It's as hard as being a soldier. The Moroccans were very **savage**. One day the rumor passed that they were coming to destroy the village. You may remember that night. I sent you and your brothers and sisters away with your mother to Da Nang."

"You didn't go with us!" My voice still held the horror of that night. I thought I had lost my father.

Think About It

Why does the father say that taking care of the farm is as hard as being a soldier?

French colonial forces moving through a swamp during the 1950s.

"Right! I stayed near the village—right on this hill. I had to keep an eye on the enemy and on our house. If they really wanted to destroy the village, I would save some of our things. That way, we could start over. Sure enough, that was their plan.

"The real problem was to keep things safe and keep from being captured. Their patrols were everywhere. Sometimes I went so deep in the forest that I feared I would get lost. All I had to do, though, was follow the smoke from the burning huts. Then I could find my way back.

"Once, I was trapped between two patrols. They had camped on both sides of a river. I had to wait in the water for two days before one of them moved on. When I got out, my skin was **shriveled** like an old melon's. I was so cold I could hardly move. From the waist down, my body was black with leeches. But it was worth all the pain. When your mother came back, we still had some furniture and tools to work the earth. Many people lost everything. Yes, we were very lucky."

My father drew me out to arm's length and looked me squarely in the eye. "Now, Bay Ly, do you understand what your job is?"

I squared my shoulders and put on a soldier's face. "My job is to get even for my family's sufferings. To protect my farm by killing the enemy. I must become a woman warrior like Phung Thi Chinh!"

My father laughed and pulled me close. "No, little peach blossom. Your job is to stay alive. You must keep an eye on things. Your job is to find a husband and have babies and tell the story of what you've seen to your children. Tell it to anyone else who'll listen. Most of all, your job is to live in peace and tend the **shrine** of our ancestors. Do these things well, Bay Ly, and you will be worth more than any soldier who ever took up a sword."

Keys to Literature

What does the **idiom** *squared my shoulders* mean here?

Think About It

Why does Le Ly's father tell her that her job is to tell stories and have children?

Meet the Author

LE LY HAYSLIP *(Born 1949)*

When Le Ly Hayslip was twelve, the Vietnam War arrived at her small village in Vietnam. She was the youngest of six children. Her brothers fought for both sides. She was accused of spying, was tortured, and spent time in prison. Hayslip married a U.S. citizen working in Vietnam. She and her husband left for the United States in 1970.

Life was hard for Hayslip in the United States. Both her first and second husbands died. She raised three children on her own. She worked as a housekeeper, factory worker, and restaurant host. She also began writing her life story. It was published as *When Heaven and Earth Changed Places* in 1989. The book led to a movie called *Heaven and Earth*. Today, Hayslip still writes. She also helps people in Vietnam.

Check Your Prediction

1. Look back at the answer you gave for the Predict question. Would you change your answer? Explain.

Understand the Autobiography

2. Why does the father take his daughter to the top of the hill?

3. Why does the father say he got his land from his wife?

4. Why did the father send his family to Da Nang and stay behind?

Think About the Autobiography

5. The father tells the author to "keep an eye on things." What does this idiom mean?

6. What did the father mean when he told Le Ly to be like Phung Thi Chinh?

7. How can you tell that this selection is an autobiography?

8. What kind of relationship does Le Ly have with her father? Explain.

Extend Your Response

Imagine that Hayslip is telling her own children about their grandfather. What words do you think she would use to describe him? Make a list and share it with a partner.

Learn More About It

VIETNAM

Land

Vietnam is a country in South Asia. It is surrounded by China, Laos, Cambodia, and the Gulf of Tonkin. Mountains cover parts of Vietnam. Most people, however, live in flatter areas near its two main rivers. Vietnam's climate is mostly warm and rainy. This climate is especially good for growing rice.

People

More than 80 million people live in Vietnam. Many are farmers. Others work in an industry such as mining or tourism. Almost all people there speak Vietnamese.

History

The people of Vietnam have had a long history of foreign rule. During the late 1800s, Vietnam was taken over by France. Rebels in Vietnam eventually defeated the French in 1954. After this, Vietnam was divided into two parts. The north was more communist and the south more democratic. The division was supposed to last just a couple of years. Instead, a war broke out between the government of the south and groups from the north. The United States supported the south. U.S. troops spent many very difficult years there. In 1973, U.S. troops pulled out. By 1975, Vietnam was one country with a communist government. Today, it has a good trade relationship with the U.S.

Apply and Connect

What effect has Vietnam's long history of foreign rule had on its people?

BEFORE YOU READ
"Grandfather's Photograph"

Keys to Literature

free verse: poetry that is not written in a regular pattern; the words do not rhyme.

>   Example: *There's just one picture of him / hanging on an old discolored wall*

comparison: showing how two things are alike

>   Example: *Something in me resembles him ...*

Did You Know?

There are over 18 languages commonly spoken in India. This poem was first written in Hindi, one of the more popular languages. Many Indians also speak or write in English because of Great Britain's long control over the country.

Words to Know

discolored	stained
composed	calm, peaceful
alms	money given to the poor
ordinariness	the state of being average or common

Genre: Poetry

   "Grandfather's Photograph" is a poem. Read more about poetry on page 467 of the Genre Guide.

Grandfather's Photograph

BY MANGALESH DABRAL

READ TO FIND OUT...
What can a photo of a grandfather tell a person about himself?

Grandfather wasn't fond of being photographed
or didn't find time perhaps
There's just one picture of him
hanging on an old **discolored** wall
5 He sits serious and **composed**
like a cloud heavy with water

All we know of Grandfather is
that he gave **alms** to beggars
tossed restlessly in sleep
10 and made his bed neatly every morning
I was just a kid then
and never saw his anger or

Keys to Literature

You can tell this poem is written in **free verse** because the lines are not written in a regular pattern and do not rhyme.

his **ordinariness**
Pictures never show someone's helpless side
15 Mother used to tell us that
when we fell asleep surrounded
by strange creatures of the night
Grandfather would stay awake inside the picture

I didn't grow as tall as Grandfather
20 not as composed or as serious
Still something in me resembles him
An anger like his
an ordinariness
I too walk with my head bent down
25 and every day see myself
sitting in an empty
picture frame.

Meet the Author

MANGALESH DABRAL *(Born 1948)*

Mangalesh Dabral was born in a small village
in the hills of the Himalayan Mountains of India.
Dabral has spent his adult life in cities, such as
Delhi. He still feels strong ties to the countryside,
though. He grew up speaking and writing Hindi.

Dabral is close to the traditions of Hindi poetry,
but he was brought up in the 1960s and 1970s.
Those were times when Hindi poets were
experimenting with new ways. His poetry shows
both old and new ways of thinking.

Understand the Poem

1. How did Grandfather feel about having his picture taken?

2. What do we know about Grandfather from the poem?

3. Why doesn't the speaker in the poem know much about Grandfather?

4. How old is the speaker in the poem when he writes this? How do you know?

Think About the Poem

5. How does the mother use Grandfather's picture to calm the children?

6. What is the comparison in the poem between Grandfather and grandson?

7. Do you think free verse is a good form for this poem? Why or why not?

8. Do you think Grandfather was a kind man? Why or why not?

Extend Your Response

Find a photograph of yourself as a child. Write what you were doing, thinking, and feeling when the photograph was taken. Tell how the person in the photograph is different from you today.

Chapter 11 Review

Summaries

The Old Grandfather and His Little Grandson The little grandson's parents mistreat his grandfather. When the grandson suggests that someday he will treat his parents the same way, the parents see their mistake.

When Heaven and Earth Changed Places Le Ly Hayslip fondly remembers her father in this autobiography. He cares for her when her mother is gone. He tells her stories of their ancestors' love of the country. He also tells her how he protected his family and farm during war. He helps Le Ly understand her role in protecting her family and the country.

Grandfather's Photograph One photograph is all the speaker has of his grandfather. It is enough, though, to help the speaker form a strong connection with his relative.

Vocabulary Review

For each sentence write *true* if the underlined word is used correctly. If it is not used correctly, change the underlined word to make the sentence true.

1. Her hands had been in the dishwater so long they were as <u>shriveled</u> as an old leaf.

2. When his mother saw that he had finished his homework before dinner, she <u>scolded</u> him.

3. The girl wrote a paper, but it was not good enough to <u>merit</u> an A.

4. A spilled cherry drink <u>discolored</u> the tablecloth.

5. Jacki felt <u>ashamed</u> that she had won the race.

Chapter Quiz

Write your answers in one or two complete sentences.
Use a separate sheet of paper.

1. The Old Grandfather and His Little Grandson What happens after the grandfather breaks the bowl?

2. The Old Grandfather and His Little Grandson Why is the little boy making a wooden dish?

3. When Heaven and Earth Changed Places Why is the father proud of his ancestor, Phung Thi Chinh?

4. When Heaven and Earth Changed Places Why did the father send the rest of the family to Da Nang?

5. Grandfather's Photograph Why is there only one picture of Grandfather?

6. Grandfather's Photograph How does the speaker of the poem grow up to be different from Grandfather?

Critical Thinking

7. The Old Grandfather and His Little Grandson Why does the son's making a dish cause the parents to change their ways?

8. When Heaven and Earth Changed Places Why does the father think Le Ly's marrying and telling what she has seen is worth more than what a soldier does?

Chapter Activity

Think of someone in your family who is important to you, like the father in *When Heaven and Earth Changed Places* or Grandfather in "Grandfather's Photograph." Write a few paragraphs or a poem describing that person. Tell what he or she is like and what he or she means to you.

Unit 5 **Review**

On a separate sheet of paper, write the letter that best completes each sentence below.

1. In "Horses," the speaker says he will never forget
   A. Berlin.
   B. the winter.
   C. the horses.
   D. World War II.

2. The puppies in "Eight Puppies" are just beginning to
   A. bark.
   B. see.
   C. learn tricks.
   D. drink water.

3. In "The Trout," Julia is troubled that
   A. The Dark Walk is so long.
   B. the trout has so little room to move.
   C. people will see her setting the trout free.
   D. her brother does not sleep well.

4. "Four Haiku," "Green Creek," and "The Cedar Chest" include descriptions of
   A. mountains, plains, and a cow.
   B. rivers, birds, and a village.
   C. seasons, a creek, and a tree.
   D. the ocean, sunrise, and a chest.

5. In "Morning," day awakens
   A. a dog.
   B. two children on a bus.
   C. a rooster.
   D. a father asleep in bed.

6. In "The Old Grandfather and His Little Grandson," the grandson
   A. gets angry with his parents.
   B. takes a photograph.
   C. makes a bowl.
   D. cooks dinner.

Making Connections

On a separate sheet of paper, write your answers to the following questions.

7. *When Heaven and Earth Changed Places* was made into a movie. Do you think that this selection would make a good movie scene? Why or why not?

8. Compare and contrast yourself and a family member. Use the comparison of the speaker and his grandfather in "Grandfather's Photograph" as a model.

Writing an Essay

Choose one theme from this unit that is important to you. Explain why it is important.

Unit Six

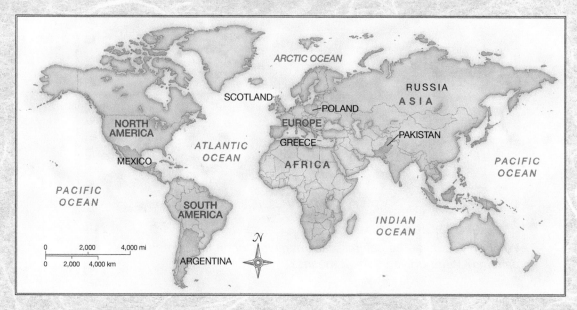

Le Chateau des Pyrenees by René Magritte (1890–1967) copyright © 2005 C. Herscovici, Brussels/Artists Rights Society (ARS), New York

What do you think the painter was imagining when he painted this painting? What do you think it means?

Chapter 12 Imagine

Learning Objectives

- Recognize a metaphor.
- Identify the atmosphere of a poem.
- Identify the narrative hooks in a story.
- Recognize foreshadowing to predict events.
- Understand what an epic is.

Preview Activity

Think of a place you have always wanted to visit. Now imagine yourself there. Write what it is like. Then, share what you've imagined with a classmate.

Theme Preview: Imagine

Each of us sees the world differently. Sometimes this leads us to imagine different things. The stories in this chapter explore what happens when writers imagine: a bicycle joins a herd of goats, a man on an empty street senses someone behind him, and a Greek hero battles a fearsome monster.

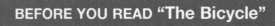

Keys to Literature

metaphor: a comparison of two things that does not use *like* or *as*

> Example: *pillows of clouds*

Did You Know?

Early bikes were dangerous and uncomfortable. They had hard wooden wheels and were called *boneshakers*. Few people used them. Then, in 1888, an Englishman invented rubber tires. Soon, bicycles were everywhere. In 1895, 20 million bicycles were sold.

Words to Know

romps	active play
glade	an open area of the woods
buck	a male goat
poacher	a person who hunts illegally
trophy	a prize that shows success in hunting or other activities

Genre: Poetry

"The Bicycle" is a poem. Read more about poetry on page 467 of the Genre Guide.

The Bicycle

BY JERZY HARASYMOWICZ

once
forgotten by tourists
a bicycle joined
a herd
5 of mountain goats

with its splendidly turned
silver horns
it became
their leader

10 with its bell
it warned them
of danger

with them
it partook
15 in **romps**
on the snow covered
glade

the bicycle
gazed from above
20 on people walking;
with the goats

it fought
over a goat,
with a bearded **buck**

25 it reared up at eagles
enraged
on its back wheel

it was happy
though it never
30 nibbled at grass

READ TO FIND OUT...
What happens when a
bicycle comes to life?

Keys to Literature

A **metaphor** compares
two things without using
like or *as*. What are the
bike's handlebars
compared to here?

or drank
from a stream
until once
a **poacher**
35 shot it

tempted
by the silver **trophy**
of its horns

and then
40 above the Tatras was seen
against the sparkling
January sky

the angel of death erect
slowly
45 riding to heaven
holding the bicycle's
dead horns.

▶ The Tatras are mountains in Eastern Europe.

Meet the Author

JERZY HARASYMOWICZ *(1933–1999)*

Jerzy Harasymowicz lived in Krakow, a city in southern Poland. After World War II, the Polish government limited freedom of speech. Many books were censored. Some writers left Poland. However, Harasymowicz continued to live and work there.

Harasymowicz is famous for his great imagination. Many of his poems tell fantastic stories. Some of these are based on Polish folklore. Others tell stories about nature. One of his best-known books of poetry is *I Live on a Raft.*

Understand the Poem

1. Who leaves the bicycle behind?

2. Why does the bicycle become the leader of the goats?

3. How does the bicycle use its bell?

4. How does the bicycle die?

Think About the Poem

5. Why do you think the bicycle enjoys its life with the goats?

6. The poet says a poacher was "tempted by the silver trophy of its horns." What is the poet referring to in this metaphor?

7. How does the reader know the bicycle is dead?

8. Do you think the goats are sad to lose the bicycle? Why?

Extend Your Response

Imagine that you are a tourist visiting the mountain. You see the bicycle leading the goats. Write a diary entry describing what you see.

Keys to Literature

atmosphere: the general mood of a piece of literature

> Example: Words such as *blind, blackness,* and *doorless* create a dark atmosphere.

Words to Know

stumble	trip
pursue	chase after; follow

Genre: Poetry

"The Street" is a poem. Read more about poetry on page 467 of the Genre Guide.

The Street

BY OCTAVIO PAZ

A long and silent street.
I walk in blackness and I **stumble** and fall
and rise, and I walk blind, my feet
stepping on silent stones and dry leaves.
5   Someone behind me also stepping on stones, leaves;
if I slow down, he slows;
if I run, he runs. I turn: nobody.
Everything dark and doorless.
Turning and turning among these corners
10   which lead forever to the street
where nobody waits for, nobody follows me,
where I **pursue** a man who stumbles
and rising and says when he sees me: nobody

READ TO FIND OUT...

What is hidden in the darkness of the street?

Keys to Literature

What **atmosphere** does the author create in the first two lines?

Think About It

The speaker in the poem says the corners "lead forever to the street." What is really happening?

Houses of Peasants in the Moonlight, Dieppe by Fritz Thaulow 1894

Meet the Author

OCTAVIO PAZ *(1914–1998)*

Octavio Paz was born in Mexico City. He published his first book of poetry when he was 19 years old. Paz was a writer, teacher, and diplomat. He was also Mexico's ambassador to India from 1962 to 1968.

Paz wrote poems and essays. His work often focuses on love, loneliness, and politics. He won the Nobel Prize for literature in 1990. He was the first Mexican to win that honor.

Understand the Poem

1. At what time of day does this poem most likely take place? How do you know?

2. What does the speaker in this poem think is happening?

3. What is the street like? Give details from the poem.

4. Where does the speaker say all the corners lead to?

5. What does the speaker see when he turns around?

Think About the Poem

6. Describe the atmosphere in this poem. Give an example of words that help create this atmosphere.

7. What is the speaker in this poem feeling? How can you tell?

8. Do you think there is someone following the person in the poem? Explain your answer.

Extend Your Response

Tell about a time that you felt frightened by noises on a street or in your house. What did you imagine was happening? What really happened? Describe your experience.

Keys to Literature

narrative hook: a point in a story at which the author grabs your attention

Example: The author grabs our attention when Odysseus says "the best plan I could think of was this."

foreshadowing: hints about what might happen later in a story

Example: Odysseus' saying "It would have been better if I had agreed" hints at trouble to come later in the story.

Did You Know?

The Odyssey was first told as a very long poem in the eighth century B.C. People did not read it. Instead, they listened to performers say it. Over the centuries, the performers changed the language of *The Odyssey* as the way people spoke changed.

Words to Know

woes	terrible troubles
fierce	violent
savage	cruel, wild, or unkind
kids	young goats
fuddled	confused

Genre: Epic

"The Cyclops" is the retelling of part of an epic, *The Odyssey*. Read more about epics in the Learn More About It on page 365 or page 466 of the Genre Guide.

The Cyclops

BY HOMER, *retold*

I am Odysseus, son of Laertes. The whole world talks of my skill in battle, and my fame has reached the heavens. My home is under the clear skies of Ithaca. Let me tell you now of our voyage as we came home from Troy. It was a terrible voyage, for the gods sent me many **woes**.

First, the wind brought me to the land of the Cicones. My men and I fought the Cicones in the city of Ismarus. We killed the men in battle. Then we divided up the wealth. Each of my men got his share. I said we must escape right away. But my men wanted to stay. Meanwhile, the people of the city sent for help from their neighbors. More Cicones came to fight. Many of my men were killed. We sailed away from Ismarus with heavy hearts. We were sad for the loss of our dear friends, but glad of our own escape.

READ TO FIND OUT...
What trials await Odysseus on his long journey home?

▶ Odysseus [oh-DEE-see-uhs]

Keys to Literature

A **narrative hook** grabs the readers' attention. What is the narrative hook in this paragraph?

▶ Cicones [key-CONE-es]

We set sail for home, but the winds blew us off course. For nine days I was chased across the seas by those winds. But on the tenth day, we reached the country of the lotus-eaters. This is the race of people who eat the flowery lotus fruit. I sent two men to find out what kind of people the lotus-eaters were. The lotus-eaters gave them lotus to taste. Once the men had eaten the lotus, they had no wish to come back to the ship. All they wanted was to stay with the lotus-eaters, eat the lotus fruit, and forget all thoughts of coming home. I had to use force to bring them back to the ship. I ordered my men to leave the land of the lotus-eaters as fast as they could.

We sailed on with heavy hearts. We came to an island where there were a great number of wild goats. We took our bows and long spears from the ship and began shooting at the goats. Then we sat down to a fine meal. As we sat, we looked across the water to the nearby island of the Cyclops. The people on the island of the Cyclops are **fierce**. They have no laws. They never lift a hand to plant or plow food. They just leave everything to the gods.

The next morning, I set out for the island of the Cyclops. When we arrived, I took twelve of my best men with me. The rest stayed to guard the ship.

As I set out, I took some food and filled a goatskin with sparkling water. The water had a special potion that would make a man or beast drowsy. I had to be prepared. I had a feeling we would find ourselves face to face with some **savage** being of great strength.

We came to the cave of a Cyclops, but he was away with his goats and sheep. We went inside and looked in amazement at everything. There were baskets of cheeses, pails and bowls for milking, and many lambs and **kids**.

Predict

What do you think will happen between the Cyclops [SY-klahps] and Odysseus and his men?

▶ In Greek myths, the Cyclops is a monster. It has a single eye in the middle of its forehead.

My men begged me to take some of the cheeses and the lambs and kids back to the ship and sail away. It would have been better if I had agreed. But I wished to see the owner of the cave. I hoped to receive some friendly gifts from him.

At last the Cyclops came with his flocks of sheep and goats. He carried a huge bundle of wood and threw it down with a great crash. We were so frightened we ran to the back of the cave. The Cyclops picked up a huge stone and closed the entrance to the cave. Then he began to milk his sheep and goats. When he had finished, he lit the fire and saw us.

In a booming voice, he said, "Strangers! Are you traders or pirates?"

The voice and the sight of the monster filled us with panic. But I managed to answer him. I said, "We are on our way back from Troy. We hope to be your guests, good sir. Remember, it is your duty to the gods, especially Zeus. He is the friend of guests."

The Cyclops said, "Stranger, you must be a fool. We Cyclops care nothing for Zeus or the rest of the blessed gods. We are much stronger than they are."

The cruel monster jumped up. He reached out to my men and snatched a couple. He dashed their heads against the floor as though they had been puppies. Then he tore them to pieces and ate them. We watched, weeping. We lifted our hands to Zeus in horror at the terrible sight.

When he finished his meal, he lay down to sleep. At first, I thought I would gather my courage and stab him with my sword. But then we would be trapped inside the cave. The door was impossible to move. So with sighs and groans we waited for the blessed light of day.

Keys to Literature

It would have been better if I had agreed **foreshadows** what is to come. What do you think will happen?

▶ In Greek mythology, Zeus [ZOOS] rules all the gods.

Predict

What do you think
Odysseus is planning?

As soon as Dawn appeared, the Cyclops milked his ewes and goats. Then he snatched up a couple of my men for his meal. When he had eaten, he drove his sheep and goats out of the cave. I watched him go, with murder in my heart. I tried to think of how to pay him back. The best plan I could think of was this.

In the pen, the Cyclops had a huge staff of green olive-wood. I told my men to smooth it down. I sharpened it to a point. Then I hardened it in the fire and hid it under some loose rocks.

Evening came, and with it came the Cyclops. He drove in his flocks and closed the great stone door. After he milked his sheep and goats, he snatched up two more of my men and ate them.

I went up to him with the sparkling water I had brought in the goatskin. I said, "Here, Cyclops, I brought you a cool drink. I hope you will take pity on me and help me on my way home."

The Cyclops took the sparkling water and drank it up. The delicious drink gave him such pleasure that he said, "Give me more, please, and tell me your name."

Think About It

What do you think the
potion will do to the
Cyclops?

I handed the Cyclops another bowl of the sparkling water. Three times I filled the bowl for him. Three times the fool drank every bit. When the special potion had **fuddled** his wits, I said, "I'll tell you my name. In return, give me the gift you promised me. My name is Nobody."

The Cyclops said, "I will eat Nobody last. This shall be your gift."

Think About It

Odysseus must have a
reason for telling the
Cyclops his name is
Nobody. How do you think
this fits into Odysseus'
plan for escape?

As soon as he had spoken, the Cyclops fell over. I went at once and put the olive-wood pole in the fire to make it hot. My men gathered around me. A god now gave them great courage. Taking the pole, we drove the sharp end into the Cyclops' eye.

The Cyclops gave a terrible shriek. He pulled the pole from his eye and threw it away from him. He shouted for other Cyclopes to come. The Cyclops' neighbors gathered outside the cave. They said, "What on earth is wrong with you, Polyphemus? Is somebody trying to kill you?"

Polyphemus said, "O my friends, it is Nobody."

The neighbors said, "If Nobody is hurting you, you must be sick. All you can do is pray to your father Poseidon."

The neighbors went away. Polyphemus moaned in pain. He pushed away the stone from the doorway and stretched out his arms. He was hoping to catch us as we slipped out of the cave. He must have thought I was a fool!

Meanwhile, I was trying to hit on some way to save us. I thought up plan after plan. This was the plan that finally seemed best. I wove together willow twigs from the Cyclops' bed. With these, I tied groups of rams together. Under the chests of the rams, we tied the men. For myself, I chose one big ram who was the pick of the whole flock.

▶ Polyphemus [po-LEE-fee-muhs] is the name of the Cyclops.

When Dawn came, the goats and rams ran out of the cave. The Cyclops ran his hands along the backs of each animal as it passed him. But the idiot never noticed my men were tied under the chests of his own rams.

When we were all a little distance from the cave, I untied my men. We drove Polyphemus' flock of goats and sheep onto our ship. The men took their places at the oars and began to row.

Before we had gone very far, I shouted out to Polyphemus, "Your crimes have caught up with you! Now Zeus and the other gods have paid you!"

The Cyclops was in a rage. He tore the top from a great rock and threw it at us. The rock fell just ahead of our ship. The water rose up in a great swell and drove us back toward the beach. My crew rowed as fast as they could. We escaped once more.

My men tried to hold me back, but my temper was up. I shouted once more to the Cyclops: "It was I who put your eye out, Cyclops! I am Odysseus, the son of Laertes!"

The Cyclops gave a groan. He cried, "Alas! A great prophet warned me that a man called Odysseus would rob me of my sight." The Cyclops lifted his hands to the starry heavens. He said, "Hear me, Poseidon. If I am your son, let Odysseus never reach his home. Or if he does, let him come late, in terrible woe. Let him find trouble in his home."

▶ Poseidon is the Greek god of the sea.

Once again the Cyclops picked up a huge boulder and threw it. But this one made a wave that carried us farther away. We reached the island, where the rest of my men and ships were waiting. We unloaded the Cyclops' flock and divided it among us.

As soon as Dawn appeared the next day, we set sail once more. We were sad for the dear friends we had lost, but glad at our own escape from death.

Meet the Author

Homer, (n.d.) anonymous

HOMER (lived circa 750 B.C.)

Homer was a poet who lived in ancient Greece. Scholars think he lived around 750 B.C., but they don't know much about him. They believe he was blind. They also think he traveled widely, reciting his poems. The two long epic poems for which he is famous are *The Iliad* and *The Odyssey*. Both tell of the adventures of Greek heroes.

Homer composed these epics before Greek was a set written language. At the time, poets said or sang their poems to audiences. People liked them so much that they passed them from one generation to the next. Eventually, people wrote down the epic poems we know today.

Check Your Predictions

1. Look back at the answers you gave for the Predict questions. Would you change your answers? Explain.

Understand the Epic

2. Where are Odysseus and his men headed?

3. Why does Odysseus stay in the cave on the island of the Cyclops when he knows fierce people live there?

4. How do Odysseus and his men wound the Cyclops?

5. How do Odysseus and his men escape from the Cyclops?

Think About the Epic

6. How do the narrative hooks interest the reader in the story?

7. What does Odysseus' comment that he should have listened to his men foreshadow?

8. Describe some of Odysseus' character traits. Tell what makes it clear he has those traits.

Extend Your Response

Draw a comic strip to tell the story of Odysseus and his visit to the Cyclops. Each frame of your comic strip should contain an important event.

Learn About It

GENRE STUDY: EPICS

Epic poems are long poems that tell a story. At the center of an epic is a hero. Usually the hero must face difficult trials. He does not always survive. Epics are often written in very formal language. However, many epics we read today are translations. They are often written in story form. This is true of the two epics in this book.

Ulysses and the Sirens, detail (4th Century)

This image shows a scene from The Odyssey *where Odysseus and his men meet nymphs known as the Sirens.*

Epics also tell about the history and feelings of a country. For example, *Beowulf* tells of a Scandinavian king. We can't be sure that Beowulf existed. And certainly, we doubt that Beowulf conquered dragons. However, scholars believe that much of the history in the epic is correct. They also believe that it tells about the values of the Scandinavian people at that time. The same is true of Homer's *The Odyssey* and *The Iliad*. *The Iliad*, for example, tells of the war between Greece and Troy. Some parts of the story are clearly not true. However, historians believe the war did happen.

Many of the epics we read today are ancient. Yet poets today continue to write in this form. In addition, some poets use the epic form for satire.

> **Apply and Connect**
> What about "The Cyclops" might be true? What is imaginary?

Chapter 12 Review

Summaries

The Bicycle A bicycle joins a herd of wild goats. The bicycle becomes the leader of the herd. The bicycle's happiness ends when it is shot by a poacher, though. The angel of death rides the bicycle to heaven.

The Street The speaker is on a dark street. Frightened, he thinks someone is behind him. He notices the person moving and stopping as he does. However, there is no one there.

The Cyclops Odysseus and his men are sailing home from Troy. They reach the island of the Cyclops and are trapped in a Cyclops' cave. The Cyclops kills and eats several of Odysseus' men. Odysseus thinks of a clever plan to help them escape. Odysseus and his men blind the Cyclops. Then they escape by hiding beneath rams that are tied together. The blinded monster chases the men, but they sail away.

trophy

stumble

pursue

fierce

Vocabulary Review

Complete each sentence with a word from the box. Use a separate piece of paper.

1. Be careful not to _____ over the crack in the sidewalk.

2. We were unable to _____ the car, and the thief got away.

3. We had a _____ dog that would growl and scare anyone who came into our yard.

4. Sam's team got a _____ for winning the soccer tournament.

Chapter Quiz

**Write your answers in one or two complete sentences.
Use a separate sheet of paper.**

1. The Bicycle What things happen to the bicycle in this poem?

2. The Bicycle Why does the poacher shoot the bicycle?

3. The Street Why does the speaker in the poem think
   someone is behind him?

4. The Street What happens when the speaker turns around?

5. The Cyclops In what two places does Odysseus lose men?

6. The Cyclops Why does Odysseus tell the Cyclops his name is
   "Nobody"?

Critical Thinking

7. The Bicycle In what ways does the bicycle act like a goat?

8. The Cyclops At the beginning of this story, Odysseus says,
   "The whole world talks of my skill in battle, and my fame
   has reached the heavens." Do you think Odysseus deserves
   his fame?

Chapter Activity

Write a letter home from one of Odysseus' men. As you
plan your letter, think about how the man's view of these
events might be different from Odysseus' view.

Paris Through the Window (1913) by Marc Chagall

What story does this fantasy painting tell?

Chapter **13** / **Fantasy**

Learning Objectives

- Recognize the external conflicts that shape the plot of a story.
- Identify and understand characters' motivations.
- Recognize allegory in fiction.
- Understand the denotations and connotations of words.
- Identify figurative language in a poem.

Preview Activity

What if animals could speak? How would the world be different? Make a list of ideas. Talk them over with a friend. Would you like the changes or not?

Theme Preview: Fantasy

How far can our imaginations take us when we let them run free? Writers all over the world have explored their own imaginations by writing fantasies. In each of these fantasies, we learn about a whole new world. Sometimes stories like these help us learn more about our own world as well.

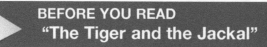

Keys to Literature

external conflict: a struggle that a person has with another person, with society, or with nature

> Example: In this story, a hungry tiger demands that a farmer give him something to eat.

motivation: the reason a character behaves as he or she does

> Example: *Still, he did not want to give up his oxen for the tiger's meal.*

Did You Know?

Bengal tigers roamed Pakistan as recently as 150 years ago. However, there are none in Pakistan today. About 3,000 remain in India. They are endangered. They are losing hunting grounds as people take over more and more land.

Words to Know

thrashed	flapped wildly about
turban	a scarf wrapped around the head to form a kind of hat
slashed	cut with rough, long strokes
jackal	a wild dog usually found in Africa or Asia

Genre: Folktale

"The Tiger and the Jackal" is a folktale. Read more about folktales on page 466 of the Genre Guide.

The Tiger and the Jackal

RETOLD BY ETHEL JOHNSTON PHELPS, *adapted*

There once was a farmer who went out with his oxen one morning to plow his field.

He had just finished plowing one row when a tiger walked up to him. The tiger said, "Good morning, friend. How are you today?"

"Good morning, sir. I am very well, sir," said the farmer. He was shaking with fear, but he thought it wise to be polite.

"I see you have two fine oxen," said the tiger. "I am very hungry. Take off their yokes at once, please. I plan to eat them."

READ TO FIND OUT...
Why would a jackal and a tiger tie their tails together?

Keys to Literature

What **external conflict** does the farmer face?

Keys to Literature

Motivation is the reason a character does something. Why does the farmer offer his wife's cow to the tiger?

The farmer's courage returned to him. Now he knew the tiger did not plan to eat him. Still, he did not want to give up his oxen for the tiger's meal.

"My friend," said the farmer, "I need these oxen to plow my field. Surely a brave tiger like you can hunt for a good meal elsewhere."

"Never mind that!" said the tiger angrily. "Take the yokes off the oxen. I will be ready to eat them in a moment." The tiger began to sharpen his teeth and claws on a stone.

"The oxen are very tough and will be hard to eat," pleaded the farmer. "My wife has a fat young milk cow at home. Spare my oxen, and I'll bring you the cow."

The tiger agreed to this. He thought a tender young cow would make a much easier meal for him than tough oxen. So he said, "Very well. I will wait here in the field while you go home and get the cow. But bring the cow back as quickly as you can. I'm very hungry."

The farmer took the oxen and went sadly to his home.

"Why do you come home so early in the day?" asked his wife. "It is not time for dinner!"

"A tiger came into the field and wanted to eat the oxen," said the farmer. "But I told him he could have the cow instead. Now I must bring him the cow."

"What!" she cried. "You would save your old oxen and give him my beautiful cow? Where will our children get milk? How can I cook our food without butter?"

"We'll have no food at all unless I plow the field for my crops," said the farmer angrily. "Now untie the cow for me."

"No, I will not give up my cow to the tiger!" said his wife. "Surely, you can think of a better way to get rid of the tiger!"

"No, I cannot. He is sitting in my field waiting for me, and he's very hungry."

His wife thought a moment. Then she said, "Go back to the tiger and tell him your wife is bringing the cow. Leave the rest to me."

The farmer did not like to go back to the tiger without the cow. But he had no better idea, so he walked slowly back to the field.

"Where is the cow?" roared the tiger angrily.

"My wife will bring the cow very soon," said the farmer.

At this, the tiger began to prowl about. He growled and **thrashed** his tail. The poor farmer's knees shook in terror.

In the meantime, his wife dressed herself in her husband's best clothes. She tied a **turban** very high on her head to make her look very tall. She took a long knife from the kitchen and put it into her belt. Then she put a saddle on their pony and rode off to the field.

As she drew near, she called out to her husband in a loud voice. "My good man, are there any tigers about? I've been hunting tigers for two days, and I'm hungry for tiger meat!" She **slashed** the air above her head with the knife in a very threatening way.

The farmer was so surprised he could not answer.

"Aha!" cried his wife. "Is that a tiger I see hiding in the grass? I ate three tigers for breakfast the other day. Now I'm hungry for more!" She started to ride toward the tiger.

These words frightened the tiger. He turned and bolted into the forest. He ran so fast he knocked over a **jackal**. The jackal had been sitting and waiting to feast on the oxen's bones when the tiger had finished his meal.

"Why are you running away?" called the jackal.

Predict

What will the farmer's wife do?

Keys to Literature

The farmer's wife rides into the field on a horse carrying a knife. What is her **motivation** for doing this?

Think About It

Who is smarter: the tiger or the jackal? How do you know?

"Run! Run for your life!" cried the tiger. "There is a terribly fierce horseman back in the field! He thinks nothing of eating three tigers for breakfast."

"That was no horseman," laughed the jackal. "That was only the farmer's wife dressed up as a hunter."

The tiger came back slowly. "Are you sure?"

"Did the sun get in your eyes? Didn't you see her hair hanging down from the turban?" asked the jackal impatiently.

The tiger was still not sure. "He looked like a hunter, and he swung that big knife as if he were going to kill me!"

"Don't give up your meal so easily," cried the brave jackal. "Go back to the field. I will follow and wait in the grass."

The tiger did not like that idea at all. "I think you want me to be killed!"

"No, of course not," said the jackal. He was hungry and eager for a meal. "If you like, we will go together, side by side."

The tiger was still not sure of the jackal's purpose. "You may run away and leave me after we get there."

"We can tie our tails together," said the jackal. "Then I can't run away."

The tiger thought this a good idea. So they tied their tails together in a strong knot. Then they set off together for the field.

Predict

How will the knot in their tails affect the tiger and the jackal as the story continues?

The farmer and his wife were still in the field. They were laughing over the trick she had played on the tiger. Suddenly they saw the tiger and the jackal trotting toward them with their tails tied together.

The farmer shouted to his wife, "Now the tiger has a jackal with him. Come away! Hurry!"

The wife said no, she would not. She waited until the tiger and the jackal were near. Then she called out, "Dear Mr. Jackal, how very kind of you to bring me such a nice fat tiger to eat. After I eat my fill, you can have the bones."

When the tiger heard this, he became wild with terror. He forgot the jackal, and he forgot the knot in their tails. He leaped for the tall grass. Then off he ran, dragging the jackal behind him over the stones and through thorn bushes.

Think About It

What does the wife's reaction show about her?

The jackal howled and cried for the tiger to stop. But the howls behind him only scared the tiger more. He ran on until they both dropped in a heap. They were more dead than alive.

As for the farmer, he was very proud of his wife's clever trick. The tiger never came back to their field again.

Meet the Reteller

ETHEL JOHNSTON PHELPS (1914–1984)

Ethel Johnston Phelps lived and died in New York state. She worked at a publishing company and took up writing as a hobby. She wrote plays and retold folktales.

Phelps wrote two books of folktales. She collected her stories from all over the world. She said she hoped they would stretch people's imaginations. Like "The Tiger and the Jackal," the tales feature strong, clever women.

Check Your Predictions

1. Look back at the answers you gave for the Predict questions. Would you change your answers? Explain.

Understand the Folktale

2. Why doesn't the farmer want to give his oxen to the tiger?

3. Why doesn't the farmer's wife want to give the tiger her cow?

4. Why do the tiger and jackal tie their tails together?

5. How does the farmer's wife make the tiger run away a second time?

Think About the Folktale

6. Why does the farmer take his wife's advice and return to the tiger empty-handed, even though he doesn't want to?

7. How would you describe the farmer's wife?

8. How does the external conflict between the humans and the tiger in this folktale mirror a real-life problem?

Extend Your Response

What would have happened if the farmer had given his oxen to the tiger? Write a new ending for the folktale.

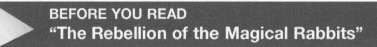

BEFORE YOU READ
"The Rebellion of the Magical Rabbits"

Keys to Literature

allegory: a story in which the characters and events stand for something else

> Example: In this allegory, the Wolf King stands for human dictators who try to make everyone believe the same things they do.

denotation: the actual meaning of a word

> Example: *Thing* means any real object or substance.

connotation: an idea or feeling suggested by a word

> Example: "*How come you didn't notice that this ... this thing was there?*" The word *thing* refers to a rabbit and also gives readers the feeling it's something unacceptable.

Did You Know?

Wolves chase down and eat big animals, such as deer. However, they also eat smaller animals, such as rabbits and squirrels. Wolves will even eat mice if other food is scarce.

Words to Know

rebellion	a fight against the government or other authority
existed	lived somewhere in the world
adviser	a person who gives information to someone else
traitor	someone who betrays the government
darkroom	a place where film is turned into pictures

Genre: Short Story

"The Rebellion of the Magical Rabbits" is a short story. Read more about short stories on page 467 of the Genre Guide.

The Rebellion of the Magical Rabbits

BY ARIEL DORFMAN, *adapted*

READ TO FIND OUT...
When a wolf declares himself king, what will the rabbits do?

When the wolves took over the land of the rabbits, the leader of the pack declared himself King. Then he said that the rabbits no longer **existed**. It would now be against the law to even say their name.

To be on the safe side, the new Wolf King went over every book. With a big black pencil, he crossed out every word about rabbits. He also tore out every picture of a cottontail. He did not stop until he felt sure that no trace of his enemies was left.

But an old gray fox, the Wolf's **adviser**, brought bad news.

"The birds, Your Wolfiness, keep saying that they have seen some ... some of those creatures."

"So how come I don't see anything from way up here, on my throne?" asked the Wolf.

Think About It
How does the Wolf King feel about the rabbits?

Predict

Why does the Wolf want the monkey to take photos? What will happen next?

▶ In folktales and fantasies, children are often the ones who see the truth.

Think About It

Why is the monkey afraid when he hears his daughter talk about the rabbits?

"In times like these," answered the fox, "people must see to believe."

"Seeing is believing? Bring me that monkey who takes photos, the one who lives nearby. I'll teach those birds a lesson."

The monkey looked at his wife and daughter. "What can the Wolf of all Wolves want with me?" he asked.

The monkey's daughter had an answer. "He must want you to take a picture of the rabbits, Dad."

"Quiet, quiet," said her mother. "Rabbits don't exist."

But the monkey's daughter knew that rabbits did exist. True, the rabbits no longer came to visit her as they had before. She had not seen them since the wolves had taken over. But in her dreams she still heard their voices singing nearby. When she awoke, there was always a small gift beside her bed.

"That's why I sleep well," said the little girl. "That's why that General Wolf must need the photo. Then he can sleep well. You'll bring me a picture of the rabbits, won't you, Dad?"

The monkey felt fear crawl up and down his fur. "Send this little girl to her room," he told his wife. "Keep her there until she understands that we just don't talk about certain things."

The King of the Wolves was not in the best of moods when the monkey came in. He said to the monkey, "You're late. I'm in a hurry. I need a picture of each important act in my life. All my acts, let me tell you, are of the greatest importance. Can you guess what we're going to do with those pictures? You can't? We're going to put one on every street, inside every bush, in every home."

The monkey was shaking so hard that no words came out.

The Wolf King said, "Now the birds will think twice before talking any nonsense about rabbits. Understand?"

The monkey understood very well. His shaking paw immediately clicked the button of the camera. He had taken the first picture.

"Go," roared the Wolf, "and develop it. I want it on every wall in the kingdom."

The monkey returned some minutes later. He did not dare enter the throne room. Instead, he asked one of the soldiers to call the Wolf's adviser, the fox. Without a word, the monkey passed the fox the picture he had just taken.

The fox blinked once. Then he blinked again. In a corner of the photo there was something. It was not the strong, fierce figure of the King. In the corner was the beginning of an ear.

"You blind monkey!" said the fox. "How come you didn't notice that this … this thing was there? Can't you aim that camera of yours?"

"If it could get into the picture," the monkey answered, "it was because you and your guards let it get close."

"It won't happen again," the adviser promised. "Rub out that … ear before His Wolfiness finds out."

From his bag, the monkey took out a special liquid. He used it to remove anything that might bother his customers. The annoying ear began to disappear.

The King of Wolves was pleased with the picture. He ordered it sent all over the kingdom. Two hours later he went on a tour of his kingdom. He wanted to make sure that not a single window was without his picture. "Not bad," he said, "but this photo is already getting old. People should see my latest deeds. Take another. Quick. Show me scaring these pigeons—right away. Bring it to me immediately. You took too long last time."

Think About It

What kind of ear is in the photo?

But the monkey wasn't able to obey this time either. Once again he had the adviser called secretly.

"Again?" asked the fox. "It happened again?"

Except that now it was worse than before. A whole corner of the new picture was filled with the face of a rabbit winking an eye.

"We've got to do a better job of guarding the King," muttered the fox. "Meanwhile, rub that out."

"Wonderful," shouted King Wolf when finally he was given the picture. "Look at the frightened faces of the pigeons trying to escape. I want a million copies. I want them on milk cartons and on the coupons inside cereals. Onward. Onward. Let's go and smash up a dam. Come on, monkey. Fame awaits us both."

Keys to Literature

In an **allegory**, the people and events in the story stand for things in real life. How are the Wolf King's actions like something in the real world?

The beavers had been working summer and winter for three years. They were building a beautiful dam to get water to a distant valley.

The Wolf of Wolves climbed a tree. "I want you to shoot the exact moment when my feet crash into the middle of the dam. If you miss the shot, next time I'll fall on top of you. Then I'll have to get myself another photographer. Are you ready?"

Not only was the monkey ready, but so was the adviser. The fox was breathing down the old monkey's back. He was staring over his shoulder, watching, listening. Nothing could escape those alert eyes.

So neither the monkey nor the fox could believe it when they saw the picture. There at the bottom was a rabbit resting on his side as if he were relaxing at a picnic. Next to him, another rabbit had raised her paw and was boldly thumbing her nose.

"They are everywhere," said the fox. "Let me tell you, our lives are in danger."

"Let's start rubbing them off," the monkey said wearily.

His Wolfhood the King yelped with pleasure when he saw the picture. There was not a single shadow of a rabbit.

"Send it out!" he shouted. Then the King said, "What are we going to do now for some fun?"

"We could rest," the monkey suggested. His paws were peeling from the strong fluid he used on the pictures.

The Wolf looked at him as if he were a stone. The Wolf said, "Who asked you for an opinion? I'm in charge here. That's why I was born with these teeth. We'll go on until there's no more light."

Think About It

What do the positions of the rabbits in the picture tell you about how the rabbits feel about the king?

In each new photo, there were more and more rabbits. The King Wolf did many terrible things. He destroyed sugar mills. He shook squirrels out of their trees and hid their nuts. He stripped ducks of their feathers. As the King became more frightful, his pictures changed. More rabbits of every color danced around the edges of the photographs.

The pictures the monkey took were beginning to look strange. There were blank spaces everywhere. The monkey knew that the only solution was to get his Wolfiness to sit up high on a raised throne. Rabbits live underground. They wouldn't be able to wiggle their way into the frame of the photograph.

The next morning the monkey and the fox rushed to see the new throne. The King's seat was now set high on top of four huge wooden legs.

"I want two shots," His Wolfhood demanded. "One will be of me approaching my throne. The other will be of me sitting on it, enjoying the fresh air."

This time, when the photos were developed, there was not so much as a sign of a rabbit.

"Didn't I tell you? Didn't I tell you the rabbits don't exist?" the adviser asked the monkey. He was thrilled. "It was just a matter of your aiming the camera properly."

For the next few days, there were no more unpleasant surprises. The Wolf of Wolves felt happy. He let his officers run things while he posed for pictures. He was pictured giving commands, making speeches, and signing laws. He looked over the shots carefully. "Congratulations," he said to the monkey. "You're being more careful. I don't see any more of the white spots that spoiled my first pictures."

But one morning, the monkey was awakened by his daughter's voice. "They're back, Dad," she whispered in his ears. "Those pictures you took sure are magical."

Think About It

What are the blank spaces on the photos?

Keys to Literature

What is the **denotation**, the actual meaning, of *wiggle*? What is the **connotation**, the idea or feeling, of *wiggle*?

▶ The adviser is convincing himself that what he wants to believe is true.

In one set of photos, there was a small army of rabbits at the foot of the towering throne.

The adviser was waiting. The monkey could see he was upset.

"How many this time?" the monkey asked.

"The photos are being taken care of," the fox said grimly. "But the birds have got wind of what happened. Now they're telling everyone that those … those awful animals exist. His Wolfiness said if those birds didn't keep quiet, he would make them disappear."

But the adviser had another idea. The Wolf of All Wolves should make a recording of one of his latest speeches. Then he should tie it around the necks of the birds. They would have to carry not only the photos, but also the King's words, all over the kingdom. Nobody would be able to hear any of their songs.

"Hearing is believing," blared His Wolfiness.

The old monkey's life had become more than he could stand. In every picture, there was a rabbit part. Sometimes it was a curious nose. Sometimes it was a pair of furry ears. There were even pictures with white whiskers.

The monkey felt dizzy.

Then one night, very late, the old monkey was awakened by an angry shake. It was the adviser with fierce soldiers at his side. The King Wolf had sent for him.

The Wolfiest of Wolves was waiting for the old monkey. The King Wolf was sitting on his throne. Around each leg of the throne, hundreds of guards kept watch.

"Monkey, you are a **traitor**," thundered the King. "Your pictures are being used by people who say that rabbits are plotting against me. I hear they are

Predict

What will happen to the monkey?

planning this very night to overthrow me. Tonight, you are going to take another picture. If a single rabbit shows its nose, I will make you eat the picture. Then I'll eat you and not only you, but your wife and your daughter. Now. Take that picture."

The monkey stood behind his camera. He aimed it at the throne. He let out a moan. Up until then, the rabbits appeared only when the picture was developed. Now the rabbits were directly in front of the camera. They chewed away at King Wolf's throne. They also chewed the swords of the guards.

"What's the matter?" bellowed the King Wolf. He did not look down. He wanted his picture to be perfect.

The monkey moved the camera nearer to the throne. He hoped that this way the rabbits would not show up in the picture. The rabbits moved faster than he did. They scrambled up the legs of the throne.

"Hurry up!" ordered the Wolf of Wolves.

The monkey closed his eyes very tightly. It was better not to see what was going to happen. The very moment he clicked the camera, he heard a very loud noise. He knew what he was going to see when he opened his eyes. Still he could not believe it. Like an old tree rotten to the core, the throne came crashing to the ground. With it came the King of Wolves. The monkey blinked. There at his feet lay the Biggest, Baddest, the Most Bragging Wolf in the World. His ribs were broken. His black fur was torn by the fall. His yellow eyes were red. He was wailing in pain.

"Monkey," squeaked the would-be Wolferor of the World. "This picture ... you have my approval not to show it."

At that moment, all the lights in the palace went out. The monkey grabbed his camera and his bag. Clutching them to his chest like a treasure, he fled.

▶ The Wolf King's throne is compared to a rotten tree. The roots of his power are as rotten as the roots of an old tree.

His daughter was waiting for him at the door of the house.

"Wait," he said to her. "Wait. I've brought you something. Without another word, he raced into his **darkroom** to develop the last picture.

When he came out a few minutes later, his daughter and wife were standing on chairs. They were taking down the pictures of the Wolf King.

"Here," the old monkey said to his daughter. "Here, this is the picture you've been asking for all this time. I've finally brought you your present."

"Thanks, Dad," the little girl said. "But I don't need it anymore."

She pointed around the room. She pointed toward the street and across the fields. There the sun was beginning to rise. The world was full of rabbits.

Think About It

Why are the monkey's wife and daughter taking down pictures of the Wolf King?

Meet the Author

ARIEL DORFMAN (Born 1942)

Ariel Dorfman was born in Argentina and lived in the United States as a child. Then his family moved to Chile when he was 12. In 1973, the government of Chile was overthrown. A dictator took over. Dorfman, like many other writers, was thrown out of the country.

Dorfman has written in a variety of genres, including plays, poetry, fiction, and nonfiction. His plays have won many awards. Most of his writing tells what happens when a government limits people's political freedom. "The Rebellion of the Magical Rabbits" clearly shows how Dorfman feels about dictators.

Check Your Predictions

1. Look back at the answers you gave for the Predict questions. Would you change your answers? Explain.

Understand the Story

2. What does the Wolf King do to make everyone believe that rabbits do not exist?

3. Why does the Wolf King want to post pictures of himself all over the land?

4. As the Wolf King acts worse and worse, what happens to the pictures the monkey takes?

5. What does the Wolf King do when he finds out about the rabbits in the photos?

Think About the Story

6. Once he is in power, the wolf crosses out the word *rabbit* and tears rabbit pictures out of books. What real-life event might this stand for?

7. Why doesn't the monkey show the pictures he takes to the Wolf King?

8. The Wolf King is called the "biggest" wolf in the world. What is the actual meaning of the word *biggest* and what idea does it represent in the story?

Extend Your Response

Imagine that a rabbit becomes king. He tells all the animals five ways the country will be different from now on. Write a list telling what the Rabbit King will say.

Keys to Literature

figurative language: words that describe something by comparing it to something else. Similies and metaphors are types of figurative language.

> Example: The nose in this poem is compared to *a factory packed with scents.*

Did You Know?

Nikolai [NIH-koh-leye] Gogol was a Russian writer who lived during the 1800s. In 1836 he wrote a story called "The Nose." In it, a nose leaves its owner and behaves like a person. That story inspired this poem.

Words to Know

flower	become as good as possible; reach full growth
scents	nice smells
bowling	rolling quickly
staggered	moved or walked unsteadily

Genre: Poem

"The Nose (after Gogol)" is a poem. Read more about poetry on page 467 of the Genre Guide.

The Nose (After Gogol)

BY IAIN CRICHTON SMITH

The nose went away by itself
in the early morning
while its owner was asleep.
It walked along the road
5 sniffing at everything.

It thought: I have a personality of my own.
Why should I be attached to a body?
I haven't been allowed to **flower**.
So much of me has been wasted.

10 And it felt wholly free.
It almost began to dance
The world was so full of **scents**
it had had no time to notice,

when it was attached to a face
15 weeping, being blown,
catching all sorts of germs
and changing color.

But now it was quite at ease
bowling merrily along
20 like a hoop or a wheel,
a factory packed with scent.

And all would have been well
but that, round about evening,
having no eyes for guides,
25 it **staggered** into the path
of a mouth, and it was gobbled
rapidly like a sausage
and chewed by great sour teeth—
and that was how it died.

La Bonne Aventure (1937) by René Magritte Copyright 2005 © C. Herscovici, Brussels/Artists
Rights Society (ARS), New York

Meet the Author

IAIN CRICHTON SMITH *(1928–1998)*

Iain Crichton Smith grew up in Scotland. He was often ill as a boy, lying in bed, dreamily listening to the sounds outside his house. When he grew up, he became a high school English teacher.

Smith wrote over 40 books. They included novels and plays, but he is best known for his poetry. He won many awards for his writing. Like "The Nose," most of his poems explore unusual ideas.

Learn More About It

SATIRE AND THE ABSURD

The poem "The Nose" is based on a story by Gogol. Gogol was known for his satires. Satire is a type of writing that pokes fun at human wrongs. "The Nose" is also absurd. Something that is absurd makes no sense. For example, in one absurd play, a whole town of people turns into rhinoceroses. This kind of writing is both serious and humorous. It is also a clever way to criticize governments. Writers living in places that censor, or restrict what can be published, sometimes use this kind of writing to get their points across.

Understand the Poem

1. What does the nose like to do as it travels?

2. Why has the nose left its owner?

3. How does the nose feel about being on its own?

4. How does the nose die?

Think About the Poem

5. Why didn't the nose notice all the world's scents while it was attached to a face?

6. How do you think the phrase "gobbled rapidly like a sausage" affects how readers visualize the nose's death?

7. What do you think the mouth is doing on the road?

8. Is the nose in any way like someone you know? How?

Extend Your Response
Write a note to your nose. Give it a few good reasons for staying on your face.

Summaries

The Tiger and the Jackal A hungry tiger wants to eat a farmer's oxen. He agrees to eat a cow instead. The farmer's wife is not willing to give up the cow, so she scares the tiger off. A jackal explains the wife's trick to the tiger. Together, the animals return to try to get a meal, but the farmer's wife tricks the tiger yet again. He runs off, dragging the jackal behind him.

The Rebellion of the Magical Rabbits Wolves conquer the land of the rabbits. Then the Wolf King declares that rabbits no longer exist. He hires a monkey to take his picture many times. That way, everyone will see exactly what he wants them to see. However, rabbits keep showing up in the pictures. After a time, the magical rabbits topple Wolf King's throne and he loses his power.

The Nose (After Gogol) A nose leaves its owner and goes traveling. When it was attached to a face, the nose was busy weeping, being blown, changing color, and catching germs. Now it can travel and sniff all the world's wonderful scents. Unfortunately, the nose dies when it bumps into a mouth that chews it up.

adviser

scents

slashed

staggered

traitor

Vocabulary Review

Match each word in the box with its meaning. Write the word next to its meaning on a separate sheet of paper.

1. cut with rough, long strokes

2. moved or walked unsteadily

3. someone who gives information to someone else

4. someone who betrays the government

5. nice smells

Chapter Quiz

Write your answers in one or two complete sentences.
Use a separate sheet of paper.

1. **The Tiger and the Jackal** What does the farmer first plan to do about the tiger's demand for food?

2. **The Tiger and the Jackal** Why does the jackal help the tiger?

3. **The Rebellion of the Magical Rabbits** What does the Wolf King want to do with the photos the monkey takes?

4. **The Rebellion of the Magical Rabbits** How do the rabbits overthrow the Wolf King?

5. **The Nose (After Gogol)** How is the nose unusual?

6. **The Nose (After Gogol)** How does the nose die?

Critical Thinking

7. **The Tiger and the Jackal** What lesson about fear does this folktale teach us?

8. **The Rebellion of the Magical Rabbits** What external conflict does the monkey face in this story?

Chapter Activity

Which fantasy in this chapter did you like best? Write a letter to a friend about the story or poem. Explain what you found most interesting about it.

Unit 6 **Review**

On a separate sheet of paper, write the letter that best completes each sentence below.

1. In "The Bicycle," the bicycle acts as if it is

  A. a motorcycle.
  B. a horse.
  C. a goat.
  D. a human.

2. In "The Street," the speaker thinks he hears

  A. thunder.
  B. a lost dog crying.
  C. a garbage truck rumbling.
  D. someone following him.

3. In "The Cyclops," Odysseus and his men escape by

  A. killing the Cyclops.
  B. hiding underneath the rams.
  C. telling the Cyclops that he is a prophet.
  D. making friends with the Cyclops.

4. The wife in "The Tiger and the Jackal" dresses as a

  A. peddler.
  B. milkmaid.
  C. hunter.
  D. farmer.

5. In "The Rebellion of the Magical Rabbits," the monkey tries to

  A. help his daughter find rabbits.
  B. tell the Wolf King that rabbits exist.
  C. erase the rabbits from the photos.
  D. convince the rabbits to hide.

6. In "The Nose (After Gogol)" the nose dies when it

  A. is gobbled by a mouth.
  B. escapes from the face.
  C. is hit by a car.
  D. smells something bad.

Making Connections

On a separate sheet of paper, write your answers to the following questions.

7. Which selection in this unit do you think is the most fantastic or imaginative? Explain why.

8. Which selection in this unit do you think has the best ending? Explain why.

Writing an Essay

Choose two animal characters in this unit. How are they alike? How are they different? Give examples.

Unit Seven

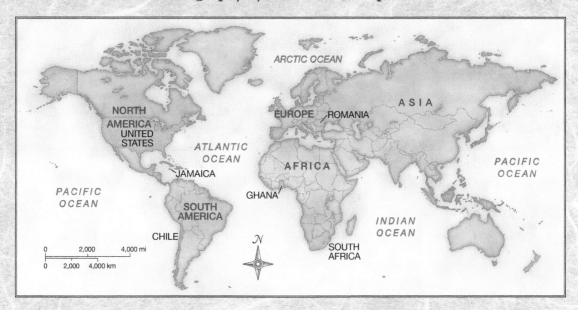

Cup of Immortality of the Benefactor of Thebes (The Wishing Cup), photograph by Erich Lessing

What wishes do you think ancient Egyptians used this "wishing cup" for?

Learning Objectives

- Understand figurative language.
- Explain what a narrative is.
- Identify dialogue in a play.
- Understand the use of stage directions in a play.
- Understand what drama is.
- Recognize a character's motivation in a story.
- Identify internal conflict.

Theme Preview: Wishes

Wishes can give us the motivation to make changes in our lives. They can help us to set goals and go after them. Wishes can also be dangerous. Wishing for things we do not have can make us less appreciative of the many things we do have. The selections in this chapter explore both kinds of wishes.

Keys to Literature

figurative language: words that describe something by comparing it to something else. Similies and metaphors are types of figurative language.

Example: *It is as clear as ice in my mind.*

narrative: a story; a report of what has happened

Example: "Young Hunger" is a narrative about Fisher's visit to her godparents at age 18.

Words to Know

wince	draw back in pain or distress
despair	hopelessness
godparents	people who sponsor or agree to be partly responsible for a child
inactive	not active
hesitate	pause
appetite	desire for food

Genre: Autobiography

"Young Hunger" is one of several essays that form M. F. K. Fisher's autobiography. Read more about autobiographies on page 466 of the Genre Guide.

Young Hunger

BY M. F. K. FISHER, *adapted*

It is very hard for people over fifty to remember the hunger of the young. They forget their own youth when dealing with the young people around them. I have seen older people helpless with anger over finding an empty cupboard or refrigerator. All because the cupboard was stripped by one, two, or three youths who could have eaten their fill at dinner.

I am not too old to remember how it feels to be young and hungry. I understand when I see a fifteen-year-old boy **wince** at the thought of waiting hours for food. His guts howl for meat—bread—candy—fruit—cheese—milk—ANYTHING TO EAT.

I remember my own **despair** when I was about eighteen. I was staying overnight with my elderly **godparents**. I had come home alone from France through a cruel storm. It had made me hollow with hunger. The night on the train seemed even rougher than the one on the ship. By the time I reached my godparents' home I was faint.

READ TO FIND OUT...

How does the hunger of the young differ from the hunger of the old?

Predict

Look at the title and the first sentence. What do you think this selection will be about?

Keys to Literature

The author uses **figurative language** here. She compares the boy's "guts" to an animal by saying they "howl."

This **narrative** begins with Fisher's trip from France to England. What was it like?

I got there just in time for lunch. It is as clear as ice in my mind. Before me were a little cup of weak broth, a cracker, and a half piece of thin toast. Then, ah then, came a whole waffle, crisp and brown. A piece of butter melted in its middle. The maid skillfully cut it into four pieces! She put one on my godmother's plate. The next two, after a nod from my godmother, she put on mine. My godfather ate the fourth.

There was a tiny pot of honey. I dutifully put a dab of it on my piggish serving. We all nibbled away and drank a cup apiece of tea with lemon. Both of my godparents left part of their waffles.

Think About It

Does the author really believe that her serving is "piggish"? Explain.

It was simply that they were old and **inactive**. They were quite out of the habit of eating a big meal with younger people. It was a good thing for them, but not for me. I did not have the sense to explain how starved I was. I would not **hesitate** doing so now. Instead, I prowled around my bedroom while everyone else in the house took an afternoon nap. Dare I sneak into the strange kitchen for something, anything, to eat! I would rather die than meet the maid or my godmother.

Later we walked slowly down to the village. All the while I was thinking passionately of double ice-cream sodas at the corner store. However, there was no possibility of such heaven. Back at the quiet house, the maid brought my godfather a tall glass of rich milk. On the saucer was a handful of dried fruit because he had been ill. We sat and watched him unwillingly eat it.

His wife said softly that it was a short time until dinner. She was sure I did not want to spoil my **appetite**. I agreed with her because I was young and shy.

Keys to Literature

What does the author compare in this use of **figurative language**?

When I dressed, I noticed my hip bones. They stuck out like two bricks under my skirt. I looked like a scarecrow.

Dinner was very long. All I can remember, though, is the main course. It was half of the tiny boiled chicken that made the broth for lunch. My godmother carved it carefully. We each got part of the breast. I, as the guest, should have the leg. First a bit had to be sliced off for her husband. He liked dark meat too.

There were hot biscuits, yes, the smallest I have ever seen. There were two apiece under a napkin on a silver dish. Because of them we had no dessert. It would be too rich, my godmother said.

Predict

What do you think dinner will be like?

We drank little cups of coffee on the porch in the hot night. When I went up to my room, I saw a large glass of malted milk beside my poor godfather's bed.

My train would leave before five in the morning. I slept little and sadly. I dreamed of the breakfast I would order. Of course, when I saw it twinkling on the silver dishes, I could eat very little. I was too hungry and too angry.

I felt my godparents had been very rude to me. They had been selfish and stupid. Now I know they were none of these things. They had just forgotten about any but their own shrinking need for food. They had forgotten about being hungry, being young, being....

Think About It

What does the narrator realize about her godparents' actions?

Meet the Author

M. F. K. FISHER *(1908–1992)*

M. F. K. Fisher was born in Michigan and grew up in California. Her full name was Mary Frances Kennedy Fisher. From the time she was young, Fisher loved cooking and writing about cooking. In 1929, she moved to France. There she began to learn more about food.

Fisher's first book came out in 1937. It was both a storybook and a cookbook. Her many works include a play, articles, nonfiction books, and novels. She also wrote a children's book. Food is the main theme in Fisher's writing. However, her writing is really about appreciating all life has to offer. Fisher won many awards. She was elected to the American Academy of Arts and Sciences in 1991.

Check Your Predictions

1. Look back at the answers you gave for the Predict questions. Would you change your answers? Explain.

Understand the Autobiography

2. To what does the author compare her hip bones? Why?

3. What details show how small the lunch seems to Fisher?

4. How does the author describe her godparents?

5. How do Fisher's feelings toward her godparents change?

Think About the Autobiography

6. Why do you think that the author now understands that her godparents were not being rude?

7. How can the differences between old and young hunger be applied to life in general?

8. What do you think the author means by "They had forgotten about being hungry, being young, being...."

Extend Your Response

Work with two other students to write a brief dialogue that the author might have had with her godparents. Base the dialogue on the ideas that the author presents in her essay. When you finish, read it aloud with each group member taking the role of one of the characters.

Keys to Literature

dialogue: a conversation between characters in a story or play; words that characters actually say

> Example: The words after each character's identification are the dialogue of the play.

stage directions: instructions to a play's actors that tell them what to do and explain a play's setting

> Example: *Character 1 points to the characters standing on the chairs.*

Did You Know?

Chile led Latin America in experimental and revolutionary theater. But when Pinochet came to rule in 1973, he censored the theater companies. He would not allow anti-government works. When the military government was overturned, the theater resumed its progress.

Words to Know

illuminates	brightens with light
exchange	trade
impressed	affected or influenced
distribute	give out
attractive	appealing

Genre: Play

"Luck" is a play. Read more about plays in the Learn More About It about drama on page 415 or on page 467 of the Genre Guide.

uck

BY ELENA CASTEDO

READ TO FIND OUT...
How do people's outlooks affect their lives?

CHARACTERS

A minimum of two actors and unlimited maximum, always divided into two groups

PROPS

As many chairs as half the number of characters

Pieces of paper representing money, about the same number as there are characters

Two spotlights with yellow light from above

COSTUMES

Any, but each of the two groups must have costumes of more or less the same color in order to identify the two groups.

The following version is written for ten characters. Thus it requires five chairs and about ten pieces of paper representing money.

Think About It
What do the descriptions of the characters and the costumes tell about the play?

ACT 1

*(As the play opens, Characters 6 to 10 are standing on the five chairs, arranged in an uneven row toward the back left side of the stage. They are making motions as if talking, but in silence. A spotlight of yellow **illuminates** them. The other spotlight illuminates the area at the front right side of the stage. Characters 1 to 5 come onto the stage and arrange themselves at the front right area of the stage, also as if they are talking. Then the light illuminating that area dims.)*

Keys to Literature
In a play, the **dialogue**, or what the characters say, is in regular type. The **stage directions**, or what the characters do, are in italic type.

Character 1: We are in shadows here already. Look, the mountain back there still has sunshine. *(Character 1 points to the characters standing on the chairs.)*

Character 2: That's why I hate living down here in the valley; it's dark in the morning and dark in the evening.

Character 3: And we don't get any views down here.

Character 4: Up there on the mountain, they get all the summer breezes. *(Character 4 moves arms to indicate breezes.)*

Character 5: Why should they get all the luck? It's not fair.

Character 1: There must be something we can do.

Character 2: Why don't we move to the mountain?

Character 3: Because there are only five houses up there, and they took them all. *(Character 3 motions to the characters on the chairs.)*

Think About It

How would you describe the outlook of these characters?

Character 4: Maybe we can **exchange** our houses for theirs. *(Character 4 moves arms to make a motion of exchange.)*

Character 5: What a great idea! *(Character 5 lifts her arms.)*

Character 3: Naw. They probably won't want to do that.

Character 4: Maybe we should pay them some extra money.

Character 2: How much money do we have?

(They take out bills from their pockets, count, and share.)

Character 1: We'll make them an offer they can't refuse.

(Characters 1 to 5 stir; some leap, some push one another, and they all move toward the chairs.)

Characters 1 to 5: Yes, yes, what a great idea. Let's go. Let's go ask them!

ACT 2

(Characters 1 to 5 stand in front of the characters standing on the chairs and greet them with many hellos.)

Character 1: Hi, we are the people from the valley. We are interested in exchanging houses; our houses are very nice.

(Characters 1 to 5 nod, make noises of agreement.)

(Characters 6 to 10 look at one another with surprise.)

Character 6: Hi, thank you for your offer, but we don't want to exchange houses.

Character 7: We like it up here on the mountain. We get a lot of sunshine.

Character 8: And breezes in the summer.

Character 9: And we like the beautiful view of the valley.

Think About It
What is the characters' plan?

Think About It
How do the people on the mountain feel about their houses?

Character 10: The air is very clean up here.

Character 7: We are so lucky to be here on the mountain.

Character 6: We are sorry you got the idea we wanted to exchange houses.

(Characters 1 to 5 get together, whisper to one another, search their pockets, give bills to Character 1, then face the characters standing on the chairs.)

Character 2: Our houses are in better shape than yours; it would be a very good deal for you.

Character 1: And we are prepared to pay you extra. *(Character 1 hands the wad of bills to Character 6.)*

*(Character 6 takes the bills and counts them. Character 6 is **impressed**. Character 6 passes them on to the other characters standing on the chairs, who count them and are equally impressed. They whisper to one another, back and forth, leaning over, and finally nod to one another and **distribute** the bills.)*

Think About It

What does the idiom *in better shape* mean?

Character 6: Okay. We'll exchange houses.

(Characters 6 to 10 step down from the chairs and move toward the front right area of the stage, which represents the valley.)

(Characters 1 to 5 shake hands to congratulate one another and smile and make winning gestures as they climb on the chairs.)

Predict

How do you think the two groups of characters will react to their new homes?

ACT 3

(Characters 1 to 5 are standing on the chairs as if talking to one another, in silence. They make gestures of being cold and tired.)

(Characters 6 to 10 are talking in the area that represents the valley.)

Think About It

What is happening now?

Character 6: I had no idea life was so pleasant down here in the valley.

(Characters 1 to 5, now standing on the chairs, stop making gestures as if "talking" to one another and now make gestures to urge one another to listen to the other group, first putting a finger to their lips, then putting a hand behind an ear or leaning forward to indicate they are listening.)

Character 7: Me, too. These wells are full of delicious water.

Character 8: It doesn't cost much to keep houses warm in the valley.

Character 9: It's lovely not to have so much wind.

Character 10: Have you noticed how easy it is to plant a garden?

Character 6: The view of the mountains is beautiful.

Character 8: Everything is so much easier than going up and down slopes.

Character 7: We are so lucky to be here in the valley.

Keys to Literature

Is the **dialogue** realistic? Explain.

Keys to Literature

What do the **stage directions** tell about Characters 1 to 5?

(Characters 1 to 5 make more gestures of discontent, of being tired and cold, whisper to one another, nod in agreement, search their pockets, give bills to Character 1, then step down from the chairs and move toward the group in the valley.)

Character 1: We would like to get our houses back.

Character 6: These are our houses now, and we like them.

Character 2: You said before that you liked living on the mountain.

Character 3: We are prepared to pay extra.

Character 1: We think you'll find this very **attractive**. *(Character 1 hands the wad of bills to Character 6.)*

(Character 6 takes the bills and counts them. Character 6 is impressed. Character 6 passes them on to Characters 7 to 10, who count them and are equally impressed. They whisper to one another, back and forth, leaning over, and finally nod to one another. They distribute the bills.)

Character 6: Okay. We'll exchange houses.

(Characters 6 to 10 move toward the chairs and climb on them.)

(Characters 1 to 5 shake hands to congratulate one another but without as much enthusiasm as before. The light illuminates the characters on the chairs.)

Character 6: How nice, we still have sunshine; look, down in the valley it's all in shadows already. *(Character 6 points to the characters in the valley.)*

Character 9: The air is so fresh here.

Character 10: What a beautiful view!

Character 8: And we have lots of money that the people from the valley gave us.

Character 7: The main thing is, we are so lucky to be here on the mountain.

Meet the Author

ELENA CASTEDO *(Born 1937)*

Elena Castedo spent her early childhood in Spain. Her family moved to Chile during the Spanish Civil War to escape a dictator. In Chile, Castedo worked first as a fashion model and as an art researcher. She also worked as a social worker. She then moved to the United States. Here she received degrees in Spanish from UCLA and Harvard University. She has taught in Chile and in the United States.

While teaching and working as an editor, she has also written a number of articles, poems, and stories. Her most famous book is *Paradise*. *Paradise* was nominated for a National Book Award in 1990. It is about a family that leaves Spain to escape the Spanish Civil War. Castedo has said her interest "is in human experience and emotions."

Check Your Prediction

1. Look back at the answer you gave for the Predict question. Would you change your answer? Explain.

Understand the Play

2. How do Characters 6 to 10 feel about their mountain homes?

3. How do Characters 1 to 5 feel about their valley homes?

4. What plan do Characters 1 to 5 make?

5. Why do Characters 1 to 5 eventually decide to return to the valley?

Think About the Play

6. How do you think Characters 1 to 5 will feel about their original homes?

7. Why do you think the author chose to use so few props and limited characters? Explain.

8. What is the author saying about luck in this play?

Extend Your Response

Work with a small group of students to role-play a talk show interview. Imagine you are one of the characters from the play. Tell your story from that character's perspective.

Learn More About It

GENRE STUDY: DRAMA

Some of history's greatest writers, such as Shakespeare, have written plays. In fact, drama is one of the world's oldest genres. Long before short stories or novels were popular, people wrote and performed plays. Some of the first known plays were written by the ancient Greeks. They usually wrote either tragedies or comedies. A tragedy is usually about a hero who suffers. A comedy usually pokes fun at people and their customs. It is meant to be entertaining.

Plays today often combine the characteristics of tragedy and comedy. They are usually divided into sections called acts and scenes. These are a bit like units and chapters in a book. During a performance, there is often a break, or intermission, between acts. In a written play, the characters' actions are described in stage directions. The directions also tell what props, or stage materials, to use. Directors and actors interpret these directions for their performances.

Most performances we see today are in theaters like the one pictured on this page. There is usually a curtain, a stage, and rows of seats on different levels. In ancient times, many theaters were outdoors and were more like small sports arenas. Shakespeare's theater, the Globe, was also round and in the open. Today a copy of it is located in London.

Apply and Connect

If you were to direct "Luck," what props would you use? What directions would you give the actors?

Keys to Literature

motivation: the reason a character behaves as he or she does

> Example: The men in this story behave cautiously because they got in trouble for treating the female cadets badly at first.

internal conflict: a struggle a person has with himself or herself when trying to make a decision

> Example: In this story, Akuba struggles with her own self-doubts as well as the doubts of the men at the Academy.

Did You Know?

Women were not allowed to work in many units of the Ghanaian armed forces until the mid-1990s. For training pilots, the army relied on help from other nations, such as Great Britain, India, Israel, and Nigeria.

Words to Know

cockpit	the place from which an airplane is steered
recruits	people who have just joined the military
candidates	people who are likely to be chosen for something
futuristic	very modern
tarmac	paved runway

Genre: Short Story

"Heavy Moments" is a short story. Read more about short stories on page 467 of the Genre Guide.

Heavy Moments

BY AMA ATA AIDOO, *adapted*

Akuba opened the door to the toilet near the **cockpit**. She had almost waited too long. Because she was now having to do a little *tinawale* jig. Left foot down. Right foot up. How could this happen to her? And at this time? Once she had finished, she flushed the toilet. She washed her hands, shut the door of the toilet, and returned to the cockpit. She sat down, smiled at her co-pilot, and took the controls. The captain nearly made some comment about women. But he bit his tongue. Biting his tongue had become a habit in the past couple years that he had those two among his **recruits** at the Air Force Academy. Before, you could say anything you liked about women. These days you had to watch everything: your step, your mouth, and over your shoulder.

READ TO FIND OUT...

How does one woman change the feelings of the Ghana Air Force Academy?

Think About It

What is happening here?

Keys to Literature

What **motivation** does the captain have for not making *some comment about women*?

Earlier the men had thought it wouldn't matter. But it had come to matter. Terribly. At first, an alarm had sounded through the Academy when first the rumors had come out. Two of the very best **candidates** that year were women.

"Women?" asked people who had heard the rumors.

"Women," others replied.

"But … but … but …"

"What do they want here?" asked one man.

"What do they want here?" asked another man.

"What do they want here?" asked yet another.

Everybody asked the same questions. From retired Group Captains to those recruits who were as new to the Academy as the young women themselves. It had never occurred to the questioners that Akuba Baidoo and Sarah Larbi wanted from the Academy what they too had gone there for. That if being a flying soldier was something to be enjoyed, then other people— including women—could want it too. They had even tried to ignore the young women recruits and carry on as if they were not around at all. Or at best, they would act as if the two too were men. So during the first term, even those men who would ordinarily not have been telling jokes about women, went around looking for some to tell. Especially when "Cadet Baidoo" and "Cadet Larbi" were around. And no one had liked it that "the girls" did not laugh.

At the end of the first term, Akuba and Yaa Sarah had complained to the director of the Academy. He himself had been one of the worst offenders. But the girls did not know this. He had listened them out. Then he tried to pretend that he had not the slightest idea of what they were talking about. It didn't work. So he had promised he would do something about it. He later called his lieutenants and asked them to speak to

Predict

What do you think will happen to Akuba at the Academy?

Think About It

How do Akuba and Yaa Sarah react to the jokes about women?

their men. Then there followed a period when, except when necessary, virtually no one spoke to them at the Academy. When they compared notes during that time and later, each of them admitted that if she had been alone, she would have given up and left. But luckily they were two. So sticking it out had been a little easier.

And now here is Akuba handling the manual controls of an air force plane, as though she had been born flying. Good God, a woman. Wonders would surely never cease.

Actually, Akuba had been born flying. Except that in her environment, no one had known that except herself. Her maternal grandparents' village lay in the path of the planes that flew over coastal West Africa.

Think About It

Why might it have been a little easier for the women since there were two of them?

Think About It

What challenge does the main character face?

They went from southern and central Africa on their way to North Africa and beyond to Europe. Others flew from those northern places to the south. One of the strongest memories of her childhood was of her and a group of children from the neighborhood watching those planes.

Yet unlike the other children, *she had wanted to fly the planes.*

The desire had been in her for so long, she could not tell how young she was when she became aware of it. All she knew was that one night—it must have been deep, deep in the night—she had woken up suddenly to what was unmistakably the sound of a passing plane. And then she knew she wished she was up there flying it. When the sound of the plane died, she started to cry. When her big mother Mam'Panyin, or Mampa for short, asked her what the matter was she couldn't speak. She just sat there wailing and could not stop, no matter what Mampa did. This, in turn, made Mampa very angry. It was a terrible, terrible night. Both of them had slept again only in the early hours of the morning.

But she had never forgotten that night. Now here she was actually flying a plane! She was lucky. At mid-morning in September, the sky was brilliantly blue. At about fifteen thousand feet up, they could see into everywhere and forever. Ahead, the sea that was the Gulf of Guinea reflected the brilliance of the sky. To the right and left, the forest was giving way to low savannah. She knew she would have to get ready to land the plane very soon. She was almost sorry. Not almost. She wished the plane was one of those **futuristic** self-fuelling machines that could go forever on ordinary air. Or at least one of those then being planned for American presidents that designers claimed would be able to refuel in midair, and then fly non-stop for eight days or something monstrous like that.

Keys to Literature

What is Akuba's **motivation** for entering the Academy?

▶ The Gulf of Guinea is on the western side of Africa. It is part of the Atlantic Ocean. The Equator runs through it.

Supposing she failed? She panicked so much she nearly made a mistake. She bit her lips. Her hands were shaking. She soon began to sweat. She told herself not to be silly. If she failed, she would take the exam again. Then she reminded herself that given their environment, getting a place in the Academy at all was hard enough. She was not sure they let people stay there forever, taking their own good time to graduate. And had she forgotten she was a woman? One of the first two ever in the history of the Academy? How much would her failure be regarded as personal and nothing to do with her gender? All in all, she had better pass this test.

Keys to Literature

Akuba now faces an **internal conflict**. She doubts herself. How does this internal conflict affect her?

Until she came to understand it all later, she had always assumed that Mam'Panyin was her grandmother. But it had turned out she was not. She was her mother's older sister. That was why everyone called her Big Mother. She was the oldest of eight more children, and was like a mother to them.

Mampa had also been like a mother to Akuba. After moving back and forth from the town to the village with her mother, Akuba left home. Her stepfather was a cruel man and Akuba could not live under the same roof with him. So Akuba returned to the village and decided that if she had to have parents in this world it must be Mam'Panyin for a father and Mam'Panyin for a mother. But as a kid, she had never been able to say "Mam'Panyin." She had arbitrarily abbreviated it to "Mampa." And so that's how the whole village came to call Mam'Panyin "Mampa."

It was all very well for Mampa to complain about Akuba behaving as though she belonged in the air. But the fact was that Akuba had never felt rooted. She had never felt like she belonged on the ground. No, the skies had to be better.

Think About It

Why was Mampa upset about Akuba's entering the Academy?

Of course there was a bit of a crisis when Akuba went to tell Mampa that she had been accepted at the Air Force Academy. Mampa thought it was all too much.

"I say," Mampa said, "if I told people that you are going to learn to drive a lorry, a taxi, or a bus, they would think it a strange, but brave achievement for a woman. But how do you expect me to go and tell anybody that you are actually going to drive an airplane through the skies and be believed? And if they won't believe me, what's the use in trying to tell them? Eh, my lady?!"

The Academy had planned everything. It was risky. You took such chances only with the best of the cadets, since you had to be able to guarantee success. But then Akuba was one such cadet. They were very sure of her. And Cadet Larbi and a few male cadets had said how much Akuba loved her aunt, her Mampa, and was always talking about her. So the administration had decided that since it was going to be a rare enough occasion, testing a female cadet pilot, they might as well go all the way and do something extra special. They would let Mampa know about Akuba's test flight: the date, the time, everything. Yes, they would alert her, and leave it to her to decide whether to come to the air force base or not.

Predict

Do you think Mampa will show up for Akuba's test? Why or why not?

The voice from the control tower came over the radio clearly, helping, guiding. She began to gently nose down.

Then she was actually taxiing on the airstrip. She brought the plane to a stop. She realized that there was quite a crowd waiting for her. In no time at all, the captain and everyone who had been on board were already on the **tarmac**, looking up at her as she came down. And they started clapping. Then the small crowd on the edge of the airstrip was also clapping. All her colleagues were there. Each one of them. Those who had already had their tests, and the rest who had

Think About It

How has Akuba performed on the test?

been scheduled to come after her. They were all there. Waiting. Then someone broke into that mad English song; "For she is a jolly good fellow." Everyone took the song up. And she wanted to tell them, "Silly, can't you see that I am not a 'fellow' at all? Jolly or not?" How had these men managed to change so much within such a short time? Akuba wondered. After all they put her and Yaa through? How could they show their joy for her so clearly? And by the way, where was Cadet Yaa Sarah Larbi? Where was Yaa Sarah? Akuba wanted to burst into tears with both joy and disappointment. But where was Yaa Sarah? Someone was opening a bottle of champagne. Then she could see Sarah coming out of the crowd. Oh, what a relief! And with her an older woman. Who was it? Mampa, yes, Mampa!

Think About It

How do you think Akuba feels when she sees Mampa?

Meet the Author

AMA ATA AIDOO *(Born 1942)*

Ama Ata Aidoo was born in what is now Ghana, on the west coast of Africa. She grew up in a royal house in Ghana and attended the University of Ghana. There she began her career as a writer. After university, she continued writing and also began teaching. She has worked at universities in several countries, including America.

Aidoo's short stories, plays, and poetry have won many awards. She has been awarded the Commonwealth Writer's Prize for Africa and the Nelson Mandela Prize for Poetry. She also directs a group that helps African women writers.

Check Your Predictions

1. Look back at the answers you gave for the Predict questions. Would you change your answers? Explain.

Understand the Story

2. How do the men first respond to the news that women have been accepted into the Academy?

3. What do Akuba and Yaa Sarah do about their unfair treatment by the men?

4. What is Akuba's motivation for joining the Academy?

Think About the Story

5. What is Akuba's internal conflict?

6. How does Akuba feel about Mampa?

7. What does the response of the cadets to Akuba's passing the test show?

8. What do you think the theme of this story is?

Extend Your Response

Write a short newspaper article about Akuba passing her test. Provide an interesting headline, as well as information about the struggles she faced to achieve her victory. Be sure to use newspaper style in your writing.

Summaries

Young Hunger The author remembers what it means to be young and hungry. During a visit to her godparents, she is fed only tiny bits of food. She reflects on her feelings of anger at her godparents and explains how that anger has changed into understanding.

Luck In this play, two groups of characters talk about their homes. One group lives on the mountain. The other lives in the valley. The group in the valley sees only the worst. They ask the group living on the mountain to switch homes with them. But after the valley group moves, they are still not happy. The other group is happy wherever they live.

Heavy Moments Akuba is taking her flight test to graduate from Ghana's Air Force Academy. She has struggled to be accepted by the men there. Even her closest relative, Mampa, has not been very supportive of her career. But after Akuba passes her test, she sees that the men have come to respect her. Mampa, too, has shown her pride by coming to see Akuba's test.

illuminates
impressed
candidates
appetite
despair
recruits

Vocabulary Review

Match each word in the box with its meaning. Write the word next to its meaning on a separate sheet of paper.

1. hopelessness
2. people who are likely to be chosen for something
3. desire for food
4. brightens with light
5. affected or influenced
6. people who have just joined the military

Chapter Quiz

**Write your answers in one or two complete sentences.
Use a separate sheet of paper.**

1. Young Hunger Why is the author so hungry at first?

2. Young Hunger Why do her godparents give her only
   a little food?

3. Luck Why do the characters on the mountain at first agree
   to move?

4. Luck Why do the characters in the valley at the beginning
   want to exchange houses with the characters on the mountain?

5. Heavy Moments What is the setting of the story?

6. Heavy Moments How do the men at the Academy treat the
   women over the course of their time there?

Critical Thinking

7. Luck What words or sayings might make a good title for
   this story?

8. Heavy Moments What can you infer about the main
   character's personality?

Chapter Activity

Think about the wishes expressed in these selections. Then, think
about one of your own wishes. Write about your wish in an essay,
poem, or short story. Be creative in your writing.

Little Girl Playing with Doll in Car, detail (2001) by Ondrea Barbe

What memory does this picture capture?

Chapter 15 Memories

Learning Objectives

- Recognize first-person point of view in an autobiography.
- Understand how details support a main idea.
- Understand what a stanza is.
- Recognize personification.
- Understand symbolism.
- Identify mood.

Preview Activity

What is your favorite memory? Think of a happy, exciting, or surprising time in your life. Write a paragraph describing your memory of that time in detail.

Theme Preview: Memories

We all have memories. The first day of school, a special trip, meeting someone new—our memories make us who we are. These selections all show how important memories are to us and how they affect our lives.

Keys to Literature

first-person point of view: when a narrator tells the story using *I* to refer himself or herself

> Example: *I should like ... to describe one day of my life in the Crimea.*

details: pieces of information that help to create a more complete picture for the reader

> Example: *There was the poultry to pluck and prepare for cooking.*

Did You Know?

Russia fought the British, the French, and the Turks in the Crimean War from 1853–1856. Russia wanted to expand into the Ottoman Empire. The other countries joined to stop Russia. Balaklava, where Mrs. Seacole went, was in the middle of the areas of fighting.

Words to Know

canteen	place where military people go for rest, food, and refreshment
poultry	birds raised to be eaten, such as chickens
joints	large cuts of meat
substitute	something used in place of another
frostbitten	damaged by extreme cold
descended	came down
excess	going beyond regular behavior
provost-marshal	military police officer
opposition	being against

Genre: Autobiography

Wonderful Adventures of Mrs. Seacole in Many Lands is an autobiography. Read more about autobiographies on page 466 of the Genre Guide.

from *Wonderful Adventures of Mrs. Seacole in Many Lands*

BY MARY JANE SEACOLE, *adapted*

READ TO FIND OUT...
What is it like to run a business in a war zone?

*Mary Jane Seacole was a woman of African descent born free during the 1800s in Jamaica. Her mother was Jamaican. Her father was Scottish. As a young woman, she strongly wished "to succeed in life." She traveled widely and worked as a shopkeeper. When the Crimean War broke out, she went to Balaklava, which is in what is now Ukraine. There she began the British Hotel at Spring Hill. The British Hotel contained a store, **canteen**, lunch hall, and doctor's office that served the officers and men of the British army. This excerpt describes Seacole's daily life at the British Hotel.*

I should like, with the reader's permission, to describe one day of my life in the Crimea. They were all pretty much alike. They were only different when there was fighting upon a large scale going on. Then duty called me to the field.

Keys to Literature

Autobiographies are always written from the **first-person point of view.** The author tells the story of his or her life using *I* and *me*.

Nurses Bound for the Crimean War (1854)

Fisherwomen carry luggage for nurses going to the Crimean War.

Keys to Literature

Details help create a more complete picture. Sometimes they support a main idea. What idea is supported by the details about plucking the poultry and mixing the medicines?

Predict

What will Mrs. Seacole do next?

Keys to Literature

What **details** tell about the sick patients?

▶ The Land Transport Corps was set up to help bring supplies to soldiers. The hospital of the Land Transport could handle serious cases.

I was generally up and busy by daybreak, sometimes earlier. There was plenty to do before the work of the day began. There was the **poultry** to pluck and prepare for cooking. There were the **joints** to be cut up and got ready for the same purpose. There were the medicines to be mixed. There was the store to be swept and cleaned. Of very great importance were the few hours of quiet before the road became alive with travelers. By seven o'clock in the morning, coffee would be ready, hot and refreshing. Army officers and workers who were building roads to the front or carrying supplies were eager for my coffee. There was always a great demand for coffee by those who knew its refreshing and strengthening qualities. I could not give them milk. (I kept it in tins for special occasions only.) But they had it hot and strong, with plenty of sugar and a slice of butter. Believe me, butter is an excellent **substitute** for milk.

From that time until nine, officers on duty in the neighborhood would come in for breakfast. At about half-past nine, my sick patients began to show themselves. In the following hour they came thickly. Sometimes it was past twelve before I had got through this duty. They came with every variety of suffering and disease. The cases I most disliked were the **frostbitten** fingers and feet in the winter.

That over, there was the hospital to visit across the way. It was sometimes overfilled with patients. I was often there. When possible, I would take over books and papers, which I used to borrow for that purpose from my friends and the officers. Someone wounded or sick would be glad to see me ride up with the comforts he was most in need of. During the day, if any accident occurred in the neighborhood or on the road near the British Hotel, the men generally brought the sufferer to that hospital. If the hurt was serious, he would be moved to the hospital of the Land Transport. When

The village of Balaklava during the Crimean War.

visiting the sick or wounded officers, I used to think of
their family at home. They would have given so much
to be in my place.

Until evening the store would be filled with
customers wanting supplies and food. At eight o'clock,
the curtain **descended** on that day's work. Then I
could sit down and eat and relax. It was no easy thing
to clear the store, canteen, and yards. But we were
determined to stick to the rule that nothing should be
sold after that hour. We succeeded. Anyone who came
after that time came simply as a friend. There could be
no necessity for anyone, except on extraordinary
occasions, to purchase things after eight o'clock.
And drunkenness or **excess** were not allowed at Spring
Hill. Indeed, my few unpleasant scenes began mainly
from my refusing to sell liquor. I allowed neither
drunkenness among the men, nor gambling among the
officers. Whatever happened elsewhere, drunkenness,
cards, and dice were never to be seen within the British

Think About It

Why does Mrs. Seacole
say life in the Crimea
would kill me easily now?

Hotel. My rules were well known. A kind-hearted officer, who was much there, undertook to be my **provost-marshal**. But his duties were very light.

At first we kept our store open on Sunday from sheer necessity. But after a little while, many stores were established at Kadikoi and elsewhere. Then Sunday became a day of much needed rest at Spring Hill. This step also met with **opposition** from the men. But again we were determined, and again we were successful. I am sure we needed rest. I have often wondered since how it was that I never fell ill. I am afraid that I was not thankful enough. I was so happy then. But although I never had a week's illness during my time in the Crimea, I have never since felt as strong and hearty as I was then. It would kill me easily now.

Meet the Author

MARY JANE SEACOLE *(1805–1881)*

Mary Jane Seacole was born in Kingston, Jamaica. Her father was Scottish. Her mother was Jamaican. At that time, people of African descent were enslaved in America and parts of the Caribbean. Seacole, however, was born free.

As a young woman, Seacole traveled widely around the Caribbean and England. In 1855, Seacole left England for Balaklava to aid the British in the Crimean War. There she set up a store and canteen. She also helped nurse the soldiers. After the war, she returned to England. She struggled at first with financial and health problems. But she also wrote her autobiography, *Wonderful Adventures of Mrs. Seacole in Many Lands*. Its publication was a huge success and helped her financial troubles. She was honored both for telling her story and for her efforts in the Crimean War.

Check Your Prediction

1. Look back at the answer you gave for the Predict question. Would you change your answer? Explain.

Understand the Autobiography

2. What jobs did Mrs. Seacole do at the British Hotel?

3. What were some rules of the British Hotel?

4. Why did the British Hotel need a provost-marshal?

5. When was the British Hotel able to close on Sunday?

Think About the Autobiography

6. How do you know this selection is told from the first-person point of view?

7. What details show how difficult life was for Mrs. Seacole in the Crimea?

8. Why do you think Mrs. Seacole was so "strong and hearty" during her time at the British Hotel?

Extend Your Response

Imagine you are a soldier walking into the British Hotel for the first time. Write a paragraph describing the British Hotel and Mrs. Seacole.

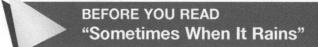

BEFORE YOU READ
"Sometimes When It Rains"

Keys to Literature

stanza: a group of lines in a poem set apart from other groups of lines

    Example: The first five lines of this poem are the first stanza.

personification: giving human characteristics to something that is not human

    Example: *cold angry winds*

Did You Know?

For many years, the laws of apartheid forced white and nonwhite people in South Africa to live separately. Nonwhite Africans were treated as lesser citizens. In 1990, a new government changed this. Even today, though, there are differences in how white and nonwhite South Africans are able to live.

Words to Know

drum	a large container for water shaped like a drum
fetch	go after and bring back
squatter	person who settles somewhere without permission
mercy	forgiveness or kindness

Genre: Poetry

    "Sometimes When It Rains" is a poem. Read more about poetry on page 467 of the Genre Guide.

Sometimes When It Rains

BY GCINA MHLOPHE

Sometimes when it rains
I smile to myself
And think of times when as a child
I'd sit by myself
5 And wonder why people need clothes

Sometimes when it rains
I think of times
when I'd run into the rain
Shouting "Nkce — nkce mlanjana
10 When will I grow?
I'll grow up tomorrow!"

READ TO FIND OUT...
What memories can a rainstorm trigger?

Keys to Literature

A **stanza** is a group of lines set apart in poetry. Each stanza in this poem is a separate thought or memory.

▶ The poet translates "Nkce—nkce mlanjana" in the next line.

Sometimes when it rains
I think of times
When I watched goats
15   running so fast from the rain
While sheep seemed to enjoy it

Sometimes when it rains
I think of times
When we had to undress
20   Carry the small bundles of uniforms and books
On our heads
And cross the river after school

Sometimes when it rains
I remember times
25   When it would rain hard for hours
And fill our **drum**
so we didn't have to **fetch** water
From the river for a day or two

Sometimes when it rains
30   Rains for many hours without break
I think of people
who have nowhere to go
No home of their own
And no food to eat
35   Only rain water to drink

Sometimes when it rains
Rains for days without break
I think of mothers
Who give birth in **squatter** camps
40   Under plastic shelters
At the **mercy** of cold angry winds

Sometimes when it rains
I think of "illegal" job seekers
in big cities
45   Dodging police vans in the rain
Hoping for darkness to come
So they can find some wet corner to hide in

Think About It
Why does the speaker in the poem usually get water from the river?

Keys to Literature

Personification is giving human characteristics to something that is not human. What non-human object is the poet personifying here?

Sometimes when it rains
Rains so hard hail joins in
50 I think of life prisoners
in all the jails of the world
And wonder if they still love
To see the rainbow at the end of the rain

Sometimes when it rains
55 With hail stones biting the grass
I can't help thinking they look like teeth
Many teeth of smiling friends
Then I wish that everyone else
Had something to smile about.

> **Keys to Literature**
>
> How are hailstones **personified** here?

Meet the Author

GCINA MHLOPHE *(Born 1959)*

Gcina Mhlophe was born in South Africa. She was named Gcina, or "the last," since she was the last of many children. She began writing in Xhosa while in high school. As a young adult, she began writing in English as well. She also established herself as an actress and playwright.

Mhlophe has written poetry, plays, short stories, and children's books. She has won awards for her plays as well as for her CDs. Her CDs feature both music and stories. She is also a well-respected storyteller. Mhlophe hopes that her work as a writer and storyteller will encourage both adults and children to read.

Understand the Poem

1. What kind of community do you think the speaker lived in while growing up?

2. Why did the speaker undress and carry books on her head during the rain?

3. Why do the "illegal" job seekers hope for darkness?

4. What sad things does the rain make the speaker think of?

5. What does the speaker notice about goats and sheep in the rain?

Think About the Poem

6. Compare the first stanza to the sixth stanza. How are the subjects of the two stanzas different?

7. How is the wind personified?

8. What does the speaker wish for?

Extend Your Response

What memory do you have of rain? Think of a time you were caught in the rain. Write a paragraph or a poem that tells what your thoughts were then and what happened.

Learn More About It

APARTHEID IN SOUTH AFRICA

South Africa is a political and economic leader in Africa. However, South Africa's people faced many challenges to become the nation it is today.

Nelson Mandela

From 1948–1994, the government enforced a policy called apartheid. White people were separated from nonwhite people. "White areas" included the best farmland, cities, and business areas. It was "illegal" for nonwhites to be in these areas without a special pass to work. Nonwhites had few rights and could not participate in the government.

Many groups protested apartheid. One leader, Nelson Mandela, was sent to prison for his protests. People all over the world heard about Mandela. Leaders spoke out against apartheid. Finally, in 1990, President F. W. de Klerk announced that apartheid had failed. He released Nelson Mandela from prison. Mandela and de Klerk worked together to create a new constitution. The new constitution gave whites and nonwhites the same rights. The two men were awarded the Nobel Peace Prize in 1993. Mandela was elected president of South Africa in 1994.

Apply and Connect

What memories described in the poem might refer to events during apartheid?

Keys to Literature

symbolism: using something to stand for something else

> Example: In this autobiography, the watch stands for several different things.

mood: the feeling you get from reading a story

> Example: *Those who lived there became gravediggers. We were digging wildly in the yard, the garden, and the cellar.* These sentences suggest a frightening, dark mood.

Did You Know?

Having a bar mitzvah [bahr-MITZ-vah] is an important ceremony in the life of a Jewish boy. He studies Hebrew and religion for several years. At the age of thirteen, he leads a religious service. That bar mitzvah ceremony marks his joining the adult Jewish community. In some communities, women also have a ceremony, called a bat mitzvah.

Words to Know

bar mitzvah	a ceremony celebrating the beginning of adulthood for a 13-year-old Jewish boy
Torah	written Jewish law and literature, including the first five books of the Bible
cemetery	a place for burying the dead
Shabbat	the period from Friday evening to Saturday evening, a time of Jewish rest and worship
rabbi	the leader of a Jewish house of worship
looter	someone who steals openly
Holocaust	the killing of Jewish and other peoples in Europe by the Nazis during World War II
Talmud	a collection of ancient writings that make up Jewish law
Hasidim	a group of people who follow the teachings of an eighteenth-century Jewish leader

The Watch

BY ELIE WIESEL, *adapted*

READ TO FIND OUT...
How can a watch bring
back a time 20 years ago?

For my **bar mitzvah**, I remember, I had received a
splendid gold watch. It was the usual gift for this event.
The watch was meant to remind each boy that he was
now an adult. From now on, he would have to answer
for his acts before the **Torah** and its timeless laws.

But I could not keep my gift. I had to part with it
the day my town became the pride of Hungary. This
was the day it chased from its borders every single Jew.
The glorious masters of our city were thrilled. They
were rid of us. There would be no more strangely
dressed people on the streets.

The time was late April, 1944.

Keys to Literature

Symbolism is
something that stands
for something else.
What does the watch
symbolize here?

A view of Sighet, Romania during the 1920s or 1930s.

A Jewish family being sent from their home in Sighet, Romania.

Think About It

Why does the author say that the Jewish part of the city has changed into a cemetery?

Keys to Literature

Mood in literature is the feeling you get from a story. What is the mood in this paragraph?

▶ Tziporah [tsee-PAW-rah]

The early morning hours followed a sleepless night. On that day the Jewish part of the city changed into a **cemetery**. Those who lived there became gravediggers. We were digging wildly in the yard, the garden, and the cellar. We were giving all we had left to the earth for just a time, we thought.

My father took care of the jewelry and important papers. His head bowed, he was silently digging near the barn. Not far away, my mother stooped on the damp ground. She was burying the silver candle holder she used only on **Shabbat** eve. She was moaning softly. I avoided her with my eyes. My sisters dug near the cellar. The youngest, Tziporah, had chosen the garden, like me. Thoughtfully shoveling, she turned down my help. What did she have to hide? Her toys? Her school notebooks? As for me, my only belonging was my watch. It meant a lot to me. I decided to bury it in a dark, deep hole, three steps from the fence. The thick leaves of a tree seemed to offer a safe cover.

All of us planned to get back our treasure. On our return, the earth would give them back. Until then, they would be safe.

Twenty years later, I am standing in our garden. It is the middle of the night. I remember the first and last gift I ever received from my parents. I need to see it. I want to see if it was still here in the same spot. I want to see if it has by some luck survived. I only think of this. I do not think of my father's money or my mother's candle holder. All that matters is my watch.

In spite of the darkness, I easily find my way to the garden. Once more I am the bar mitzvah child. Here is the barn, the fence, the tree. Nothing has changed. To my left, the path to the Slotvino **Rabbi**'s house. The Rabbi, though, had changed.

But I mustn't think of him, not now. The watch, I must think of the watch. Maybe it was saved. Let's see, three steps to the right. Stop. Two forward. I know the place. Automatically, I get ready to act out the scene I recall. I fall on my knees. What can I use to dig? There is a shovel in the barn. Its door is never locked. But by fumbling around in the dark, I risk stumbling and waking the people in the house. They would think I was a **looter**, a thief. They would hand me over to the police. They might even kill me. Never mind, I'll have to get along without a shovel or any other tool. I'll use my hands, my nails. But it is difficult. The ground is so hard and frozen. It is as if it did not want anyone to know its secret. Too bad, I'll punish it by being the stronger.

Emotionally, wildly, my hands claw the earth. I do not feel the cold. I do not feel tired. I do not feel pain. One scratch, then another. No matter. Continue. My nails inch ahead. My fingers dig in. I bear down. My every muscle shares in the task. Little by little the hole deepens. I must hurry. My head touches the ground. Almost. I break out in a cold sweat. I am soaked, dazed. Faster, faster. I shall rip the earth from end to end, but I must know. Nothing can stop or frighten me.

Predict

What do you think the narrator will do now?

▶ The rabbi did not live through the war.

What time is it? How long have I been here? Five minutes, five hours? Twenty years. This night is timeless. I am digging for the watch. I am also digging to bring back the time that has passed. I was working to dig up not an object but time itself.

Suddenly a chill goes through me. A sharp feeling, like a bite. My fingers touch something hard. It is metal and has four sides. So I have not been digging for nothing. The garden is spinning around me. I stand up to catch my breath. A moment later, I'm on my knees again. Carefully, gently I take the box from its tomb. Here it is, in the palm of my hand. I am holding the only remaining symbol of everything I have loved. A voice inside me says: "Don't open it. It contains nothing but emptiness. Throw it away and run." I cannot obey the warning. It is too late to turn back. I need to know, either way. A slight push of my thumb and the box opens. I hold back the cry rising in my throat. The watch is there. Quick, a match. And another. Briefly, I catch a glimpse of it. The pain is blinding. Could this thing, this object, be my gift, my pride? My past? It is covered with dirt and rust. It is crawling with worms. I sit there staring at it. I begin to feel deep pity. The watch, too, lived through the war and **Holocaust**. In its way, the watch is also a survivor. It also has old memories. Suddenly I feel the urge to carry it to my lips, dirty as it is. I want to kiss and comfort it with my tears.

Predict

What do you think the narrator will do now?

I touch it. I stroke it. I feel thankful. The people I expected to live forever are gone. My teachers, my friends, my guides had all left me. Only this lifeless thing had survived. Its only purpose was to welcome me on my return and to give a final chapter to my childhood. I feel a need to tell it about myself. In turn I would listen to its story.

It is growing late. The eastern sky is turning a deep red. I must go. The people in the house will be waking. They will come down to the well for water. No time to lose. I stuff the watch into my pocket and cross the garden. I enter the courtyard. From under the porch a dog barks. Then he stops. The dog knows I am not a thief. I open the gate. Halfway down the street I feel a great deal of sadness. I have just committed my first theft.

I turn around. I go back through the courtyard and the garden. Once again I kneel beneath the poplar tree. Holding my breath, my eyes refuse to cry. I place the watch back into its box and close the cover. My first gift once more finds safety deep inside the hole. Using both hands, I smoothly fill in the earth.

Breathless and with pounding heart, I reach the still empty street. I stop and ask myself about the meaning of what I have just done. I find I cannot explain it.

Looking back, I tell myself that probably I simply wanted to leave behind something to show that I had been there. One day, a child would play in the garden. The child would dig near a tree, and stumble upon a metal box. He would learn that his parents had taken what was not theirs. He would learn that Jews and Jewish children once lived in this town. The Jewish children were robbed of their future.

The sun was rising. I was still walking through the empty streets. For a moment I thought I heard the singing of schoolboys studying **Talmud**. I also thought I heard the prayers of **Hasidim** reading morning prayers in thirty-three places at once. Yet above all these chants, I heard clearly the tick-tock of the watch. The sound seemed far away. I had just buried it according to Jewish custom. It was, after all, the very first gift a Jewish child had once been given for his very first celebration.

▶ Talmud [TAHL-muhd]
Hasidim [hah-SEHD-eem]

Since that day, the town of my childhood has stopped being just another town. It has become the face of a watch.

Meet the Author

ELIE WIESEL *(Born 1928)*

Elie Wiesel was born in Eastern Europe, in what is now Romania. During World War II, Wiesel and his family were sent to concentration camps. Wiesel survived the camps, but most of his family did not. After the war, Wiesel lived in France. There he began to write, at first as a journalist. Later he moved to the United States.

Wiesel became famous for his first book, *Night*. *Night* tells what it was like for a teenage boy in the concentration camps. His later novels and memoirs also deal with the Holocaust and the Jewish tradition. Wiesel has received many awards, both for his writing and his efforts to fight for human rights. He received the Nobel Peace Prize in 1986.

Check Your Predictions

1. Look back at the answers you gave for the Predict questions. Would you change your answers? Explain.

Understand the Autobiography

2. How did the narrator get the watch?

3. Why do the narrator and his family leave their home?

4. Where does the narrator hide the watch?

5. What does the narrator finally do with the watch?

Think About the Autobiography

6. What is the mood at the end of this piece of writing?

7. How does the symbolism of the watch change over the course of the autobiography and Wiesel's life?

8. Why do you think the narrator reburies the watch?

Extend Your Response

Imagine that years after this, someone digs up the watch. On the watch is written the date and why the watch was a present. Write a paragraph telling what happens when the person digs up the watch.

Chapter 15 / Review

Summaries

Wonderful Adventures of Mrs. Seacole in Many Lands A young Jamaican woman opens the British Hotel for soldiers during the Crimean War. She tells about her challenging daily life there. She works hard as a cook and a storekeeper. She also nurses the soldiers. Despite the challenges, she recalls being healthy, happy, and strong.

Sometimes When It Rains The rain reminds the speaker of the poem of days in her childhood. Then the speaker thinks of others in the rain. She thinks of the homeless and of those without jobs. She wishes that everyone could have something to smile about.

The Watch The narrator gets a wonderful present, a watch. It is to celebrate becoming an adult in the Jewish faith. Then World War II comes. The narrator buries the watch and is forced to leave his town. He returns years later to where he buried the watch and digs it up. Then he decides to bury the watch again. He is at first unsure why he buries it. Then he decides it will be a reminder of the Jewish community that once lived in the town.

poultry
rabbi
substitute
fetch
mercy
looter

Vocabulary Review

Match each word in the box with its meaning. Write the word next to its meaning on a separate sheet of paper.

1. forgiveness or kindness
2. something used in place of another
3. birds raised to be eaten, such as chickens
4. the leader of the Jewish house of worship
5. someone who steals openly
6. go after and bring back

Chapter Quiz

Write your answers in one or two complete sentences.
Use a separate sheet of paper.

1. Wonderful Adventures of Mrs. Seacole in Many Lands Describe a day in Mrs. Seacole's life at the British Hotel.

2. Wonderful Adventures of Mrs. Seacole in Many Lands Why does the British Hotel close on Sundays?

3. Sometimes When It Rains What difference does the rain make to the chores the speaker has to do when she is young?

4. Sometimes When It Rains Give an example of how the rain is not pleasant for some people in this poem.

5. The Watch Why does the narrator call the watch "a survivor"?

6. The Watch When does the narrator return to find the watch?

Critical Thinking

7. Wonderful Adventures of Mrs. Seacole in Many Lands What can you tell about the character of Mrs. Seacole from this selection?

8. The Watch How do you know this selection is from an autobiography?

Chapter Activity

Choose one of the selections from this chapter. Make a list of five questions you would like to ask the author or speaker of the poem. Then write the answers he or she might give.

Unit 7 **Review**

On a separate sheet of paper, write
the letter that best completes each
sentence below.

1. In "Young Hunger," the author
   is fed

   A. only bread and water.
   B. something she is allergic to.
   C. too little.
   D. nothing.

2. The theme of "Luck" is that

   A. happiness depends on how a
      person sees things.
   B. being at the top of a mountain
      is unpleasant.
   C. only a few people can be lucky.
   D. it's best to avoid taking
      chances.

3. After her flight test in "Heavy
   Moments," Akuba is surprised
   to see

   A. the Director.
   B. Mampa.
   C. Yaa Sarah.
   D. the other cadets.

4. In *Wonderful Adventures of Mrs.
   Seacole in Many Lands*, Mrs. Seacole
   runs the

   A. ambulances.
   B. bank.
   C. hospital.
   D. British Hotel.

5. The speaker in "Sometimes When
   It Rains" wishes that

   A. she did not have to cross
      the river.
   B. it would stop raining.
   C. everyone had something to
      smile about.
   D. people understood her better.

6. The author of "The Watch"
   reburies the watch

   A. because it no longer works.
   B. so another child can play
      with it.
   C. because he is afraid his sisters
      will take it.
   D. to show that he has been there.

Making Connections
**On a separate sheet of paper, write
your answers to the following
questions.**

7. How are wishes you have like the
   wishes in the selections in this
   unit? How are they different?

8. Which selection had the most
   realistic details? Explain why.

Writing an Essay
Write about a special or powerful
memory. Use one of the selections in
this unit as a model.

Appendix

Glossary of Words to Know

Note: These definitions fit the way the word is used in the selection. See a dictionary for more information about the words.

adviser a person who gives information to someone else

alms money given to the poor

ancestor a person who lived long ago and is related to someone living many years later

ancestors the family or group a person comes from

Anglo-Indian English and Indian

anvil an iron block on which hot pieces of metal are hammered into shapes

appetite desire for food

apprentice a person who works for an experienced worker to learn a skill

arena an open space used for sports or events

armor a covering that protects a fighter in battle

ashamed feeling guilty or sorry for something done wrong

attractive appealing

azaleas bushes with bright flowers

baboon a type of large monkey

bait something, often food, that attracts animals to a trap

bamboo a tropical plant with hollow woody stems

bar mitzvah a ceremony celebrating the beginning of adulthood for a 13-year-old Jewish boy

beckoning calling

bellowed shouted very loudly

bellows a machine operated by hand that makes a stream of air so a fire will burn hotter

blade a single stem of a plant, especially grass

bleats the cries of a goat, sheep, or calf

bolted ran away

bounds jumps forward quickly

bowling rolling quickly

brambles prickly bushes

brigade a group of people organized for a purpose

brim the top edge of a jar or container

buck a male goat

bulwarks strong supports

candidates people who are likely to be chosen for something

canteen place where military people go for rest, food, and refreshment

captured caught

career the work a person chooses to do in life

cast off thrown away; sent away

cemetery a place for burying the dead

challenged called to a fight or contest

chuckling quietly laughing

civilized educated or having manners

civil service part of the government or public service

clatter a rattling noise

clever smart and quick

clumsiness awkwardness

cockpit the place from which an airplane is steered

collapsing caving in or falling down

collide crash or bump into

composed calm, peaceful

condemnation strong disapproval

congregation a group of people who attend a church

cottage a small house in the country

cowardly lacking courage

crackles makes a crisp snapping sound

criticized blamed; found fault with

crossbow a weapon similar to a bow and arrow

crumple crush into a ball or pile

cubbyhole small shelf or cupboard used for storing things

custom a way of doing things or a practice that's gone on for a long time

cypress a kind of evergreen tree

darkroom a place where film is turned into pictures

dazzling bright

dedicated devoted

deluge flood

dense thick or crowded

descended came down

deserted empty; left behind

deserts abandons; leaves someone in need

despair hopelessness

dikes dams

discolored stained

disgruntled unhappy; irritated

dishonest not honest; likely to cheat or lie

distribute give out

dowry money or belongings that a bride brings to her new husband

drought a long period of time with no rain

drum a large container for water shaped like a drum

engulfed covered completely

escorting taking someone from place to place

excess going beyond regular behavior

exchange trade

exhibit present for viewing

exile a person forced to leave a country

existed lived somewhere in the world

explanations answers or reasons that make something clear

failings faults or weaknesses

felled cut down

fetch go after and bring back

feud a long quarrel between families

fierce violent

firmness steadiness; unchangeable manner

flesh the soft parts of an animal's body that are covered with skin

flexible easy to bend

flower become as good as possible; reach full growth

forbid order not to do something

fragrance a sweet or pleasing smell

frostbitten damaged by extreme cold

fuddled confused

furiously fiercely; intensely

futuristic very modern

game wild animals hunted for sport or for food

gauze very thin cloth used for bandages

gazelle a small, fast antelope

generations spans of time between the birth of parents and the birth of their children

glade an open area of the woods

glimpse a fleeting look or glance

glittered sparkled or shined

goblets heavy drinking cups with stems

godparents people who sponsor or agree to be partly responsible for a child

gourds fruits with thick skins or rinds

gradually slowly

grieve to feel or show great sadness

groaned made a deep, pained sound

grudge bad feeling toward someone who is supposed to have done something wrong

guarded cautious or watchful

gulp a large swallow or sip

hallowed holy

harness the leather straps and metal pieces used to connect a horse to a plow or wagon

Hasidim a group of people who follow the teachings of an eighteenth-century Jewish leader

headmaster a male school principal

headmistress a female school principal

hemp a strong, fibrous plant

hesitate pause

hesitated stopped for a moment

hobble walk with a limp

Holocaust the killing of Jewish and other peoples in Europe by the Nazis during World War II

homespun loosely woven homemade cloth

houseboy a boy or man hired to do housework

huddled crowded closely

humbly with meek or modest feeling

illuminates brightens with light

imitate try to be like

immortal living forever

impressed affected or influenced

inactive not active

innocence freedom from guilt

insult something said that hurts someone's feelings

intense very strong or deep

intruder a person who does not belong in a place

jackal a wild dog usually found in Africa or Asia

joints large cuts of meat

judgment a decision

kids young goats

lantern a covering for a light with see-through openings

lashed moved suddenly or violently

lawsuit a disagreement brought to court

lever a rod or bar used to lift things

loaf pass the time doing little

lodger a person who rents a room

loom a machine on which cloth is woven

looter someone who steals openly

lucid clear

mangled cut and bruised

mannequin a model of the human form

mansion a very large house

manure animal waste

marketplace a place where goods are bought and sold

meddle to get involved with another person's business

mercy forgiveness or kindness

merit cause, earn

messenger person who carries news or other information

milky like milk in color or form

ministers people who help run the government of a country

mischief action that bothers or annoys others

misery great pain; suffering

misplaced wrongly given importance

nobility outstanding qualities; high moral character

oaths promises to speak the truth

obliterated erased; forgotten

ooze soft mud at the edge of a body of water

opposition being against

ordinariness the state of being average or common

outcast a person whom other people do not accept

pagan having to do with ancient religion

panting breathing rapidly in short gasps

parched very dry

peddler a person who sells things, often door to door

penalty punishment

perished died

plank a heavy, thick board

poacher a person who hunts illegally

porter a person who carries things for other people

possibility chance

poultry birds raised to be eaten, such as chickens

priceless of great worth

prodded moved to action

proper correct

proposed offered marriage to someone

provost-marshal military police officer

pumice a type of rock, sometimes used to scrub away dead skin

pursue chase after; follow

quarrel an argument

rabbi the leader of a Jewish house of worship

rabble a crowd of people who are hard to control

rasping scratchy, harsh

reassure make a person feel comfortable or confident

rebellion a fight against the government or other authority

rebels people who are working against the ruling government

recruits people who have just joined the military

reef a ridge of coral in the sea

reel a spool attached to a fishing rod used for winding and storing the fishing line

remains stays behind

reserves extra supplies

riddled filled with

romps active play

routines regular ways or patterns of doing things

sacred holy

sacrifices offerings of valued objects

satin a smooth, shiny material

savage cruel, wild, or unkind

scarcely hardly

scents nice smells

scolded told someone angrily what he or she did wrong

scuffed scratched or scraped

scuttling running in a hurry

serene calm and peaceful

severed separated, broken apart

Shabbat the period from Friday evening to Saturday evening, a time of Jewish rest and worship

shabby old and worn

shelter a place to live

shrine a place where people pay respect to a god

shriveled wrinkled, sometimes from being in water

shuttle a card or spool that moves thread back and forth to weave cloth

slashed cut with rough, long strokes

slender thin

slimy slippery, wet, and smooth

slithered slid; moved like a snake

sneer an expression that shows dislike

sneering curling the upper lip in an unpleasant way

snout a long nose

solemnly very seriously

soy a salty, thin brown sauce made from soybeans

splendor grandness

spring a source of water flowing from the ground

sprouted began to grow

squabbled argued noisily

squatter person who settles somewhere without permission

staggered moved or walked unsteadily

stale not fresh; tasteless

steppe a large area of flat grassland

stingy unwilling to spend money

stubborn firm; unchanging

stumble trip

substitute something used in place of another

superior better or more important than others

swiftest fastest

Talmud a collection of ancient writings that make up Jewish law

tantrum a display of bad temper or anger

tarmac paved runway

thatched covered with straw, grass, or leaves

thrashed flapped wildly about

thrifty not wasteful; careful with spending

thrive to grow; to be healthy

Torah written Jewish law and literature, including the first five books of the Bible

torso trunk

traitor someone who betrays the government

tripod a stand with three legs

trophy a prize that shows success in hunting or other activities

turban a scarf wrapped around the head to form a kind of hat

tusk a long, curving tooth that usually grows in pairs out of the sides of the mouths of certain animals

twilight faint light after sunset

unwitting innocent; unaware

veranda a large, open porch

wake a track left behind

wallaby a small kangaroo

warehouse a place where food or other products are stored

water chestnuts plants found in watery marshes of Asia and Africa

wearily in a tired way

weariness tiredness

whirlpool fast-moving water that turns in a circle

whitewash a mixture used like paint to make something white

whitewashed painted white

wince draw back in pain or distress

withered dried up, shriveled

witness a person who sees or hears something

woes terrible troubles

worthy having value or honor

wretch a person who is looked down on as worthless

writhed squirmed; twisted and turned

Keys to Literature: A Handbook of Literary Terms

allegory a story in which the characters and events stand for something else

alliteration repeating the same consonant sound

atmosphere the general mood of a piece of literature

character a person in a story

character clues the thoughts, actions, and words in a story that help you understand what a character is like

character traits qualities that a person has, such as bravery or honesty

climax the high point in a story when the outcome is decided

colloquial language everyday language people use when talking to friends

comparison showing how two things are alike

concrete words words that describe things that the reader can see, hear, feel, smell, or taste

conflict a problem that needs to be solved in a story

connotation an idea or feeling suggested by a word

denotation the actual meaning of a word

details pieces of information that help to create a picture for the reader

dialogue a conversation between characters in a story or play; words that characters actually say

external conflict a struggle that a person has with another person, with society, or with nature

fable a short story that teaches a lesson. In fables, animals and other natural things act and talk like people.

figurative language words that describe something by comparing it to something else. Similes and metaphors are types of figurative language.

first-person point of view when a narrator tells the story using *I* to refer to himself or herself

foreshadowing hints about what might happen later in a story

form the structure of a poem. A poem can be open form (free verse) or closed form.

free verse poetry that is not written in a regular pattern; the words do not rhyme.

hero the main character in a story who acts with great courage or kindness

idiom a phrase or expression that has a different meaning from what the individual words usually mean

imagery colorful words that appeal to the senses

internal conflict a struggle a person has with himself or herself when trying to make a decision

irony a result that is the opposite of what is expected; it is often unfortunate.

metaphor a comparison of two things that does not use *like* or *as*

mood the feeling you get from reading a story

motivation the reason why a character behaves as he or she does

narrative a story; a report of what has happened

narrative hook a point in a story at which the author grabs your attention

narrator the person telling the story

omniscient point of view when the narrator knows what all the story characters do, say, and feel. An omniscient narrator uses *he, she,* and *they* to refer to the characters.

onomatopoeia the use of words that imitate sounds

personification giving human characteristics to something that is not human

plot the action of a story or a play. Most stories have a problem and, at the end, a solution.

realism a style of writing in which people and events are presented the way they actually are in life

repetition words or sentences used over and over to create a feeling or mood

rising action the buildup of excitement in a story

sensory details details that show how something looks, sounds, smells, tastes, or feels

setting the time and place of the action in a story

simile a comparison of two things using *like* or *as*

speaker of the poem the one who is describing or telling about something in the poem

stage directions instructions to a play's actors that tell them what to do and explain a play's setting

stanza a group of lines in a poem set apart from other groups of lines

story-within-a-story a story told inside another story. A character from the outer story tells the inner story to another character.

suspense a feeling of uncertainty about what will happen next in a story. Suspense can keep readers curious and interested.

symbolism using something to stand for something else

theme the main idea of a story, novel, play, or poem

tone the feeling a writer shows toward his or her subject

turning point the event in a story that leads to a solution to the problem

Index of Authors and Titles

Index of Fine Art and Artists

Genre Guide

Autobiography

In an autobiography, the author tells the story of his or her own life. The author uses *I* and *me* (first-person point of view) to tell what happens. A person may write an autobiography near the end of his or her life. The author might also choose to tell about part of his or her life.

Diary

A diary tells a person's thoughts, feelings, and descriptions of events. Most diaries are not written to be published. Diaries can tell us a great deal about a person or a period of time.

Epic

An epic is a long poem that tells a story. It usually tells about a hero's adventures. The hero may have been a real person, but the person's deeds are often exaggerated. Today, many epics are translated into English. Many of these translations are no longer in poetic form.

Fable

A fable is a short story that teaches a lesson. In fables, animals and other natural things act like people.

Fiction

Fiction comes from a writer's imagination. Fiction can be realistic. It can describe people and events that could happen in real life. It can also describe things that could not happen in real life, as in science fiction and fantasy. Folktales, myths, novels, and short stories are examples of fiction.

Folktale

A folktale is a type of oral literature. It was once told aloud and passed on from teller to teller. Folktales are often quite old and usually have no known author. They may have colorful characters and an exciting plot. Folktales also may include repetition, which helps the reader remember the story.

Haiku

Haiku is a poem with three lines. This form began in Japan. Traditionally, the first and third lines have five syllables each. The second line has seven syllables. Haiku typically describe nature and the emotions.

Memoir

A memoir is a type of nonfiction. As with an autobiography, the author tells his or her own story. However, it often focuses on a specific event or part of a person's life.

Myth

Like folktales, myths were originally told aloud. Some explain why the world is the way it is. Others tell how certain things came into being. Often, these stories include gods or goddesses. Most ancient cultures of the world have told myths. Some, such as the ancient Greeks, have left behind hundreds of stories about their gods and goddesses.

Nonfiction

Nonfiction tells a true story or describes something real. Nonfiction includes autobiography, memoir, and diary. Nonfiction also includes scientific and historic works.

Novel

Novels are book-length works of fiction. They often have many characters and take place over a long period of time. As in short stories, the plot revolves around a conflict or problem, which is resolved at the end of the novel. In a novel, there may also be several small related plots, called subplots.

Play

Plays are written to be performed. They are made up of dialogue and stage directions. The dialogue is the words the characters speak. The stage directions tell what the characters do and how they act. They also tell how the stage should look. There are different types of plays. Comedies are funny or light-hearted. Dramas are more serious. Musicals include song and dance.

Poetry

Poetry is arranged in lines on a page. Poetry often has rhythm and may also rhyme. Some poems describe people, places, or real events. Other poems tell stories. The language in a poem creates strong images and feelings. This sets the mood, or general feeling, of the poem.

Short Story

A short story is a short work of fiction. Usually it has fewer than twenty pages. Most short stories have only a few characters and take place over a short period of time. They often have a problem or a conflict that is resolved at the end of the story.

Acknowledgments

page 4: "The Fly," from *The Toad Is the Emperor's Uncle* by Mai Vo-Dinh. Doubleday & Co. Inc, 1970. Reprinted by permission of Mai Vo-Dinh.

page 12: All pages from "By Any Other Name" from *Gifts of Passage* by Santha Rama Rau. Copyright © 1951 by Santha Rama Rau. Copyright renewed © 1979 by Santha Rama Rau. Reprinted by permission of HarperCollins Publishers, Inc. "By Any Other Name" originally appeared in *The New Yorker*.

page 24: "The Small Cabin" from *Selected Poems 1966–1984*, by Margaret Atwood. Copyright © 1990 Oxford University Press Canada. Reprinted by permission of the publisher.

"The Small Cabin" from *Selected Poems 1966–1984* by Margaret Atwood. Copyright © 1975 by Margaret Atwood. Reprinted by permission of Houghton Mifflin Company. All rights reserved.

page 32: "Arachne" from *Greek Myths*. Copyright © 1949 by Olivia E. Coolidge; copyright renewed © 1977 by Olivia E. Coolidge. Reprinted by permission of Houghton Mifflin Company. All rights reserved.

page 40: "Lather and Nothing Else" reprinted from *Américas*, a bimonthly magazine published by the General Secretariat of the Organization of American States in English and Spanish. Used by permission.

page 66: "The Mountain of the Men and the Mountain of the Women" a Cambodian folktale told by Touch Neak, translated by Samoi Tan, and retold by Alice Lucas. Copyright © San Francisco Study Center. Used by permission.

page 76: Copyright © 1968 by Esther Hautzig. Used by permission of HarperCollins Publishers.

page 98: "The Heroic Fisherman," pp. 172–175 from *Time Before Morning: Art and Myth of the Australian Aborigines* by Louis A. Allen. Copyright © 1975 by Louis A. Allen. Reprinted by permission of HarperCollins Publishers Inc.

page 114: "Unanana and the Elephant" from *Tales from Africa* retold by Kathleen Arnott (Oxford University Press, 2000), copyright © Kathleen Arnott 1962, used by permission of Oxford University Press.

page 128: "The Good Brother's Reward," from *Tales of a Korean Grandmother* by Frances Carpenter. © 1973 by Charles E. Tuttle Co., Inc. Reprinted by permission of Charles E. Tuttle Co., Inc. of Boston, Massachusetts, and Tokyo, Japan.

page 140: From *Harvest* by Selma Lagerlöf, translated by Florence and Naboth Hedin, copyright © 1934, 1935 by Doubleday, a division of Random House, Inc. Used by permission of Doubleday, a division of Random House, Inc.

page 156: "The Story of Washing Horse Pond." Reprinted by permission of HarperCollins Publishers Ltd. Copyright © He Liyi 1985.

page 176: "The Friends of Kwan Ming," from *Tales of Gold Mountain*, text copyright © 1989 by Paul Yee. First published in Canada by Groundwood Books, Ltd. Reprinted by permission of the publisher.

page 192: "Things I Forgot Today," from *Raven Tells Stories: An Anthology of Alaskan Native Writing*, edited by Joseph Bruchac. Copyright © 1991 by Martha Malavansky. Reprinted by permission of the publisher.

page 202: "Clever Manka: The Story of a Girl Who Knew What to Say" from *The Shoemaker's Apron: A Second Book of Czechoslovak Fairy Tales and Folk Tales*, copyright © 1920 by Parker Fillmore and renewed 1948 by Louise Fillmore, reprinted by permission of Harcourt, Inc.

page 212: "A Piece of String," from *The Best Short Stories of Guy de Maupassant*. Copyright © 1968. Reprinted by permission of Airmont Publishing Company, Inc.

page 224: "Dead Men's Path," from *Girls at War and Other Stories* by Chinua Achebe. Copyright © 1972, 1973 by Chinua Achebe. Used by permission of Doubleday, a division of Random House, Inc.

Reprinted by permission of Harold Ober Associates Incorporated. Copyright © 1972, 1973 by Chinua Achebe.

page 240: Reprinted with the permission of Simon & Schuster Adult Publishing Group, from *Anne Frank Remembered: The Story of the Woman Who Helped to Hide the Frank Family* by Miep Gies with Alison Leslie Gold. Copyright © 1987 by Miep Gies and Alison Leslie Gold. All rights reserved.

page 250: From *The Diary of a Young Girl: The Definitive Edition* by Anne Frank. Otto H. Frank & Mirjam Pressler, editors, translated by Susan Massotty, copyright © 1995 by Doubleday, a division of Random House, Inc. Used by permission of Doubleday, a division of Random House, Inc.

page 262: Reprinted with permission of The Estate of Lyll Becerra de Jenkins c/o Mary Jack Wald Associates, Inc. This is an adapted abridgement of chapters six, seven, and eight of *The Honorable Prison* by Lyll Becerra de Jenkins published by Lodestar Books/Penguin USA, 375 Hudson Street, New York, NY 10014. Copyright © 1988 by Lyll Becerra de Jenkins.

page 280: "Horses" from *Extravagaria* by Pablo Neruda, translated by Alastair Reid. Translation copyright © 1974 by Alastair Reid. Reprinted by permission of Farrar, Straus and Giroux, LLC.

page 284: "Eight Puppies" from *Selected Poems of Gabriela Mistral* by Gabriela Mistral. Adapted and translated by Doris Dana. Copyright © 1961, 1964, 1970, 1971 by Doris Dana. Used by permission.

page 288: "The Trout" copyright © by Devin-Adair Publishers, Inc., Old Greenwich, Connecticut, 06870. Permission granted to reprint "The Trout" by Sean O'Faolain. All rights reserved.

page 300: The translation of the Chiyo haiku "After a Long Winter" is used with permission of the copyright holder, David Ray. The poem first appeared in the anthology *For Rexroth: The Ark 14*, The Ark Press, New York, N.Y., 1980, edited by Geoffrey Gardner.

"Autumn," "Heat," and "Winter" from *An Introduction to Haiku* by Harold G. Henderson, copyright © 1958 by Harold G. Henderson. Used by permission of Doubleday, a division of Random House, Inc.

page 306: Wang Wei, "Green Creek," from *Laughing Lost in the Mountains*. Translations by Tony Barnstone, Willis Barnstone, Xu Haixin © 1991 with permission from University Press of New England, Hanover, N.H.

page 310: "The Cedar Chest," from *The Tree Is Older Than You Are* by Naomi Shihab Nye. Translation by Judith Infante. Reprinted by permission of Judith Infante.

page 314: "Morning" from *Earth Magic* by Dionne Brand is used with the permission of Kids Can Press Ltd., Toronto. Text copyright © 1979 Dionne Brand.

page 326: From *When Heaven and Earth Changed Places* by Le Ly Hayslip, copyright © 1989 by Le Ly Hayslip and Charles Jay Wurts. Used by permission of Doubleday, a division of Random House, Inc.

page 338: "Grandfather's Photograph" by Mangalesh Dabral. Used by permission of the author.

page 348: "The Bicycle" by Jerzy Harasymowicz, translated by Edmund Ordon from *San Francisco Review* Annual #1. Reprinted by permission of Zora Ordon.

page 352: "The Street" from *Selected Poems of Octavio Paz*. Copyright © 1966. Reprinted by permission of the publisher, Indiana University Press.

page 370: "The Tiger and the Jackal" from *The Maid of the North* by Ethel Johnston Phelps. Copyright © 1981 by Ethel Johnston Phelps. Reprinted by permission of Henry Holt and Company, LLC.

page 378: Copyright © 1986 by Ariel Dorfman, reprinted with the permission of The Wylie Agency, Inc.

page 390: "The Nose (After Gogol)" by Iain Crichton Smith from *Love Poems and Elegies*. Copyright © 1972. Reprinted by permission of Victor Gollancz, a division of the Orion Publishing Group.

page 400: From *As They Were* by M. F. K. Fisher. Copyright © 1955 by M. F. K. Fisher. Reprinted by permission of Alfred A. Knopf, a division of Random House, Inc. Used by permission of Alfred A. Knopf, a division of Random House, Inc.

page 406: "Luck" by Elena Casteda, from *You're On! Seven Plays in English and Spanish*. Copyright © 1999 by Lori Marie Carlson. Used by permission of Curtis Brown, Ltd. All rights reserved.

page 416: "Heavy Moments" reprinted by permission of the author, Ama Ata Aidoo.

page 436: "Sometimes When It Rains" from *The Heinemann Book of African Women's Poetry*. Copyright © 1987 by Gcina Mhlophe. Reprinted by permission of the author.

page 442: "The Watch" from *One Generation After* by Elie Wiesel. Copyright © 1965, 1970 by Elie Wiesel. Reprinted by permission of Georges Borchardt, Inc., on behalf of the author.

Note: Every effort has been made to locate the copyright owners of material reprinted in this book. Omissions brought to our attention will be corrected in subsequent editions.

Photo and Illustration Credits

Cover: *t.l.* © Scala/Art Resource, NY; *m.l.* © DK Images; *m.* © Michael Goldman/Taxi/Getty Images, Inc.; *b.l.* © The Granger Collection; *b.r.* © S.J. Krasemann/Peter Arnold, Inc. 2: © Fabrice Vallon/Corbis. 10: © Mai Vo-Dinh. 21: © Bettmann/Corbis. 23: © Bettmann/Corbis. 25: © Layne Kennedy/Corbis. 26: © Sophie Bassouls/Corbis. 30: © Peter Harholdt/Corbis. 33: © Cameraphoto Arte, Venice/Art Resource, NY. 36: © The Granger Collection. 38: © Erich Lessing/Art Resource, NY. 58: © The Granger Collection. 64: © Scala/Art Resource, NY. 75: © Lawrence Migdale Photography. 85: © Alinari/Art Resource, NY. 92: © Mitchell Library, State Library of New South Wales. 96: © Philadelphia Museum of Art/Corbis. 103: © Roger Ressmeyer/Corbis. 105: © Jennifer Steele/Art Resource, NY. 126: © Fine Art Photographic Library, London/Art Resource, NY. 154: *t.* © The Granger Collection; *b.* © Royalty-Free/Corbis. 168: © Images.com/Corbis. 174: *t.* © The Granger Collection; *b.* © Leonard de Selva/Corbis. 182: Courtesy, Paul Yee. 185: © Reunion des Musees Nationaux/Art Resource, NY. 188: © Reunion des Musees Nationaux/Art Resource, NY. 190: © The Granger Collection. 193: © Francis G. Mayer/Corbis. 200: © The Newark Museum/Art Resource, NY. 221: © Bettmann/Corbis. 223: © Christie's Images/Corbis. 230: Steve Miller/New York Times Co./Getty Images, Inc. 233: Chinese. Streams and Hills under Fresh Snow, XIII, Ink and color on silk, H. (entire scroll): 16-1/8 in., L.: 7 ft. 11 in. (41 x 241.3 cm). The Metropolitan Museum of Art, Gift of John M. Crawford, Jr., 1984. 234: © The British Library. 238: © Photograph Courtesy of Gwendolyn Knight Lawrence/Art Resource, NY. 241: © The Granger Collection. 245: *t.* © DK Images; *m.* © The Granger Collection; *b.* © Hulton Archive/Getty Images Inc. 247: © AP/Wide World Photo. 249: © Hulton-Deutsch Collection/Corbis. 251: © The Granger Collection. 253: *t.* © Hulton Archive/Getty Images, Inc.; *b.l.* © Hulton Archive/Getty Images, Inc.; *b.r.* © Hulton Archive/Getty Images, Inc. 259: © The Granger Collection. 260: © The Granger Collection. 278: © National Gallery Collection; By kind permission of the Trustees of the National gallery, London/Corbis. 281: © Erich Lessing/Art Resource, NY. 282: © The Granger Collection. 285: © Fine Art Photographic Library/Corbis. 286: © The Granger Collection. 294: © Jim Sugar/Corbis. 298: © Francis G. Mayer/Corbis. 301: © Giraudon/Art Resource, NY. 302: © The Newark Museum/Art Resource, NY. 303: © Snark/Art Resource, NY. 305: © Asian Art & Archaeology, Inc./Corbis. 307: © Christie's Images/Corbis. 311: © Museo Franz Mayer Mexico/Dagli Orti/The Picture Desk/The Art Archive/Kobal. 312: © The New York Public Library Photographic Services/Art Resource, NY. 315: © Royalty-Free/Corbis. 316: *t.* © Courtesy, Dionne Brand; *b.* © The Granger Collection. 320: © The Mukashi Collection/SuperStock, Inc. 324: © Michael Nicholson/Corbis. 327: © Jeremy Horner/Corbis. 331: © AP/Wide World Photo. 333: © AP/Wide World Photo. 335: *t.* © Steve Raymer/Corbis; *b.* © Robert Eric/Corbis Sygma. 337: © Macduff Everton/Corbis. 339: © Stephen Wilkes/The Image Bank/Getty Images, Inc. 346: © Herscovici/Art Resource, NY. 353: © Christie's Images/Corbis. 354: © William Coupon/Corbis. 363: © Gianni Dagli Orti/Corbis. 365: © Ruggero Vanni/Corbis. 368: © The Granger Collection. 388: © Touhig Sion/Sygma/Corbis. 391: © Banque d'Images, ADAGP/Art Resource, NY. 398: © Erich Lessing/Art Resource, NY. 404: © John Engstead/North Point Press a division of Farrar, Straus & Giroux. 415: © Owaki-Kulla/Corbis. 428: © Ondrea Barbe/Corbis. 431: © Corbis. 433: © Corbis. 434: National Library of Jamaica. 437: © Thinkstock/Royalty-Free/Getty Images, Inc. 439: © Paul Weinberg/SouthPhoto. 441: © David Turnley/Corbis. 443: © United States Holocaust Memorial Museum. 444: © United States Holocaust Memorial Museum. 448: © Mitchell Gerber/Corbis.

Illustrations: 408, 410: Paul Bachem. 227, 229, 417, 419, 423: Shawn Barber. 379, 382, 387: Bryn Barnard. 77, 79, 81: James Bentley. 371, 375: James Bernardin. 213, 214, 217, 220, 323: Denny Bond. 203, 207, 210: Susan Gaber. 171, 173: Ed Gazsi. 51, 53, 57: Ron Himler. 87, 89: Robert Hunt. 48, 83, 141, 143, 147, 149, 163, 194, 272, 340, 350, 392, 401, 403, 424: Joel Iskowitz. 67, 68, 71, 73: Laura Jacobsen. 157, 159, 161, 291, 293: Ron Mazzelon. 41, 43, 46: Kagan Mcleod. 107, 108, 111: Cliff Nielsen. 13, 17, 20: Cheryl Kirk Noll. 177, 181: Phyllis Pollema–Cahill. 357, 361, 362: Larry Schwinger. 99, 101, 102, 265, 268, 271: Marc Scott. 349: Joel Spector. 5–9, 129, 131, 133, 137: Winson Trang. 115, 116, 119, 120: Eric Velasquez. 1, 63, 125, 199, 277, 345, 397: XNR Productions.